Together and Equal

Fostering Cooperative Play and Promoting Gender Equity in Early Childhood Programs

Carol Hilgartner Schlank

Barbara Metzger

Allyn and Bacon

Boston   London   Toronto   Sydney   Tokyo   Singapore

Library of Congress Cataloging-in-Publication Data

Schlank, Carol Hilgartner.
    Together and equal : fostering cooperative play and promoting gender equity in early childhood programs / Carol Hilgartner Schlank and Barbara Metzger.
        p.   cm.
    Includes bibliographical references.
    ISBN 0-205-18155-4
    1. Play. 2. Early childhood education—Activity programs. 3. Sex discrimination—Prevention—Study and teaching. 4. Sex role in children. I. Metzger, Barbara. II. Title.
    LB1139.35.P55S35   1997
    370.19′345—dc20   96-11570
                                                                              CIP

Printed in the United States of America
10 9 8 7 6 5 4 3 2 1   00 99 98 97 96

Contents

Preface

Since the 1970s, in our work in early childhood—as teachers, administrators, consultants, and writers—we have tried to look at the roles we played in promoting gender equity and fostering cooperative play between girls and boys. In the beginning, our efforts were sporadic and unfocused, but the more we worked with children, parents, and colleagues, the more committed we became to the ideas of equality and cooperation. In the late 1980s, we began to share some of our thoughts and experiences with other early childhood practitioners, who, in turn, shared theirs. Educators told us repeatedly that they were concerned about the many children who had already developed firm ideas as to what boys and girls could and could not do, and about the excluding behavior and intolerance they often witnessed between gender-segregated groups.

To answer these concerns and to address the problems of sexism in early childhood from infancy through age 8, we decided to write this book. The activities and programmatic adaptations we have proposed are not presented as a set curriculum, but as possible extensions to any dynamic and changing one. Our ideas can be integrated into all developmentally appropriate programs and should be particularly valid for inclusion in and expansion of any antibias curriculum.

We believe that, with effort, teachers can become aware of their own gender biases and the influence these have on their teaching. Using these insights, along with a willingness to try new ideas and risk mistakes, teachers can begin consciously to strive to promote gender equity and cooperation between girls and boys. By involving parents and colleagues in understanding these goals, teachers will be more effective in facilitating change.

In the process of writing *Together and Equal*, we read many articles that suggested that since boys and girls are innately different, it is small wonder that their behavior is so different. Even given that girls and boys have different bodies and hormones and that their brains *may* differ in significant ways, we believe that, in our society, the differences between the sexes have been magnified, while the many commonalities between the genders have been minimized. Whatever the differences are between girls and boys, the behavioral differences are often greater among individuals of the same sex than they are from one sex to the other. And, of course, aside from biological influences, the effects of cultural expectations and attitudes on behavior are well established.

However these arguments are eventually resolved, educators need not wait until all the evidence is in before beginning to try to change attitudes and influence behavior. It is vital that educators work now to help each child realize her or his potential, regardless of gender, and to help children of both genders learn to work and play together. Our aim is not to change girls who prefer dolls or boys who emulate athletes or to deny the legitimacy of same-sex friendships. But we believe that sex-role stereotyping and sex segregation limit individual choices and curtail opportunities for both genders to learn to live and work together amicably and productively.

It is particularly important for girls to view themselves as worthwhile and to have the opportunity to fulfill their intellectual, social-emotional, and physical potential and for boys to be able to express a wide range of feelings, including feelings of vulnerability, gentleness, and love. We would like both boys and girls to feel as free to choose non-traditional roles as they are to choose traditional ones.

In a world where conflict and oppression are sadly prevalent, we believe that helping girls and boys respect themselves and each other as equals is imperative, and that learning to cooperate, rather than disparage or compete with the other sex, is essential. Whatever advances made now toward promoting gender equity and partnership between the sexes will have long-range implications for a more just and harmonious future for children.

ACKNOWLEDGMENTS

We wish to thank the many individuals who shared their comments and ideas and encouraged us to write this book. In particular, we wish to thank Carol Ely, Sarah Gardener, Michael Glidden, Carol Jackman, Kathleen O'Neil, Judith Van Ness, and Ann Weintraub for their help in reading and responding to the manuscript; Jim Hilgartner and Steve Hilgartner for their technical assistance; our husbands, Mel Schlank and Bernie Metzger, for their ongoing support and commitment to the endeavor; and our editor, Nancy Forsyth, for her enthusiasm for the book, her consistent support, and her perceptive suggestions.

CHAPTER ONE
TEACHING FOR CHANGE

Everyday Ways to Diminish
Gender Stereotyping and
Build Self-Esteem

From the time parents first think of having a child, they think about whether the baby will be a boy or a girl. Almost from the start, parents and others ascribe male and female characteristics to the unborn baby; for example, if the baby is active in utero, it must be a boy, and if it is quiet, a girl. As parents wait for the birth of their baby, more of them say they would prefer a boy, especially for the first born. Even today, in the rapidly changing society, males are frequently viewed as superior to females, and although many girls and women say they wish they had been born male, few boys or men say they wish they were female.

In any case, both genders start with a disadvantage: society's belief that males and females should fit (albeit in varying degrees) the stereotypic roles of their gender. Boys are burdened with the societal expectation that they will grow up strong and successful and in control of their emotions, girls with the expectation that they will marry, become mothers, and put the needs of others before their own.

As you think about your own history as a female or a male, you will no doubt realize how much it contains the seeds of who you are today. You will probably also begin to see how your experiences as a member of your sex affect your thinking, beliefs, actions, and relationships. Perhaps, like many women and men, you accepted without question the prevailing beliefs and biases of your family, culture, and society. Perhaps also, you feel you were limited or stereotyped because of your gender.

You may have already made a conscious decision to see yourself and others as individuals with freedom of choice, not as members of a particular gender with limited options. But as you think about your gender history and recall your experiences as a male or a female, you may uncover areas of gender bias previously hidden from your awareness. Since gender bias will have an impact on your ability to encourage cooperative play and gender equity in your classroom, you will want to identify attitudes and behaviors that warrant reconsideration and possible change.

In this chapter, we suggest ways to help you work to diminish sex-role stereotyping in your early childhood program and to build self-esteem in the children you teach. First, we ask you to look at your own gender history to see how your past experiences as a female or a male impact on your teaching today. Then, we go on to discuss teaching strategies for helping children develop as confident individuals who respect themselves and others regardless of gender.

BEGIN WITH YOURSELF

To help you weed out your gender bias (and everyone has some), we suggest you set aside time to reflect on the ways your life has been influenced by your gender and how you relate to the other gender. To that end, we ask you to consider the following questions.

> **What kind of family/neighborhood/culture did you grow up in? What work did the females/males in your immediate and extended family do? What chores were assigned to you and your siblings? Who was in charge of your family? Who made decisions?**

If you grew up in a family where both girls and boys took out the garbage and both boys and girls did the dishes, your parent(s) counteracted the societal stereotypes around certain work being appropriate for each sex. But if the chores in your family were assigned in a stereotypic way, you will want to be careful that you do not fall into a familiar pattern of asking or expecting that the girls and boys you teach will do certain jobs or activities based on gender.

If your parents discussed and made decisions together, you witnessed shared leadership in your home. However, if your father (or mother) made the major family decisions, such as when to move to a new neighborhood or where to go on vacation, you will want to look at how that part of your gender history has affected your ideas about who should be in charge. You may find that it is hard for you to relinquish control or that it feels awkward to assume a leadership role. And you may have to make a conscious effort to see that decision making in your early childhood program is shared by both sexes.

> **How did you get to do something you wanted to do? Did you ask permission, manipulate the situation, cry, whine, pout, argue, present your case rationally, or throw a tantrum?**

The stereotypic view is that often girls learn to manipulate or cry to get what they want, whereas boys are more likely to present their case rationally or act out in an angry way. Stereotypically, girls are more likely to ask permission, and boys are more likely to go ahead with a plan without asking for approval. If your past behavior fits any of these stereotypes, you will want to make sure that you do not expect and tacitly accept or reject certain behaviors from the children you teach based on their gender.

Did you always like being a girl/a boy? Why/why not?

If you liked or disliked being a girl/a boy, you can use this information to help you walk in the shoes of at least some of the children you teach who share your gender. To get a feel for how others of your sex might experience being a girl/a boy, try to imagine how you would have felt had your attitude about your gender been different.

How dependent/independent were you allowed to be? Was your dependence/independence limited because of your gender?

Often, girls have been discouraged from being as independent as boys, and boys have been made to feel weak if they expressed a need for dependence. You may feel you were pushed to be independent or that your independence was curtailed. You will want to think about realistic ways to encourage a reasonable balance between dependence and independence in the boys and girls you teach.

Were you encouraged to be whatever you wanted to be? To further your education? To go against the norm?

If you can answer yes to these questions, you will be in a better position to encourage the children you teach to feel free to choose who they want to be. If, like many others, you were directed in certain prescribed ways based on your gender, you will want to make a special effort to help children feel free to choose their own paths.

Were you expected to follow in your parents' footsteps or to go further than they had? Were the boys/girls treated equally in your home? If not, how were rules and expectations different?

In some families, boys are treated as future breadwinners and, as such, are expected to work harder and pursue more education than their sisters. Whether or not your family gave you equal opportunities regardless of your gender, you will want to be sure to give equal opportunities to the boys and girls you teach. Watch yourself to be sure that whenever your rules and expectations for the children you work with vary, you are thinking of the children as individuals rather than as members of either gender.

Were your ideas listened to and respected? Did you notice any difference between how the opinions of men and women were valued?

Men and boys tend to expect to be listened to and respected, whereas women and girls are often brought up to pay attention and admire. But all of us know how good it feels to have someone value our opinions and insights. You will want to be sure to give both girls and boys and their mothers and fathers equal attention and respect.

When you were a child, what were your favorite toys, games, and activities? Who were your playmates? Did you have friends of both sexes? Were you encouraged to have friends of both sexes?

If you were encouraged to try a wide variety of toys and activities and to have friends of both sexes, you will have experienced firsthand the value of diverse activities and broader friendships. Those of you who played with only "girl toys" or "boy toys" and who were encouraged to have only same sex friendships may have to work harder to break away from the familiar and open up possibilities for the children you teach to explore more areas and to experience cross-gender friendships.

If you were hurt, sick, or upset, how were you treated? Were members of the other sex treated differently? Were you encouraged to be brave and stoic, to employ a stiff upper lip? Or were you allowed to express your feelings of discomfort, pain, and upset?

Many men recall being told more than once that big boys don't cry when they are hurt, sick, or upset, whereas many women remember that their tears were likely to ensure nurturing attention. As you recall your experiences in this area, you will want to note how important it is for you as a teacher to allow both boys and girls to openly express their feelings of pain and distress.

Who were your positive role models? Why did you choose those people? Were they male or female?

If all, or nearly all, of your positive role models were the same sex, try to discern why. Perhaps your role models were national leaders (most of whom were, and still are, male); perhaps you were interested in careers that were dominated by one sex (such as science or teaching); perhaps you disregarded, distrusted, or disesteemed the other sex to such an extent that you chose few role models of that sex; or perhaps you so strongly identified yourself in terms of your own gender that you revered only those of your own sex. As a teacher of young children, you will want to introduce them to many exemplary individuals of both genders and encourage the children to view the strengths and contributions of these people as more important than their genders. You will also want to look for more ordinary role models of both sexes, such as women and men who take pride in their less extraordinary, but nevertheless worthy, achievements and contributions. (Since most people will not make it into history (or *her*story) books, it is important for you, as a teacher, to hold up the accomplishments of both men and women that may seem attainable to the children.

Was yours a traditional family? If not, how was it different?

Since few people would call their families traditional, you may find it helpful to think about how different family constellations, different family circumstances, and different cultures and social classes influence your perceptions of gender. Whether you grew up in a nuclear family, a single-parent family, a blended family, or an extended family; as a member of the dominant or of a nondominant culture; or as rich, middle income, or poor, you will look at gender bias from a unique point of view. Whatever your background, any insights you come to will likely help you understand the differences in attitudes about gender that you encounter in the families with whom you work.

How did you experience adolescence in terms of your gender?

Some of you may feel that adolescence marked a point in your lives when you became particularly aware of how your looks and abilities determined how members of the other gender viewed you. Many adolescent girls continue to feel that, in order to be liked by boys, they must be attractive and agreeable. Likewise, many adolescent boys still feel that, in order to be liked by girls, they must be handsome and athletic. Adolescent boys continue to fill more primary leadership roles (class president or treasurer), whereas adolescent girls more often hold secondary positions (class vice-president or secretary). Although most adolescents believe that being smart is important to success, even today many girls feel obliged to conceal their intelligence in order to be liked—especially by boys. As a teacher of young children, you will want to think about ways to bolster children's awareness of their unique qualities and strengths, since solid feelings of self-worth should help these children enter adolescence with enough confidence to be themselves.

How has your gender affected your adult life?

Think about the part your gender has played and may continue to play in your adult life. If you are single, think about how people treat you as a single male or female. If you are married, or live with a member of the other sex, think about who does what chores, who decides how money is spent, and whose job is deemed more important. Consider whether you generally defer to or dominate your spouse and whether you have assumed certain roles based on the expectations for your gender. Think about so called little things, such as who buys and sends greeting cards to family members, who visits Great Aunt Lila in the nursing home, and who takes charge of the plans for a family gathering. Think about who takes care of the car, the yard, and the household repairs. If you have children, think about who is in charge of their clothing, their meals, and their activities. Then ask yourself if these roles are chosen freely and are open to change, or if these roles have been assumed with little thought or awareness of stereotypes. The more you recognize any bias that is part of your own life, the better able you will be to recognize and cope with the bias you meet in your work world.

How did the world you grew up in differ from today's world in terms of gender?

Take a look at how things have changed vis-à-vis gender issues since you were a child and young person. You will probably recognize that today there are more women in science, government, higher education, and business, and that more men have opted for careers in nursing, the arts, social work, and early childhood education. Child rearing is no longer considered mainly women's work, as men have taken a larger role in parenting. You will, undoubtedly, come up with many more ways today's world differs from the world you experienced growing up, and both the progress and the continuing need for change you note should inspire you to work for further improvements.

Have your beliefs and thinking about gender issues changed during your adult years? If so, how? What conditioning or ideas regarding gender have you consciously discarded? Do you find yourself slipping back to earlier beliefs and behaviors? If so, in what circumstances?

Because of your own experiences with gender bias and gender equity, and because of your growing awareness of gender issues, you may be determined to work to eliminate sexism and to promote cooperation between the genders. You may have made a conscious decision to help today's children develop without the constraints of sex-role stereotyping and to enhance their abilities to cooperate and work in partnership with the other sex. But, for many reasons, it is easy to slip back into familiar sexist behaviors and expectations. It takes effort to change, to be more attuned to the way you use language, to address sexism in books and materials, to set the stage for cooperative play between all children, and to listen to females as attentively as you do to males. And just as it is easy to deviate from the diet or skip the exercise that you know is good for your health, it is easy to take time off from the bias watching and cooperation building that can benefit you and the children and parents in your program. Do not chastise yourself if you feel your resolve weakening; rather, try to recollect the importance of your goals and dedicate yourself once again to continuing your endeavors to promote gender equity and cooperation.

After you have thought about your gender history, you should be in a better position to listen carefully to yourself as you teach, noticing if any of your responses to children reflect the kind of stereotypical thinking that you may have experienced growing up. You will be more apt to notice if any of your responses limit opportunities for the children in your program. And you will work with more awareness to foster cooperation and shared learning among the children you teach. You will consciously begin to think of children as individuals with enormous potential, not as representatives of their gender. You will realize that although children acquire values and biases of their own through their families, their cultures, and the society in which they live, you *can* promote gender equity by showing your appreciation of individual children without reference to gender, by questioning value judgments that denigrate either sex, and by discussing differences and similarities between the sexes in a matter-of-fact way.

WHAT YOU SAY AND DO MAKE A DIFFERENCE

After deciding to work for gender equity and cooperation between the sexes, you may feel somewhat overwhelmed. How do you, as a teacher, promote gender equity and cross-gender cooperation during an ordinary day in your program? Here are some suggestions to get you started.

- Children should be treated primarily as individuals, and not primarily as members of either gender. Emphasize their shared humanity and their common characteristics, not their gender differences.

- As a teacher, you can encourage children and parents to recognize the value of both females and males and to celebrate the variety of differences within each gender. You can actively challenge gender stereotyping and excluding and belittling behaviors. Children and parents will notice how you treat the girls and boys you teach and will learn from your example.

- Whenever possible, be gender inclusive or gender neutral, not gender specific. As a teacher, make gender-inclusive comments such as, "The children like to pretend they are parents" rather than "The girls like to play with dolls"; or "The children like to make roads for the cars and trucks" rather than "The boys love to play with vehicles."

- Notice and comment when boys, as well as girls, are kind and helpful, are gentle and caring, and are playing cooperatively. Do not pass up opportunities to say things such as, "Tanya looked happy when you invited her to build with you, Ethan."

- Point out that girls, as well as boys, are smart, competent, and strong. Go out of your way to say things such as, "That was a hard puzzle you did, Sonia" or "That was a good idea, Joleen."

- It is important to acknowledge positive behaviors or to recognize a milestone by describing what you see. For instance, you might say, "Manuel and Celia are working together to make a road for all the Matchbox cars" or "Dana, that's the first time you've buttoned your coat all by yourself!" Avoid overuse of praise, however. It is much better to help children acquire skills, thus helping them toward feelings of self-worth and competence. Repeated comments such as, "What a beautiful painting!" or "Look how strong you are" can become automatic and meaningless. Children may repeat behaviors simply to please *you*, not because the behavior has meaning for them.

- Give children appropriate choices and honor their decisions. In this culture, the opinions of males are often valued over those of females; counter this tendency by asking girls what they think at least as often as you ask boys. For example, "How could we make that building safer, Keesha?" or "How long do you think it will take for this bean seed to sprout, Tameeka?"

- Deemphasize extrinsic qualities of the child. Avoid using descriptors such as *cute, pretty,* or *handsome*. Also, do not gush over physical attributes or clothing children wear ("What beautiful curls!" or "What a handsome new sweater!"). In a discussion of physical attributes, use a matter-of-fact approach as you acknowledge that Joe has curls and Jill has braids, that Nobuko has golden skin and Jose's is tan. If a child comes in with a new outfit and is eager to show it off, say something such as, "Where did you get your new clothes?" or "It's special to get something new." Talk about the color or the number of pockets rather than delivering value judgments.

- If a parent or visitor says something like, "Oh, what a pretty little girl!/ What a handsome boy," you can add, "And she's/he's friendly and smart, too."

- Be aware that girls may have a harder time being assertive about their needs, so you may need to say the words for the child to use. For example, you might say, "Maria, tell Tim, 'I had it first. You can have it when I'm done.'" Make sure that Tim is listening!

- Since boys often have a hard time expressing their feelings in words, you can help here too—for instance, "Michael, you look scared about that. Can you tell Sam how you feel?" Some boys may need you to model ways to express their feelings— such as, "Juan, tell Rachelle, 'I'm sad you tore my picture,'" and make sure Rachelle is listening.

- Validate all children's feelings. Let children know it is OK to feel angry, sad, upset, and scared, even if some of the behaviors provoked by these feelings (such as hitting a person) are not OK.

- Use the child's sense of fairness and developing empathy to help resolve conflicts—for instance, "Carla has been waiting a long time for the stethoscope. When can she have a turn, Chen?"

- Stress the positive aspects of differences. For example, you might say, "Isn't it great that everyone is different? Mary wants to fingerpaint, Nathan wants to read a book, and Crystal wants to do a puzzle."

- Make an effort to pay attention to the quiet children as well as to the demanding or disruptive ones. A recent study conducted by the American Association of University Women (AAUW) showed that boys, whether rowdy or quiet, get more teacher attention than girls. So consciously strive for attention equity in your classroom!

- Treat the children in your care as a group, not as members of different sexes. Instead of saying, "Boys and girls, . . ." use the inclusive "Children, . . ." or "Friends, . . ."

- Avoid using gender designations at transition times. For example, instead of saying, "All the girls, go get your coats; now all the boys," say, "Anyone with buttons (a zipper, red socks, overalls, sneakers), go get your coat."

- Comments about the children's "girlfriends" and "boyfriends" have no place in an early childhood classroom. Instead, recognize and support both same-sex and cross-gender friendships.

- Be alert to your own tendencies to have preferences for certain children. For example, notice if you are drawn to children who are quiet and nondisruptive, if you are particularly sympathetic to active and energetic children, or if you tend to prefer one sex over the other. Acknowledge your right to your feelings, but make sure that your preferences do not translate into unfair and unequal treatment of children.

WATCH YOUR LANGUAGE

The English language is filled with words that make assumptions based on gender. Since language affects people's perceptions of the world, it is important to listen carefully to what you are saying and to notice what messages you are sending to the children you teach and the parents with whom you work.

Word choices too often reflect unfortunate and unconscious assumptions about gender and gender roles. For example, no woman is only nurturing and emotional, and no man is only strong and silent. Be careful to speak in terms of each individual's characteristics, not in stereotypic generalities. Remember that most work can be done by both men and women. Therefore, do not assume that the doctor or dentist or boss is male or that the elementary teacher or nurse or secretary is female. Help children become aware of wider possibilities for women and men in the world of work. Point out that men can sew and clean house, women can repair machines and build furniture, and that both men and women can choose to make child care and household management their primary work.

Language Changes to Make in the Classroom

Firefighter (not fireman or firewoman)

Flight attendant (not stewardess or steward)

Sales clerk (not salesman or saleslady)

Mailcarrier (not mailman or mailwoman)

Police officer (not policeman or policewoman)

Server (not waitress or waiter)

Women (not ladies or girls [when referring to adult females])

Language Changes to Make with Older Children and Adults

Humankind or people (not mankind)

Ancestors (not forefathers)

Chairperson or coordinator (not chairman or chairwoman)

The best person for the job (not the best man or the best woman)

Member of Congress or Representative (not Congressman or Congresswoman)

Manufactured (not manmade)

Descriptive Language to AVOID

He is confident; she is full of herself.

He is caring; she is emotional.

He makes quick decisions; she makes snap judgments.

He is ambitious; she is pushy.

He is a detail person; she is a nitpicker.

She says what she thinks; he has a big mouth.

She is cooperative; he is a pushover.

She is in charge; he is a dictator.

She has high expectations; he is impossible to work for.

She is kind and considerate; he is a pussycat.

Sexist Put-Downs to AVOID

sissy

tomboy

egghead

bully

helpless female

scatterbrained dame

Gal Friday

the weaker sex

an old wives' tale

"the girls"

henpecked hubby

spinster or old maid

housewife

scaredy cat

doll

sex-pot

hunk

bimbo or babe

wimp

stud

kingpin

Females and males should both be treated with equal esteem and importance. Consider the following:

Identify individuals by name, not by gender. For example, Margaret Wise Brown is a well-known author of children's books (not Margaret Wise Brown is a well-known female author of children's books).

Identify individuals by name, not by a relationship to someone else—for example, Sheila Brown (not Hank Brown's wife).

Refer to women and men in comparable ways. For example, Gary's mother is a lawyer, and his father is a nurse (not Gary's mother could be a model, and his father is a nurse).

Refer to men and women in a parallel way using both first and last names or just last names. For instance, avoid a list like this: Kennedy, Gingrich, Dole, Moynihan, Barbara Boxer, and Hatch.

Avoid overuse of masculine pronouns (*his, he, him*). Instead of saying, "The average child spends X hours of his day watching TV," try "The average child watches X hours of TV a day." If you must use a pronoun, vary the usage of *she* and *he, her* and *him, hers* and *his.*

As you pay close attention to the language you use and hear, notice how often words divide males and females rather than focus on the commonalities of human beings. Do not become discouraged when you slip into the sexist language that pervades the culture; rather keep trying to increase your awareness and use of gender-neutral language.

CLASSROOM RULES FOR COOPERATION AND GENDER EQUITY

Our basic belief for early childhood classroom rules is this: The fewer rules, the better. Of course, some rules are necessary, but we suggest that you keep the list short and simple. This way, children can learn them easily and state the rules themselves when they need to.

Basic Rules

Children must follow safety rules. (Tailor these to your classroom situation and equipment.)

No child may hurt another person.

No child may harm another child's belongings or work. (This includes damaging as well as interfering with a child's work.)

Children must take good care of materials and equipment.

We advocate that you add these gender-inclusive rules to the Basic Rules list:

Gender-Inclusive Rules

All children may play with all toys and in all activity areas of the classroom. (Everybody may play with everything.)

No children may be kept from playing because of something they cannot change—such as gender, skin color, or disability. (In her book, *You Can't Say You Can't Play*, Vivian Gussin Paley says it simply and well!)

These two rules provide children with the freedom to explore all areas and activities and to try out many different roles. As children move more freely, you will see more cross-gender play. The rules also protect children from exclusion and/or ridicule when they want to play in an area that may be stereotypically perceived as an area for one particular sex. For example, the house corner is often seen as a place for girls to play, and the block area may be seen as boy territory. If you hear, "No girls allowed in this building" or "No boys allowed in our house," you can remind children of the rules.

Parents, students, or others who work or visit in your classroom need to know your rules too. Tell them that, as much as possible, they should allow children to work out their differences and solve their own conflicts. However, immediate action needs to be taken if a child is about to hurt another child, hurt herself or himself, or hurt equipment, work, or belongings. Also, be sure to explain the gender-inclusive rules to helpers or visitors and encourage them to question any stereotypic comments they hear children make. You may wish to post your rules in a prominent place.

SUPPORTIVE INTERVENTION

Although you will want to let children solve their own difficulties whenever possible, there are times when you will need to intervene in a supportive way to foster gender equity. For example, if you hear a child say something such as, "Girls can't do that," you might start by asking the child, "Why do you think that?" It can be helpful to know where the idea has come from before responding. Responses to consider include acknowledging that "Although some people believe that, I think . . . " or providing information that refutes the statement, such as, "Girls can become astronauts. Sally Ride and Shannon Lucid are two famous astronauts."

Whenever children are being ridiculed or left out because of gender, you can appeal to the excluders' emerging feelings of empathy and their sense of fairness. ("How do you think Angie feels when you say she can't help you build?" or "Do you think it's fair to tell Elijah he can't play Lotto with you?") This might also be a good time to invoke the rule we described earlier: No children can be kept from playing because of something they cannot change.

If a boy tells a girl she cannot be a fireman, you can state the reality that women can and do work as firefighters. If a girl tells a boy who wants to cook in the house corner that only girls can play house, again you can correct the assumption by saying something like, "Lots of dads know how to cook." (Try to have books and pictures to demonstrate these realities.) And, if necessary, you can remind the children of the rule: All children can play with all toys and in all activity areas of the classroom.

If a boy pretends to be a mommy, dressing in a skirt and going shopping, or if a girl pretends to be a daddy, dressing in a suit coat and going to work, you will appreciate that each of these children is working on understanding these roles and/or is experimenting with how it feels to be a member of the other sex. In addition, you have an opportunity to challenge the assumption that only mothers shop and only fathers go to work. If a child says, "Girls can't be daddies"/"Boys can't be mommies," you have a perfect opportunity to teach children that being female or male depends on anatomy, not on clothes or activities.

Of course, your ultimate goal is to help children arrive at a point where they can begin to challenge sexist stereotypes themselves. Strive for a group where you can hear children saying things such as, "Carlos can be the nurse," "Molly can be the bus driver," "Everybody can play in this gas station," "Omar can play house—he can be the Daddy," and "We can have two doctors. Orlando and Rhonda can work in the same office."

COPING WITH SUPERHEROES AND BARBIE DOLLS

Superhero and Barbie doll play in the early childhood setting often results in adult confusion, distress, and controversy. Almost every early childhood teacher, caregiver, or parent has been confronted with the question of what to do about children's fascination with superheroes and their weapons and/or with Barbie and her paraphernalia.

Many early childhood professionals "solve" this dilemma by making rules: No Barbie dolls, no Power Rangers, no weapons (and so on) allowed. Our concern with this solution is twofold. First, by banning this play, you lose a golden opportunity to repeatedly discuss and challenge the assumptions and attitudes implicit in the fantasy characters' behavior. Furthermore, you lose the chance to ask children to come up with alternative behaviors and solutions to problems the characters face. Could Barbie go to college and become a scientist? Could the Power Rangers settle a dispute with words rather than violence? Second, we find that children consistently break the rules that ban these toys. What teacher has not seen a child smuggle a Power Ranger figure into school, furtively fashion a Ninja Turtle sword out of bristle blocks, or use a gun-shaped unit block as a pistol? What teacher, when confronting a child who has made a pretend gun, has not been distressed by the child's obvious lie, "It's not a gun; it's a flashlight!"?

Do educators want to teach children to feel they must be sneaky and secretive, even dishonest, in order to act out what fascinates them? Don't good early childhood teachers follow the interests of the children in order to provide meaningful learning opportunities? And don't good teachers let children work out their fears and their feelings of power-lessness through play?

On the other hand, what should teachers do about the divisions into all boy and all girl groups, the sexist messages in Barbie and superhero play, and the aggression and injuries that too often result from superhero play? How should teachers deal with the repetitive, unimaginative aspects of this play? Should teachers allow children to act out violence and pretend to destroy one another? By letting children bring superhero and Barbie toys to school, are teachers fueling competition, acquisitiveness, and envy? And shouldn't teachers be talking with parents rather than spending frantic moments at dismissal time looking for a Barbie tiny swimsuit or a superhero figure?

Clearly, these are valid and complex questions. These questions could form the basis for a stimulating and thought-provoking in-service meeting that could help the staff work out possible solutions and establish policy regarding superhero, gun, and Barbie doll play. (See Chapter 7 for a sample meeting and references to readings on this topic.)

Our own experience over the years has led us to allow this play *within limits*. Banning the toys and play usually makes them even more attractive and desirable for the children and leads to a climate of deception and of "us against them." We have found that sometimes a child simply wants to make a weapon out of Legos and tuck it in a pocket to carry around. Other times we have been successful in redirecting aggressive play by encouraging children to act out new ideas rather than simply repeating TV programs they have seen.

Although we dislike the sexist repercussions of Barbie play, we have found that when we allow the dolls, children (usually girls) often abandon the play in favor of a more enticing activity. If the play continues, we question any sexist assumptions in the plots. For example, when Barbie was falling off a mountain and screaming for Ken to help, we asked, "What could Barbie do if Ken were somewhere else?"

In general, we have found that allowing the superhero play has helped children, who, at this stage of development, often feel over-whelmed by adult expectations and experience a lack of control in their real lives, become powerful and in charge in their fantasy play. (We believe it is important for girls, in particular, to feel powerful.) Through acting out roles of fantasy characters, children are helped to understand concepts of good and evil, fairness and perfidy. We also like the fact that girls and boys have an opportunity to practice negotiation and cooperation when they work out the rules for their superhero and Barbie doll play.

Ways to Handle Superhero and Barbie Doll Play

Set limits on the place and time for such play. For example, you may wish to limit active superhero play to the playground or to a particular time each day.

Invoke the rules about *not hurting others* during the play. Children often need help to figure out safe alternatives to the aggressive actions of superheroes.

Make sure that all the children involved in the superhero play are choosing to participate and are comfortable with their roles.

Check frequently to make sure that the game is not getting out of hand and redirect play before it becomes too frenzied.

Learn all you can about the superhero characters and their activities in order to help children expand and enhance the play. Give children ideas and encouragement to go beyond the stories they watch on TV. (For example, you might suggest that a group of Power Rangers build a command center out of hollow blocks and have *two* leaders representing both sexes making the decisions.)

Watch episodes of the superhero programs and discuss them with the children. Find out what they think, ask open-ended questions about what might have happened if . . . , and express your ideas as well. Let the children know how you feel about the violence and sexism that pervade the superhero scripts.

Provide activities that relate to the children's interest in superhero characters but remove the children from actual superhero play. For example, a group of Power Rangers might enjoy making an Alpha 5 robot using cartons, boxes, glue, paint, and other materials, and a group of Ninja Turtles might have fun making pizza and having a pizza party. Encourage children who are enamored of certain characters to draw pictures, tell stories, or make books about them.

Frequently point out the difference between real and pretend characters.

Make sure children understand that real weapons are dangerous and can be lethal and that pretend weapons must never be used to hurt another person.

Be aware that girls often choose or are assigned submissive, passive roles, whereas boys often take on the dominant, powerful roles. Help children exchange these roles in their play.

Make sure that in play that involves chasing others, girls have turns as the pursuers and boys experience being chased. (You can also form mixed-gender groups for chase games based on other attributes, such as color of clothing.)

Discuss and challenge sexist attitudes that permeate Barbie and superhero storylines. Help children figure out alternatives to plots that sanction male supremacy and female subservience.

If necessary, remind children that everyone can play in all areas and with all toys. For example, a boy can dress a Barbie doll and a girl can be a superhero.

Consider limiting the number of superhero and Barbie-type toys children can bring to school and/or selecting a special day for these toys.

TO SUM UP . . .

As you have read the sections in this chapter, we hope you have become more aware of how you can have a positive impact on the children you teach in terms of gender equity and cooperative play. As you focus on your gender history, the language you use, and your interactions with children, we expect that you will begin to notice obvious and more subtle positive changes in the way the children you teach feel about themselves and each other. Of course, sometimes you will catch yourself slipping into stereotypic behaviors and using sexist expressions. But do not be discouraged—recognition is the first step toward change, and small steps do make a difference.

CHAPTER TWO
ARRANGING FOR CHANGE

Setting Up Your Classroom to Encourage
Cooperative Play between Girls and Boys
and to Discourage Gender Stereotyping

As you think about how to arrange the interest areas in your classroom and what pictures and materials to choose, you will, of course, be using your knowledge and expertise as an early childhood professional to set up the room in a way that will enhance learning for all the children you teach. While you are in the process of establishing a developmentally appropriate and attractive environment in which young children can explore, interact, and learn, we urge you to keep the goals of encouraging cross-gender play and discouraging gender stereotyping firmly in mind. Pay particular attention to where you place the interest areas and what pictures and materials you choose for these areas. Remember to provide ample space for children to move freely between areas and have easy access to materials and equipment. Crowded or disorganized areas can lead to frustration and conflict and interfere with cooperative play.

In this chapter, we discuss how to set up your classroom to (1) attract *both* sexes to the area to engage in constructive, creative, and cooperative play; and (2) promote positive examples of each gender through pictures, books, and materials you place in your classroom. We include a sample room arrangement (Figure 2–1) for you to consider and adapt to your needs. Also, at the end of this chapter, you will find a list of catalogs that carry the equipment and materials we suggest you consider.

HOUSE CORNER

Names are important! If you have an area you call the Doll Corner or the Housekeeping Area, rename it the House Corner. Doll Corner and Housekeeping Area both suggest limits to the kind of play taking place there. Boys may be reluctant to enter an area that is defined by "girl toys and activities."

How to Make Your House Corner Appealing to Both Sexes

Use bright primary colors.

Furnish the house corner with a sturdy child-sized refrigerator, stove, sink, cupboard, table (a large round one can seat more children), and chairs.

Add child-sized doll beds, a child-sized rocking chair, and a high chair.

Include sturdy dishes, flatware, cookware, and plastic baby bottles.

Gather cereal boxes, coffee cans, and the like to represent real food.

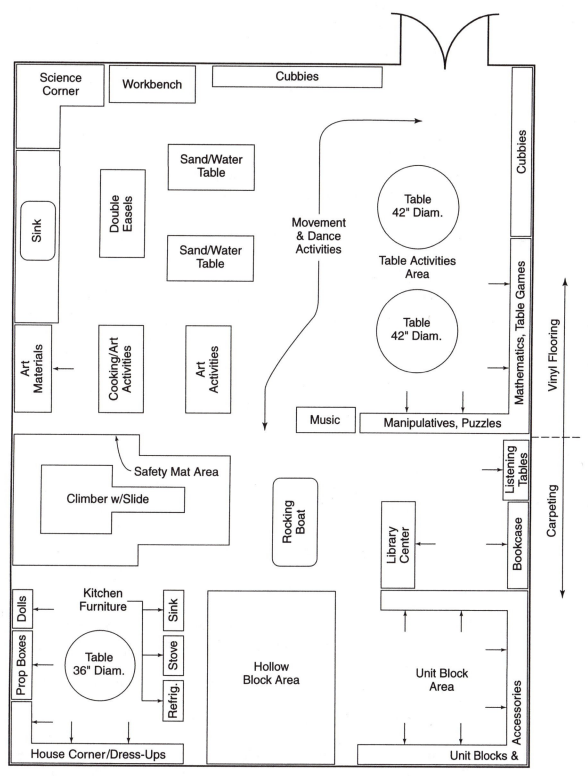

FIGURE 2–1   Sample Room Arrangement

Provide imitation life-sized fruits, vegetables, and other foods with baskets and bins for storage.

Rinse out empty detergent bottles and cleanser containers for make-believe cleaning supplies.

Add child-sized mops and brooms, dish towels, and pot holders.

Include a child-sized ironing board and toy iron.

Provide two telephones so children can talk together and pretend to talk with a "doctor," a "pizza shop owner," or a "repair person."

Consider placing a regular-sized couch or a love seat next to a bookcase, so boys and girls can read together in the house corner.

Additional Props That Will Attract Both Sexes to the House Corner

Old typewriters and computer keyboards, cash registers, calculators, and portable phones

Medical kit, bandages, blankets, and pillows

Scales for weighing babies or food

Doll carriages and strollers

Baby bathtub

Child-sized shopping carts and baskets

Toy tool kit

Anatomical Awareness

To help children develop an understanding that being male or female depends on anatomy, not on what they like to do and what they wear, it is important to provide accurate representations of the physical differences between genders. An easy way to do this is to include anatomically correct dolls in your house corner. Of course, you will want to include equal numbers of boy and girl dolls as well as racially and ethnically diverse dolls. (See the end of this chapter for catalog information.)

Be sure to include various types of gender neutral doll clothes (e.g., overalls, jeans, t-shirts, sweaters, diapers, and pajamas in colors and with decorations that do not suggest either sex) as well as the gender-specific ones you may already have. Discussions about what dolls (and children) are wearing can help children understand that anatomy, not clothing, determines gender.

Put books such as *What Is a Girl, What Is a Boy* by Selma Waxman, *The Bare Naked Book* by Kathy Stinson, and *Bodies* by Barbara Brenner on your house corner bookshelf to help children understand that anatomy determines gender. To develop children's awareness that their abilities and interests are not dictated by gender, also include books such as *Is It Hard? Is It Easy?* by Mary McBurney Green, *In Christina's Tool Box* by Dianne Homan, and *William's Doll* by Charlotte Zolotow.

DRAMATIC PLAY AREA

In this area, you will want to have dress-up clothes and accessories that encourage children to act out a variety of roles, both traditional and nontraditional. Too many dramatic play areas have a preponderance of frilly negligees, taffeta gowns, and high heels—an imbalance that suggests that dressing up is an activity primarily for girls. To attract both girls and boys to the dramatic play area, make sure you have equal numbers of gender-specific clothes as well as many that are gender neutral. Remember that all children explore different roles they are curious about. A girl may want to dress up like her father, a boy may want to experience what it is like to wear a frilly party dress. Having gender-specific clothing allows for this experimentation. You will also want to include hats, clothing, and accessories that suggest various career options. As children engage in dramatic play, remind them that in today's world, girls can be police officers, firefighters, doctors, or construction workers, and boys can be nurses, homemakers, librarians, or secretaries. Hang clothes from hooks so children have easy visual and physical access to them. Store hats and accessories on open shelves to make them readily available as well.

Suggested Clothing and Accessories for Role-Play

Soft floppy felt hats

Cowhand hats and boots, an old saddle

Firefighter hats, coats, short pieces of hoses (clear plastic tubing, vacuum cleaner hose with hard ends removed, pieces of garden hose), firefighter boots

Police officer hats, badges, jackets

Construction worker hard hats

Medical personnel outfits, medical satchel

Mail carrier hats, jackets, mailbags (large pocketbooks or tote bags can serve as mailbags)

Dresses and skirts (not too long), suit coats, ties, vests, scarves, gloves

Pocketbooks, briefcases, wallets, change purses, small pieces of luggage, backpacks, baby carriers

Aprons, server trays, chef hats

Railroad engineer hats, bandannas

Straw hats, overalls

Baby blankets

Prop Boxes

Sometimes children become involved in repetitive play or play that excludes one gender. Be prepared to introduce a prop box to encourage expanded or different activities and cross-gender play. To make a prop box, fill an ordinary carton with a few intriguing objects that relate to a specific theme and that will suggest new ideas for dramatic play to the children. When you introduce a prop box filled with materials that are new to the children, both sexes will be curious about the contents of the box and eager to explore possibilities for new play together. As you set up your room, prepare some prop boxes so as to be ready to provide enrichment when the need arises.

Sample Prop Boxes to Prepare for Use at Different Times of the Year

Housepainter box with real paintbrushes and rollers, paint trays, and painter hats

Auto mechanic box with small wrenches, new unused oil can, old spark plugs, distributor caps, air pump, and chamois cloths

Office worker box with an old typewriter and computer keyboard, envelopes and paper, deposit slips and order pads, calculator, adding machine, telephone card file, and business cards

Red felt glued on cardboard "pizzas"; felt mushrooms, pepperoni pieces, peppers, and so on; empty parmesan cheese shakers; pizza boxes; pizza pans; order pads; toy money; and cash register

Train or bus box with tickets, ticket punch, toy money, and conductor hat

Airplane box with used airline tickets, flight attendant trays, pilot hats, and earphones

Hospital box with clothes for medical personnel, elastic bandages, empty plastic bottles, stethoscopes, rubber reflex hammers, toy syringes, flashlights, and adhesive bandages

BLOCK BUILDING SITES

We like to separate the hollow block area from the unit block area, since the two kinds of blocks have distinct purposes. Hollow blocks are used for child-sized buildings, whereas unit blocks are used to build structures symbolic of the real world.

Hollow Blocks

Placing the hollow blocks in a large space next to the dramatic play area and house corner encourages cross-over play and joint use of the areas. Since boys are often drawn to the hollow blocks and girls to the house corner, cross-over play may well result in more cross-gender interaction. Children using the hollow blocks will have easy access to dress-up clothing and house accessories. With this room arrangement, children are likely to expand their role-playing and move more readily from blocks to house and house to blocks. For example, children playing in the house corner might decide to go to the park by riding on a bus that other children have made with hollow blocks.

Hollow Block Accessories

Child-sized vehicles

Blankets and pillows

Tablecloth

Baskets

Unit Blocks

In an area apart from the hollow blocks, store your unit blocks on shelves clearly marked with the block shapes for easy access and recognition. If possible, place indoor/outdoor carpeting in this area for children's comfort and to cut down on noise. To encourage cross-gender building, place a shelf with unit block-building accessories that will appeal to both sexes near the unit blocks. Girls who have previously avoided the unit blocks may become interested in building a zoo with animal figures or making structures to decorate with various accessories.

Unit Block Accessories

Multiethnic, nonstereotyped, family and community worker figures (Resources are listed at the end of this chapter.)

Animal figures, both domestic and wild

Small vehicles, airplanes, and trains

Small blocks and wooden beads for building/decorating structures

Fabric cut in squares, circles, rectangles, and ovals—in colors to represent grass, water, concrete, and so on

Corrugated cardboard, carpet scraps, and clear plastic boxes

Dollhouse furniture

MANIPULATIVE PLAY CENTER

Manipulative materials should be stored neatly on shelves that are easily accessible to children. Since both girls and boys find manipulatives intriguing, having a good collection of these will encourage cross-gender play. By changing these materials from time to time, you will renew interest in the area. (Resources are listed at the end of this chapter.)

Suggested Manipulatives

Nonsexist career puzzles

Puzzles that show females and males in nontraditional activities

Body parts puzzles (preferably ones that show accurate anatomy)

Animal, vehicle, everyday objects puzzles

Jumbo-sized floor puzzles

Pegboards with small and large pegs

Bristle blocks

Beads for stringing, sewing cards

Classifying and sorting games

Design cubes

Lego or Duplo sets

Magnet boards and magnet construction sets

Lotto and board games

Marble runs

ART AREA

An interesting art area will attract both girls and boys. Easels and shelves with art materials should be readily accessible to children on a daily basis. Try to have a special table available for art activities at all times. If possible, have your art area near a sink for easy clean-up.

Art Materials

Poster paints

Easel brushes of various widths

Child-sized scissors

Glue, paste, and tape

Collage materials

Paper of various colors, sizes, and textures

Plasticine, clay, and playdough

Markers, crayons, pastels, and chalk

Rubber stamps and ink pads

WOODWORKING CENTER

At the woodworking center, girls, as well as boys, can explore traditionally male-dominated construction activities. Although some girls may have to be enticed to approach this area, once they are pounding nails and sawing wood, they usually become enthusiastic "carpenters," with a sense of pride and accomplishment in their work.

Many teachers use this area for only part of a year. We encourage you to have a workbench available as often as possible as a way to empower girls and to facilitate cross-gender play.

Woodworking Tools and Materials

Real child-sized hammers

Nails of various lengths with large heads

Sandpaper

Soft wood pieces of assorted shapes

Saws and vise

Hand drills, screwdrivers, and screws

Assorted fasteners, braces, and other hardware

Spools, beads, knobs, and the like

Glue

Safety goggles

LIBRARY CORNER

A quiet, cozy corner away from active play will appeal to both boys and girls who want to explore books and experience a change of pace. Be sure the area is uncluttered and spacious. A carpeted area with large pillows or beanbag chairs makes a comfortable place to read and relax.

You will, of course, display the books attractively and fill the bookshelves with a variety of books, carefully selected to entice readers of both sexes. Remember to add new titles to your collection on a regular basis to stimulate and maintain interest. (See Chapter 5 for an annotated bibliography of nonsexist books.)

In addition to looking at books, children will often enjoy listening to audiotapes of books in your collection. Child-friendly tape recorders are now available, as are many commercial books on tape. (See a list of resources at the end of this chapter.) We also urge you to make your own tapes to accompany favorite books.

SAND AND WATER AREA

The sand and water area naturally attracts both girls and boys. So, if you have the space, set up both a sand table and a water table near each other. To vary the play and to provide opportunities for exploring the properties of sand and water, use only sand or only water in both tables, or use sand in one and water in the other. Or you may prefer to use a divided table with one space for sand and one for water. (Resources are listed at the end of this chapter.)

Accessories for Sand and Water Play

Scoops, measuring cups and spoons, containers and bottles, funnels, and basters

Tubing, siphons, and pumps

Sand/water wheels

Sifters, molds, and rakes

Watering can

Aprons, mops, and brooms

SCIENCE CENTER

Although a variety of science activities will occur in different areas of the classroom, it is important to have a special place where teachers, children, and parents can display natural objects and living things for hands-on exploration. Because children are innately curious, they will be attracted to this area to observe and interact with changing displays.

Things to Display in the Science Center

Shells

Stones

Bird nests and feathers

Wasps' and bees' nests

Caterpillars

Polliwogs, tadpoles, worms, snakes, frogs, and toads

Ant farm

Fish tank

Leaves, flowers, seeds, and seedlings

Plants

Science Accessories

Large and small magnifying glasses

Scales—platform and bucket balance

Rulers, measuring tapes, and measuring cups

Magnets

MUSIC AND MOVEMENT AREA

For music and movement, you will need to plan for a large open space in your room arrangement. You will also want to have a place for a record/tape player and for a display of carefully chosen songbooks, records, tapes, and accessories that will appeal to both sexes. You will want to select music for movement and circle time activities, for enhancing planned activities and spontaneous play, and for small group or individual listening. Of course, you will want to choose non-sexist songs or revise those that are sexist. (See Chapter 4 for a bibliography.)

Music and Movement Accessories

Rhythm instruments: drums, triangles, bells, maracas, jingle clogs, rhythm sticks, sand blocks, tone blocks, castanets, and so on

Xylophone

Rain sticks

Keyboard, autoharp

Listening center with headphones

Tapes and records

Scarves and streamers

INDOOR/OUTDOOR ACTIVE PLAY AREAS

In your indoor/outdoor active play areas, try to include equipment that will enhance interactive and cooperative play between both sexes—equipment such as a rocking boat that requires the children to cooperate as they work out how fast or slow to "row" or how to let a child climb on board or disembark safely. At a climber/slide, the children often engage in cross-gender play as they pretend to be firefighters scaling a building or monkeys playing on trees in the jungle. On active play equipment, children of both sexes test their skills and learn new ones from their peers. And, of course, the children need to negotiate taking turns and making rules. Equipment such as parachutes, bean bags, balls, balance beams, slides, tunnels, and vehicles encourage children to work together in order to have fun and keep everyone happy.

Suggested Equipment

Climber/slide

Gym mats (for use under indoor climbing equipment and for tumbling)

Rocking boat

Balance beam

Tunnel or tube for crawling into and through

Child-sized vehicles

Parachutes, balls, bean bags

Sandbox

ALL AREAS OF THE ROOM

In planning your room arrangement, take advantage of wall space, doors, and the backs of dividers and shelves to display pictures that will appeal to children and expand the ways girls and boys define gender roles.

Ideas for Pictures to Display

Men and boys, as well as women and girls, nurturing babies and children

Men and boys, as well as women and girls, cooking, washing dishes, doing laundry, vacuuming, and sweeping

Women and men having a good time with children

Women and men participating in comparable activities

Grandmothers working in the garden or driving a car—not just baking cookies or rocking babies

Grandfathers reading to children or changing diapers—not just playing ball or using tools

Traditional and nontraditional families engaged in a variety of activities, such as picnicking, shopping, and visiting the zoo

Girls, as well as boys, acting competent and confident

Boys, as well as girls, looking gentle and vulnerable

Girls involved in active play, boys involved in quiet activities

Girls, as well as boys, functioning as leaders and problem solvers

Boys and girls playing together cooperatively

Remember to choose pictures that reflect the real world—a world of racial and ethnic diversity and of people with a variety of physical challenges. Avoid pictures of beautiful and handsome models; search out pictures of ordinary people.

Gender-Stereotypic Pictures to AVOID

Girls having tea parties, boys fighting or roughhousing

Boys as rescuers, girls as victims

Girls in frilly party clothes, boys in sports outfits

Girls crying, boys being brave and stoic

Boys as competitors, girls as spectators

TO SUM UP . . .

Once your classroom is set up and ready to function as a place that will encourage gender equity and foster cooperative play between girls and boys, you will remain alert to the possibilities of different room arrangements or new equipment, props, and materials to further these goals. Do not hesitate to try a new room arrangement if the one you have set up seems not to be working as well as you would like, and remember to change or add materials to an area when play becomes repetitive and unimaginative. When children become interested in a specific theme, look for nonsexist pictures, books, and materials to support and extend that interest, and add them to your setting. You will be gratified to see both sexes exploring interesting changes together.

RESOURCES

The following companies provide catalogs with pictures, descriptions, and prices. We are *not* recommending everything in these catalogs; we are suggesting them as resources for many of the materials mentioned in this section. You will have to search for the nonstereotyped materials and watch out for stereotypic items. For example, the same catalog that offers nonsexist career puzzles and figures and anatomically correct dolls may offer only one nurse's outfit—one with a feminine apron and cap rather than one that is gender neutral. As you select materials and equipment for setting up your classroom, keep asking yourself if the materials are consistent with your goals for gender equity and cooperative play and whether the materials contain any obvious or subtle gender stereotypes. Make sure, too, that you choose puzzles, board games, and family and community figures with (as nearly as possible) equal numbers of females and males, as well as those that reflect the diversity of people in today's world. As you make selections, keep in mind that you want your equipment and materials to have the potential to appeal to both girls and boys and to have possibilities for extended play.

ABC SCHOOL SUPPLY, INC.
3312 N. Berkeley Lake Rd.
P.O. Box 100019
Duluth, GA 30136-9419
1-800-669-4222

BECKLEY-CARDY
905 Hickory La.
Mansfield, OH 44905
1-800-227-1178

CHILDCRAFT
250 College Park
P.O. Box 1811
Peoria, IL 61656-1811
1-800-638-1504

CHILDSWORK/CHILDSPLAY
Center for Applied Psychology, Inc.
P.O. Box 1586
King of Prussia, PA 19406
1-800-962-1141

COMMUNITY PLAYTHINGS
Box 901
Rifton, NY 12471-0901
1-800-777-4244

CONSTRUCTIVE PLAYTHINGS
1227 E. 119th St.
Grandview, MO 64030
1-800-448-4115

CREATIVE EDUCATIONAL
SURPLUS
9801 James Cir., Suite C
Bloomington, MN 55431
1-800-886-6428

DISCOUNT SCHOOL SUPPLY
P.O. Box 670
Capitola, CA 95010-0670
1-800-627-2829

J. L. HAMMETT CO.
P.O. Box 9057
Braintree, MA 02184-9057
1-800-333-4600

HAND IN HAND
Catalogue Center
Route 26
RR l, Box 1425
Oxford, ME 04270-9711
1-800-872-3841

KAPLAN SCHOOL SUPPLY
CORP.
1310 Lewisville-Clemmons Rd.
P.O. Box 609
Lewisville, NC 27023-0609
1-800-334-2014

LAKESHORE LEARNING
MATERIALS
2695 E. Dominguez St.
P.O. Box 6261
Carson, CA 90749
1-800-421-5354

NEW ENGLAND SCHOOL
SUPPLY
609 Silver St.
P.O. Box 3004
Agawam, MA 01001-8004
1-800-628-8608

SANDY AND SON
EDUCATIONAL SUPPLIES
1360 Cambridge St.
Cambridge, MA 02139
1-800-841-7529

TOYS TO GROW ON
P.O. Box 17
Long Beach, CA 90801
1-800-542-8338

CHAPTER THREE
TOGETHERNESS

Activities to Encourage
Cross-Gender Play

As a teacher, you may have noticed that during free play the children often divide into gender-segregated groups and that little cross-gender play takes place. If the girls consistently choose to draw and paint, play house, and read books, while the boys are off playing with the blocks, on the climber, and at the workbench, you will want to take steps to facilitate more cooperative interactions between the sexes.

In this chapter, we present suggestions to foster cooperative play between boys and girls and to attract each gender to areas and activities they may have avoided or neglected. As children move more freely in all the interest areas, you should see increased cross-gender play and wider exploration of materials, equipment, and roles.

HOUSE CORNER PLAY

By setting up your classroom to encourage cross-gender play (for example, having the house corner next to the hollow block area and the dramatic play area), you are more likely to see both girls and boys enjoying the house corner during free play. However, if boys shun the house corner, try introducing one of the props or prop boxes we described in Chapter 2, or design new ones to respond to the specific interests of children, to relate to field trips you have taken with the children, or to reflect the world of work. In addition, plan special activities—such as the ones that follow—activities that both boys and girls find hard to resist.

HOUSE CORNER ACTIVITIES

WASH DAY

Materials you will need

Mild detergent
Water table or dishpans
Clothesline and clothespins
Laundry basket
Aprons

Hang a clothesline in an area where drips will not cause a slippery floor. Outdoors is ideal if the weather and your setting permit; otherwise, towels can collect the drips. Let children bring doll clothes from the house corner to wash in the water table or dishpans. Show them how to rinse the soap out after lathering and scrubbing the clothes. Then let the children wring out the clothes, place them in the laundry basket, and hang them on the line to dry.

DISHWASHING

Materials you will need

Mild dishwashing detergent
Water table or dishpans
Dish drying rack
Sponges and dish towels
Aprons

Let children collect the dishes and pots and pans from the house corner to wash. Have children take turns washing and drying the dishes. Keep a mop or towels handy to wipe up spills.

HOUSE CLEANING

Materials you will need

Sponges, dust cloths
Carpet sweeper
Child-sized broom(s)
Mop, towels

Bucket with water and mild
   detergent
Aprons

Let children clean the house corner. They will enjoy washing the stove, sink, and refrigerator, dusting the other furniture, and sweeping and mopping the floor. To keep the area from getting too inundated, supervise the activity and have towels and mops available to wipe up spills.

MOVING DAY

For a variation of this activity, have a moving day, and let children rearrange the house corner furniture. For safety, have careful adult supervision of the "movers."

DRAMATIC PLAY

Since dramatic play is such an integral part of any good early childhood program (in fact, many educators believe that dramatic play is *the* most important element in early learning) you will want to encourage the children to engage freely and regularly in this activity. As children play in the hollow block area, the indoor/outdoor active play areas, and the house corner, they spontaneously take on a variety of roles. Be ready to help the girls and boys you teach expand their understanding of traditional and nontraditional roles and encourage them to cooperate as they develop increasingly complex scenarios in their make-believe play.

Look for possibilities for dramatic play in all areas of the room and playground; watch for opportunities to propose ideas for new dramatic play or to expand on undeveloped dramatic play. Keep in mind that dramatic play can grow out of stories, songs, and rhymes you introduce; field trips and special experiences children have had away from school; TV programs, videos, plays, or movies children have watched; and recordings or concerts children have heard. In short, be particularly attentive to what fascinates and intrigues the children you teach, and be ready to provide the accessories to inspire their emerging dramatizations.

Hollow Block Building

With your hollow blocks next to the dramatic play area and house corner, you will find it easy to suggest activities with the blocks that will include and overlap with these adjacent areas and that will involve both sexes. Of course, you will build on the interests of the children in your classroom as they create child-sized replicas of places from their world. But for those times when one sex is dominating the hollow block area, when interest in the area has waned, or when the block building has become repetitive, we are including some activities with the hollow blocks that are popular with both girls and boys.

HOLLOW BLOCK ACTIVITIES

THEATER/CONCERT STAGE

Materials you will need

Dress-up clothes
Props from the house corner for stage sets
Chairs for the audience
Rhythm instruments
Pretend microphones (small cylinder unit blocks work well)

Let the children make a stage with the hollow blocks. (For safety reasons, check to make sure the stage floor has blocks placed close together so children cannot fall through any cracks!) Encourage the children to create their own plays or act out favorite stories and rhymes or to act as musical performers who sing, dance, or play in a band. Use the dress-up clothes for costumes.

Children may wish to place chairs in rows for an "audience." If too few children come to the performance, suggest that the children use dolls and stuffed animals to augment the audience.

PICNIC

Materials you will need

Picnic baskets
Large blanket
Dishes
Pretend food
Tablecloths

Dress-up clothes
Hats (for protection from the
    "sun")
Dolls and stuffed animals

Let the children pack food and dishes into baskets at the house corner to take to the "picnic grounds." Children may want to build picnic tables and benches with the hollow blocks, or they may wish simply to spread a blanket out. Some children may want to build vehicles with chairs or hollow blocks to ride to the picnic. Provide the props and a suggestion or two, and let the children take it from there.

POST OFFICE

Materials you will need

Envelopes and paper
Stickers for stamps
Magazines and junk mail
Play money (children can
    make this)

Cash register
Dress-up clothes (mail carrier
    hats, tote bags or large pocket
    books for mailbags)

Let the children set up the post office, using the hollow part of the blocks as boxes for mail. They may also like to build a post office counter with a cash register and stickers for stamps. Some children may enjoy "writing" their own letters and sealing them in envelopes. The children can take turns working at the post office, being customers, and delivering mail to the house corner.

LIBRARY

Materials you will need

Children's books and magazines
Index cards for return date cards

Let the children build bookshelves with the hollow blocks and arrange books on the shelves. They can either build a check-out counter or use a table and chair. The "librarian" will check books out for the library visitors, putting a card in each book. Library visitors can then take books "home" to the house corner to read to each other and to their dolls before returning them to the library.

This is an excellent follow-up activity after a visit to your school or local library. Children will often enjoy acting out a story hour if they have experienced one.

GROCERY STORE

Materials you will need

Clean empty food boxes
Clean empty plastic containers
Clean empty milk and juice
    containers
Shopping bags

Cash register
Play money
Purses and wallets
Shopping carts/baskets
    (if available)

Let the children make shelves with the hollow blocks and stock them with pretend groceries. The children can build a check-out counter or use a table and act out the roles of both shoppers and clerks. Play will flow between the hollow block area and the house corner as children purchase groceries and take them "home" to put away and use.

PET SHOP

For a variation of this activity, let the children use stuffed animals to create a pet shop. They will also have fun making some of the "pets," such as snakes and fish, in the art area.

CAR WASH

Materials you will need

Child-sized vehicles
Plastic buckets, sponges, and rags
Pieces of garden hose or plastic tubing

Let the children work together to erect a car-wash building with the hollow blocks. The children can take turns driving their vehicles through the car wash or acting as car-wash attendants. If you are feeling brave, let the children use water and soap in the car wash, although even without water, children of both sexes enjoy this activity.

PIZZA PARLOR/ICE CREAM PARLOR

Materials you will need

Tablecloths	Cash register
Dishes from the house corner	Order pads
Napkins	Markers or kindergarten pencils
Play money	Telephone for take-out orders

This activity will attract both sexes to the hollow block area, the house corner, and the art area. Some children can make representations of pizzas or ice cream cones in the art area. (Pizzas can be simple cardboard circles colored red and decorated with pictures from magazines or colored paper to represent cheese, peppers, mushrooms, pepperoni, and onions. Ice cream cones can be simple cardboard triangles with various colored circles to represent flavors of ice cream.) Other children can set up the food parlor, using hollow blocks for counters, tables, and benches. Both boys and girls will cooperate as they act out the roles of sellers, servers, cooks, and customers. Again, as with many of these building activities, if you take a trip to an actual pizza or ice cream parlor, the children's play will be enhanced.

APARTMENT COMPLEX/HOUSING DEVELOPMENT

Materials you will need

Sheets, blankets, or large tablecloths

Let the children create places to live by arranging the blocks and other furniture to form apartments or houses for varying numbers of occupants. Drape the sheets over these arrangements to form "walls." Children will enjoy bringing dolls, stuffed animals, and dishes, into these dwellings.

This is a good activity for working out a solution to the "she/he can't play here" dilemma without having to invoke a rule. You can also use this play as an opportunity to discuss different kinds of families and different living arrangements.

UNIT BLOCK BUILDING

Children, more often girls than boys, sometimes ignore the unit block area. When this happens, you may find that it is helpful to station yourself or a colleague in that area, offering ideas and suggestions or perhaps even demonstrating the use of the blocks by building a *simple* tower or structure. We stress that any adult construction be simple in order not to overwhelm children and make them think they could never make anything that elaborate. Any adult construction should work as a catalyst for the children's own ideas, not as an example for them to copy. If possible, have a woman demonstrate block building to model that it is fine for girls, as well as boys, to build with blocks.

To attract both sexes to unit block building, be sure to set up a large, defined space for the activity and provide a wide variety of block building accessories in the area. Display pictures of both girls and boys building with the unit blocks, as well as pictures of construction workers of both sexes building actual houses, roads and bridges. In addition to these suggestions, we recommend the following activities to attract the reluctant builder.

UNIT BLOCK ACTIVITIES

TABLE BLOCK BUILDING

Materials you will need

Parquetry design blocks and patterns
Colored cubes
Table play blocks and miniature figures

Use table blocks to encourage both girls and boys to work cooperatively to create designs and miniature structures and to provide a transition to unit block play. Bring out each of these sets of table blocks at different times and let the children explore and create with these materials. In the case of the parquetry design blocks, you may wish to demonstrate how to replicate one of the simple patterns. As you see children problem solve and experience success with these small building materials, you can suggest that they might like to try working with the unit blocks.

FAMILY/DOLLHOUSE

Materials you will need

Dollhouse furniture
Multiethnic family figures
Nonsexist and multicultural community figures
Small vehicles

Let the children make houses and buildings using the unit blocks. They will enjoy furnishing them with dollhouse furniture and using the family/community figures to act out family living and community events. For example, the firefighter figures might come to put out a "fire" at the "house," or the toy school bus might take the toy children to a "school" made with unit blocks.

ROADWAYS AND TRAIN TRACKS

Materials you will need

Roadway/train set (or unit blocks to build roads and tracks)
Toy cars, trucks, and trains

We have found that those children who have not explored unit blocks or who have lost interest will often come to this area when new materials are introduced. If you add roadway/train sets to your block area, you may find that children are intrigued and eager to build railroad stations, bridges, and buildings to make a town or country setting around the roads or train tracks.

Trips to see a train station and/or a superhighway will often stimulate and enhance block building. Books on trains, vehicles, and transportation can also add interest to this area. Look for pictures and books that show women, not just men, as drivers, engineers, and conductors.

FARMS AND ZOOS

Materials you will need

Toy zoo and/or farm animals
Blue material or paper for water

Introduce these materials to the unit block area to attract new building. Children will build zoo cages and environments or farms and farm buildings with the unit blocks. At first, you may wish to introduce the zoo and farm animals separately, but later, if you introduce the animals together, children can decide where each animal belongs. This is good practice in categorization, and it gets children of both sexes involved in problem solving together. Trips to a farm and/or a zoo and books about these subjects will likely stimulate and enhance the block play.

MARINAS AND AIRPORTS

Materials you will need

Toy boats and planes
Blue material or paper for water

If you introduce these materials to your unit block area, children will build runways, airports, piers, and docks with the unit blocks and will pretend to fly the planes and steer the boats. If a child has had a recent trip on a plane or boat, this is a good time to set up this activity. For example, a girl who has recently been on a plane trip, but who has avoided block building, might get involved in playing out her experience in the block area. Again, as with other building activities, books about and trips to these places will invite and enhance block building.

DESIGNS AND FANTASY STRUCTURES

Materials you will need

Spools
Small colored cubes, blocks, and beads
Miniature figures
Material scraps
Plastic wrap and aluminum foil

Let the children create designs and fantasy structures using these materials with the standard and more unusual unit blocks. Children will respond creatively to the freedom to build and decorate something wonderful or weird. You may wish to use pictures of unusual designs and structures, such as fancy walls and gates, formal gardens, murals and sculptures, and wedding cakes to stimulate creative expression.

MANIPULATIVES/GAMES PARTICIPATION

By carefully selecting your manipulatives and games, you will draw both boys and girls into this type of play. (See the list of resources at the end of Chapter 2.) Boys and girls will often cooperate to put together a large floor puzzle, work together with the Lego blocks, build a marble run, construct a log house, string beads, solve a shape-sorting problem, or play games such as Candyland or Go Fish. To maintain high interest in manipulatives, change them frequently. Teach the children new board and card games when interest in earlier favorites wanes.

ART EXPERIENCES

Both boys and girls are usually enthusiastic artists at the easel until the novelty wears off, and many girls are interested in whatever the art activity may be. Boys, on the other hand, may be less eager to sit down at a table to engage in an art activity.

To encourage cross-gender interaction in art and to attract boys to art activities, always have paper, markers, child-sized scissors (left- and right-handed), and glue available so that all children realize that they are free to make something whenever they want to. Position these materials on low shelves that are easily accessible to children.

Consider placing two easels next to each other, so that children can talk together as they paint. Have lots of bright colors and opportunities for mixing colors at the easel. All children, regardless of gender, like to see what happens when they mix white and red, for example. To keep easel painting from becoming routine, change colors and brush sizes frequently.

Have interesting collage materials readily available. Boys, as well as girls, are likely to be interested in unusual materials such as sandpaper, styrofoam, wood shavings and pieces, feathers, and bright fabrics of different textures.

Have a variety of clays and playdough, with accessories and tools such as cookie cutters, colored pegs, and tongue depressors. Children of both sexes enjoy rolling, pounding, and shaping clay and dough.

In addition to these suggestions, you will want to plan specific art area activities that attract children of both genders. We have included some of our favorites for you to try.

ART ACTIVITIES

ME-MAPS

Materials you will need

Roll of light brown or white 36"
    sturdy paper
Large black marker or crayon
Poster paints (red, blue, yellow,
    white, and black)

Containers for mixing paints
Easel brushes (short handled
    ones work especially well)
Markers of all colors
Child-sized scissors

Cut the paper into 3½- to 4-foot lengths in advance of this activity. To begin the project, ask the children to lie down on their backs on their papers. While the children lie still, draw around their bodies with a black marker, naming body parts as you go.

Next, talk with the children about the colors of their eyes, skin, hair, and clothing and about the colors they will need to paint their me-maps. Help the children mix colors they will need to paint their me-maps. Help the children mix colors in small containers. When they are finished painting, set the me-maps aside to dry.

When the me-maps are dry, many children like to use markers to add details such as buttons, belts, barrettes, and fingernails. Some children may want to cut out their me-maps, but others may find that much cutting burdensome. Display the finished me-maps with the children's names, since children enjoy identifying each other's me-maps. This is a good time to discuss and appreciate individual differences and similarities.

Because you will need to work one on one for part of this activity, you may wish to invite some parents to help. You might also find it helpful to work on this project over several days.

BOOKS AND STORIES

Materials you will need

Construction paper
Markers
Clear contact paper

Have the children dictate stories about an event or subject that interests them. If the children wish to illustrate their stories, you can put words and pictures together as simple books. Boys who may not like art activities often are eager to illustrate their own stories. Children sometimes like to have their stories read aloud at storytime and to be recognized as authors and illustrators. Some children will put their books in the library corner for others to look at, but some will insist on taking them home. If you have access to a copier, you can make copies and cover them with contact paper for the library corner.

Make a class book with the children. Ask parents to bring in snapshots of their children at different ages. Put these in a book along with information the children wish to share. Some members of the group may want to draw self-portraits and pictures of their families, pets, or favorite activities to add to the class book. For example, the book could include a photo or two of Mark, a drawing he has made, and facts about his life. The pages might read: "Mark has two brothers. His dog is named Comet because she runs so fast. His favorite food is macaroni and cheese. Mark's favorite book is *Swimmy*."

When the class book is finished, let children in the class take turns taking the class book home for a weekend to share with family members. Parents particularly appreciate the chance to learn more about their children's friends and experiences.

WHO IS THE BABY?

Materials you will need

Baby pictures of the children in your group
Poster board
White glue

To make a group poster, ask parents to bring in baby pictures of their children. Have the children glue their baby pictures on the poster board. When the poster is dry, hang it at the children's eye level. Children of both sexes love to try to identify their classmates as babies.

FOOTPRINT MURAL

Materials you will need

Foot-sized trays of colored poster paints
Long sheet of rolled paper taped to the floor or sidewalk
Washing basins for foot baths
Soap, water, and towels

Ask barefoot children to step into the color of paint they choose and walk from one end of the paper to the other. Then ask them to step into the foot baths to wash and rinse their feet. This project produces lots of participation and giggles from both girls and boys. If you can do this activity outdoors, you will find the cleaning up afterwards easier!

HANDPRINT MURAL

To make a handprint mural, adapt the footprint mural instructions accordingly.

MURALS ABOUT DIFFERENT THEMES

Materials you will need
Pictures from catalogs, brochures, and magazines
White glue
Paper from a large roll

Choose a theme related to the children's interests—such as vehicles, farm animals, zoo animals, superheroes, or dinosaurs—and have the children choose pictures and glue them on the mural paper. Display the mural with the names of all the children who worked on it. If the theme relates to a strong interest, both girls and boys will be drawn to this activity.

CAR/TRUCK/WHEEL PICTURES

Materials you will need
Styrofoam or aluminum trays
Bright-colored poster paints
White or light-colored large construction paper
Toy cars, trucks, airplanes, and construction vehicles with tires of
    different sizes and with unusual treads
Basins with soap and water for washing paint off vehicles

Let each child choose a vehicle and dip its wheels in a pan of paint and then drive the vehicle around on the construction paper. The child may decide to use more than one vehicle and several colors of paint. The resulting designs are pleasing and the follow-up car washing is also fun. Children who like to play with vehicles and those who like art projects are attracted to this activity. In addition to individual pictures, small groups of children can cooperate to make a mural.

COLLAGES

Materials you will need

Paper of various colors,
   textures, sizes, and shapes
Beans, seeds, feathers,
   interesting fabrics, buttons,
   and so on

White glue
Child-sized scissors
Large pieces of construction
   paper, cardboard, and
   styrofoam trays

Free your imagination to think of materials that will interest children in this activity. Some of the materials you collect should be available to children at all times on easily accessible shelves. Encourage children to make their own designs by gluing collage materials onto paper, cardboard, or styrofoam trays.

You can choose to plan collage making as a specific art activity by setting out additional and unusual materials to attract the interest of both boys and girls. Or you may wish to plan a collage activity around a specific theme, such as how things feel. For a touch-and-feel collage, you can provide materials such as velvet, sandpaper, plastic, cotton balls, foil, packaging materials, and corrugated cardboard.

SUNCATCHERS

Materials you will need

Clear plastic shapes
   (lids from coffee cans
   and deli containers)
Small pieces of colored tissue
   paper and/or colored plastic
   wrap

White glue
Paper punch
Colored yarn

Suggest that the children glue overlapping pieces of tissue paper and/or plastic wrap onto clear plastic shapes. When the glue is dry, have the children punch holes in their creations, string yarn through the holes to form loops, and hang the finished products in a window to catch the sunlight. Both boys and girls delight in making these attractive suncatchers.

SPRAY PAINTING

Materials you will need
Plastic spray bottles
Poster paint slightly thinned with water
Long sheet of rolled paper
Masking tape
Newspapers or shower curtain

Tape the paper on a wall or fence. Give the children spray bottles with paint and let them squirt the paper. If you do this activity inside, protect the floor with newspapers or a shower curtain. Children of both sexes enjoy this uninhibited art activity!

Q-TIP PAINTING

Materials you will need
Egg cartons
Red, yellow, blue, and white poster paint
Q-tips
Construction paper

Fill the egg carton sections with each of the four colors. Give the children Q-tips to put in each color and extra Q-tips for mixing colors in the empty sections. Both girls and boys will be intrigued by the color mixing and will take pleasure in painting with the colors they have created.

MARBLE PAINTING

Materials you will need

Marbles	Egg cartons
Box covers	Teaspoons
Paper to fit into the box covers	Poster paints

Put different colors of paint in the egg carton sections. Let each child drop marbles in the different colors. Then ask the children to retrieve the paint-covered marbles with spoons, drop the marbles onto their papers in the box covers, and tip the covers from side to side to make the marbles roll. Pastel colors on dark paper or bright primary colors on white paper make excellent contrasts. This activity and the resulting colorful designs will appeal to both genders.

COOPERATIVE MARBLE ROLL MURAL

For a variation of this activity, use a large box cover lined with a sheet of paper to make a group marble roll mural. Four or more girls and boys can work together dipping marbles in paint and tipping the box cover to roll the marbles over the paper.

SAND SCULPTURES

Materials you will need

Powdered tempera paints (bright colors work best)

Sand

Containers to mix sand and paint

Small jars (baby food jars are perfect)

Spoons

Trays to catch excess sand

Help the children mix the sand and dry paint in large containers to make colored sand. Next, have each child place a small jar on a tray. Using spoons, the children then layer different colors of sand in their jars. Be sure the children fill their jars to the top before screwing the jar lids on tightly. To keep stripes of colored sand in place, remind the children to carry their "sculptures" with care. This activity is a winner with both genders, and the end product can be used as a gift.

MAGIC SAND PAINTING

Materials you will need

Powdered tempera paints (bright colors work best)

Sand

Containers to mix sand and paint

Spoons

Funnels

Clear empty salt shakers and spice jars with perforated lids

Trays to catch excess sand

White glue in small containers

Glue brushes

Construction paper

Help the children mix the sand and dry paint in containers to make colored sand. Using funnels and spoons, the children then fill the shakers and jars with colored sand and screw the jar lids firmly in place. Next, have the children dribble or brush glue designs on construction paper. Some children will enjoy writing their names or making a picture in glue, and others will make a "scribble" design. When the glue is on their papers, have the children shake the colored sand onto the glue. Have them tip their paper over a tray to remove excess sand. The process of mixing sand and paint and the resulting magic pictures appeal to both boys and girls.

ZIPPERED BAG PICTURES

Materials you will need

Plastic bags with zipper closures
Poster paints
Containers to hold paint
Spoons

Let the children choose two colors (and white if desired) and place two or three spoonfuls of each into their plastic bags. Then have them zip the bags closed. Moving their fingers on the outsides of their plastic bags, the children will mix the colors. Children who avoid messy paint activities will like this tidy one. The finished products look colorful when held up to the light or mounted in a window.

PRINTING

Materials you will need

Objects for printing
Poster paint
Styrofoam trays
Construction paper

Collect a variety of classifiable objects with interesting shapes and designs, such as potato mashers, funnels, pastry cutters, and whisks; sponges cut in various shapes; potatoes, carrots, celery, broccoli, and other vegetables cut for printing; spools of different sizes; and rectangular, and cylindrical, square, and triangular objects. Pour paints to cover the bottom of styrofoam trays. Let the children dip the objects into the paints and use them to print designs on the construction paper. If the objects are intriguing, both girls and boys will find this activity hard to resist.

STRAW PAINTING

Materials you will need

Poster paint watered enough to run
Short straws
Spoons
Construction paper

Let the children choose the paints to spoon onto their papers. Give them straws to blow the paint to make designs on their papers. The children will enjoy seeing what happens when colors run together.

SURPRISE PICTURES

Materials you will need
Poster paints of various colors
Construction paper
Containers to hold paint
Spoons

You or the children will fold their papers exactly in half. Then the children will open their papers and place dollops of paint on different places on their papers. Next, instruct the children to fold their papers back together and rub their hands over the tops of their folded papers. The children love to open their papers to discover the surprise designs. Some children will enjoy naming their "Rorschach" paintings.

STRING SURPRISES

For an interesting variation of this activity, have the children dip strings into the paint and lay them in loops and squiggles on their unfolded papers, leaving one end of each string exposed. Ask the children to close their papers, rub their hands over the tops of the folded papers, and then, while pressing down on their papers, pull each string out.

WOODWORKING VENTURES

Woodworking is often seen as an activity primarily for boys. But if it is presented in an engaging way, girls will enjoy it too. Here are some strategies to help make a workbench tempting for all children and for encouraging reluctant users to try woodworking.

Start with a child-sized, sturdy workbench with a strong vise attached. Have a variety of well-made tools in weights and sizes children can handle. In addition to hammers, include a sharp saw or two, drills, and screwdrivers. Safety goggles are a must.

Collect a wide variety of different-shaped and relatively smooth-edged *soft* wood such as pine, and sort the pieces into different boxes (children like to do this) for easy access to similar sizes and shapes. (Long, pointed pieces of wood suggest guns and weapons. Enough said!) Make sure you have a collection of various-sized nails (ones with large heads are easier for the children to hit), an assortment of screws, assorted grades of sandpaper, and white glue.

Before the children begin woodworking, you will need to demonstrate the proper use of the tools. Be sure to limit the number of children at the workbench. Four at a time is usually the maximum number for space and safety. Have an adult (a parent of a girl might be a good choice) supervising the area at all times. An angry child with a hammer can be dangerous! Also, an adult can provide just the right amount of assistance (perhaps simply tightening the vise one more turn) to keep a child from experiencing intolerable frustration.

To attract reluctant carpenters, as well as eager ones, enlarge your collection of materials. In addition to wood scraps, provide styrofoam pieces, bottle caps, cloth scraps, wooden and plastic spools, popsicle sticks, tongue depressors, twistees, rubber bands, string and yarn, fabric tapes, leather pieces, thick cardboard, and masking tape for children to attach to their creations.

Consider placing your woodworking center near the easels and paint area. Children often like to paint what they make at the woodworking bench.

It is important to remember that the process of sawing a piece of wood, pounding a nail, or drilling a hole is often much more important to the child than the end product. Encourage children to experiment with the various tools. Do not ask the children what they want to make, since they may wish to work with the tools and leave it at that. With this thought firmly in mind, we suggest a few somewhat structured activities for children who want to make something.

WOODWORKING ACTIVITIES

WOOD SCULPTURE

Materials you will need

Wood scraps of various shapes and sizes

Fabric scraps, buttons, toothpicks, bottle caps, popsicle sticks, and so on

White glue

Poster paint

Glue brushes and paintbrushes

Containers for glue and paint

Markers

Colored tapes, duct tape, and masking tape

This activity can be set up on a table next to the woodworking bench. This will often attract any "tool-phobic" children to the woodworking center and will also provide an interesting activity for children who are waiting for a turn to use the tools.

Let the children glue pieces of wood together and decorate their sculptures with fabric, bottle caps, and other materials as they wish.

You will find that some children will make simple sculptures; others will create elaborate ones.

CARDBOARD STRUCTURES

Materials you will need

Toilet paper rolls	Other cardboard shapes
Paper towel rolls	White glue
Small, medium, and large boxes	Glue brushes
Corrugated paper	Poster paint
Box dividers	Large paintbrushes
	Containers for glue and paint

When the workbench is being used by other children or when you have no adult available to supervise the workbench, children of both sexes will enjoy creating structures and sculptures from cardboard pieces.

Give the children the materials listed here and let them construct cardboard configurations. Some children will prefer to work on their own, but a group of children can work together to create a large-scale structure. Start with a large carton as the base and let the children take it from there. When the glue is dry, children often enjoy painting their creations.

Any cooperative ventures can be displayed in a prominent place in your room with the names of the children who worked on them printed on signs attached to the structures. In this way, you will "publicly" recognize and appreciate those children who worked cooperatively and collaboratively on a project.

STYROFOAM SCULPTURES

Materials you will need

Assorted styrofoam pieces (packaging material is a good source)
Fabric pieces, buttons, bottle caps, toothpicks, and so on
White glue
Glue brushes
Containers for the glue

As with the cardboard structures, children also enjoy creating three-dimensional works with styrofoam pieces when the workbench is not available. Give the children access to the materials listed here, and let them create either individual or group sculptures.

Children particularly delight in making a group styrofoam structure—a fantasy city or world. Add the names of the "architects" and display the creation in a prominent place.

BOAT BUILDING AND LAUNCHING

Materials you will need

Soft wood for sawing
Spools or dowels for smoke
    stacks and masts
Hammer, saw, and nails
Nonwater-soluble glue
Glue brushes

Containers for glue
Fabric cut into sail shapes
Permanent markers
Pictures of different kinds of
    boats

Talk with the children about boats and show them pictures of different types. Then encourage them to construct their own boats by using any or all of the materials listed here.

When the boats are finished and the glue (if used) is dry, let the children float their boats in the water table, in a baby bathtub, or in a child-sized swimming pool. Some children will enjoy naming their boats and having you print the names on the boats with permanent markers. Children who can print the names themselves need supervision with the permanent markers.

RUBBER BAND DESIGN BOARDS

Materials you will need

Soft wood squares at least 6" × 6"
Nails with large heads
Colored rubber bands
Pencil or marker

Make a sample model for the children to see. (Keep it simple.) Then ask them to mark with a pencil the places where they will hammer in nails. Suggest that they leave ample space between nails so the rubber bands will stretch. Explain that nails will need to go far enough into the wood to withstand the tension created by the placement of the rubber bands. Show the children how they can change their designs by using different colors and different configurations of rubber bands. Both girls and boys find this to be a wonderful toy to take home, and you will find it a creative way to help children learn about shapes.

MUSICAL CLAPPERS OR JINGLE CLOGS

Materials you will need

Soft wood approximately 2″ × 8″ × ¾″
Metal bottle caps
Nails (about 1½ inches long and of two diameters) with large heads

Have each child pound a large nail through several bottle caps to make holes in the centers of the caps, and then remove that nail and replace it with a thinner nail with a head that is larger than the holes. Next, have the child hammer the nail with the caps on it into the piece of wood. Be sure the child leaves room for the bottle caps to move along the nail to clink together and strike the wood. Make sure the nail does not go all the way through the piece of wood.

This instrument will make a nice sound when the child shakes the block or claps it against one hand. Both boys and girls will have fun accompanying a song or recording with these instruments.

MUSICAL SAND BLOCKS

Materials you will need

Soft wood, approximately 4″ × 5″ × ½″
Sandpaper pieces of the same dimensions
Spools or knobs for handles
Nails and screws
White glue

Each child will need two matching blocks, two pieces of sandpaper, two handles, and two screws or nails. Ask each child to nail a spool or screw a knob into the center of each matching block, then put glue on the smooth side of each piece of sandpaper, and press one piece of sticky sandpaper onto the flat surface of each block.

When the glue has dried, each child will be able to make a pleasant sound by rubbing the two sand blocks together. As with the jingle clogs, the children can try out their instruments in a musical group.

LIBRARY CORNER SUGGESTIONS

Since books are an important vehicle for learning and for promoting your goals for gender equity and cooperation, conscientiously leave enough free time in your program activities for children to explore the books in the library corner. In addition to planning your more formal storytime, look for opportunities to read to one or two children or to small groups. If you notice children who are at loose ends or children who seem to be getting overexcited or overwhelmed, offer to read them a book in the library corner. And, if children need a focus during transition times, suggest that they go to the library corner to look at books or listen to books on tape while they wait.

To enhance the library corner, change your books and book displays frequently. Children will often come into the library corner to look at new books you have purchased or borrowed from the public library.

Teach the children how to use audiotapes along with companion books for those times when you or another adult is not free to read to children. As you get to know the children in your group, tape books for specific children. A child who seldom visits the library corner will find it hard to resist coming to this area to listen to your voice reading a book you have taped especially for her or him. If two or more children share a particular concern or experience, tape relevant books. For example, if Gregina, Liam, and Darnell are uneasy about new experiences, they will love listening to stories about the fearful bear in Rosemary Wells's books *Edward in Deep Water* and *Edward's Overwhelming Overnight*, or if Sid and Delia have each recently been to visit their grandmothers, they might enjoy hearing a book such as *Grandma Gets Grumpy* by Anna Grossnickle Hines or *Our Granny* by Margaret Wild. In both examples, the children will benefit from hearing nonstereotypic views of both sexes, and if the children listening represent both sexes, they will be involved in cross-gender interaction.

Children who have taken part in creating a class book or who have written their own books (see the section on art experiences in this chapter) will return to the library corner frequently to see their work. If you put together a photo album of the children in your group and place it in the library corner, girls and boys will return again and again to scrutinize pictures of themselves and their friends. Once children are in the library corner, they often become interested in exploring other books.

Another way to get both genders working together in the library corner is to assign a boy and a girl to be the "librarians of the week." Ask them to see that the books are kept in order and to check for books that need repairs. You can also ask the "librarians" to categorize books on a particular subject (books about bears, families, friendship, or holidays) and to help you arrange new displays. Sometimes you might ask these helpers to choose a book to read at storytime that day. (See Chapter 5 for more on using books with children.)

SAND AND WATER PLAY

Water and sand table activities bring children of both sexes together over and over again. By introducing new activities in the tables, you will increase the interaction of girls and boys. It is important to have a variety of water and sand toys and to change these toys frequently. (See our list of accessories for sand and water play in Chapter 2.)

Having both a sand table and a water table is ideal for planning activities using both substances. However, if you have only one table, you can alternate the use of water and sand in the table. There are many ways to change and enhance water and sand play; a few of our suggestions follow.

COLOR THE WATER/SAND

Add a dollop of poster paint to your water to make brightly colored water—blue one day, green another, and red another. Let the children choose the color and help mix the paint and water. Or mix powdered paint with sand to make colored sand. Again, children will enjoy mixing the sand and the powdered paint.

COLOR EXPERIMENTATION

Set the water table up for color-mixing experiments. Use plastic containers and poster paint or food coloring. Children will be fascinated to see what happens when various colors are mixed together.

DOLL BATHS AND SHAMPOOS

Let the children bathe dolls in the water table. Provide them with shampoo bottles, soap, washcloths, and towels.

FLOAT AND SINK

Fill the water table with objects that will float and/or sink. Have the children experiment with what will make certain objects sink or float.

For example, a floating boat may sink if it is filled with water or with something heavy; a nail that sinks might float if it is cargo in a boat.

BUBBLE PLAY

Add liquid dishwashing detergent to the water in the water table. Give the children bubble pipes, plastic tubes, straws, and containers and let them blow bubbles. Be sure the children understand how to blow air *out* to make bubbles.

CAR WASH

Ask the children to collect small washable toy cars and trucks for a soapy car wash in the water table. Provide towels or rags for drying the vehicles.

WATER TABLE FINGERPAINTING

Using shaving cream, let children fingerpaint in the water table. You can add paint to the shaving cream so children can experiment with making pastels and color mixing. The clean-up is relatively easy.

WATER/SAND WHEELS AND SIEVES

Have a special day when you put out water/sand wheels, sieves, sifters, funnels, tubing, containers, and balance scales for exploration and experimentation in the sand and water tables.

MIXING SAND AND WATER

Let the children experiment with adding water to the sand in the table.

DINOSAUR DAY

Put your dinosaur collection in the sand table for prehistoric play! Of course, you can use other collections as well.

VEHICLE DAY

Dampen the sand in the sand table. Encourage the children to create hills, valleys, and roads for washable vehicles to traverse. Add bridges, trees, and buildings if desired.

HIDDEN OBJECTS

Children love to bury seashells, stones, and other treasures in the sand. They also like to take turns being the ones to hide the objects and the ones to search for them.

SAND TABLE SUBSTITUTES

Instead of sand in the sand table, try using oatmeal, rice, buttons, beads, styrofoam pieces, or sawdust.

SCIENCE EXPLORATIONS

All children, regardless of gender, are curious about the world they live in. Throughout the day, look for opportunities to encourage the children to observe, to wonder, to predict, and to check their assumptions. Make sure you involve girls as often as boys in these investigations. (Since many people still think that science is more appropriately the domain of males than of females, be particularly careful to counteract that myth.)

Let all the children make their own discoveries and formulate their own theories. If a child makes an incorrect prediction, rather than correct the mistake, ask questions that will lead to further exploration and discovery. Give the children ample time for trial and error rather than jumping in with solutions.

Although a science center is a good place to keep scientific equipment and interesting physical and natural things to explore, remember that scientific thinking takes place in all areas of your program. Be sensitive to the child exploring how water goes through a tube or how sand in one side of a bucket balance can tilt the scale. Ask the child what she thinks will happen if she puts a cork in the tube or sand in both buckets of the balance. If a child says his soup is too hot, ask him what he might do to make it cooler. When children separate the crayons from the markers, or put all the blue beads in a pile, recognize that categorization is taking place, and be ready to suggest other categories the children might explore. When the children are cooking, ask them what is changing, what they think will happen next, and how long it will take.

Be alert to opportunities to explore the natural and physical world. If the children are planting seeds in a corner of the play yard and find a worm, take advantage of the discovery to help them observe and examine the worm. Ask how the worm feels on their hands, how it moves, which end is the head, and what they think it eats. If some children are squeamish, respect their feelings, but support any efforts to participate.

As you model your own comfort with "creepy-crawlies," you will be helping children overcome their inhibitions and fears.

Although you will foster everyday scientific observation and thinking as exploration happens naturally in your classroom, we have added some specific activities to stimulate the scientific thinking of both girls and boys.

SCIENCE ACTIVITIES

COLLECTIONS

Materials you will need
Bags with handles for each child

Give each child a bag and go for a walk in the neighborhood or park to collect leaves, stones, cones, chestnuts, and so on. When you return from your walk, let the children explore their finds—describe, compare, sort and classify, count, weigh, or measure them. You can provide the labels for different categories. Other collections, such as shells, animal and dinosaur sets, magnets, and bird nests, lend themselves to similar exploration.

SHADOW PLAY

Materials you will need
Chalk or markers
Roll of brown or white 36-inch sturdy paper

On a sunny day, show children shadows and let them discover how shadows are made and how they change throughout the day. As children make shadows of themselves in various poses, draw around their shadows on the sidewalk with chalk, or outline their shadows on large sheets of paper with a marker. Put the children's names on their shadow drawings.

INDOOR SHADOWS

Materials you will need
White sheet
Floor lamp
Puppets (optional)

Hang a white sheet in the classroom and place a lamp a few feet in front of the sheet. Children will then place their hands and bodies between the light and the sheet to make shadows. As an added feature, you can introduce puppets for the children to use to make shadows and shadow plays.

WIND TOYS

Materials you will need

Paper towel and toilet paper
  rolls
Colored tissue paper
White glue

Glue brushes
Containers for glue
Child-sized scissors

You or the children will cut colored tissue paper into streamers approximately 10 inches long. Each child will then select streamers and glue them to the inside surface of one end of a paper towel roll. When these wind toys are dry, children will want to experiment with them outdoors. They will notice how the wind moves the streamers and how their own motions can create wind to move the streamers. Both girls and boys will be intrigued by this activity as they experiment with wind direction and velocity.

BLOWING BUBBLES OUTDOORS

Materials you will need

1 cup liquid dishwashing
  detergent (we like Dawn)
10 cups water
¼ cup glycerin
Pipe cleaners twisted to form
  bubble wands of various sizes
Plastic rings from a six-pack

Funnels
Rubber jar rings
Paper or styrofoam drinking
  cups with holes in the bottoms
Containers for the bubble
  mixture

Make the soap bubble mixture using detergent, water, and glycerin. Take your materials outdoors and give each child a container of bubble mixture. Let the children make bubbles with the different objects. Children love to watch their bubbles get blown by the wind. Some will chase and pop the bubbles; others will watch to see how far the bubbles will go.

FLYING KITES

Materials you will need

Real kites
Kite string wrapped around a spool or dowel

In our experience the kind of paper kites teachers often help children make do not fly and are easily torn. Try your hand at flying real kites with the children. Go to a large empty field far from power lines. If possible, bring some parents to help get the kites in the air. Once the kites are soaring overhead, all children will love feeling the tug and pull of the wind as they keep the kites airborne.

SNOW AND ICE

Materials you will need

Snow
Water
Buckets
Ice cube trays
Containers of varying sizes

If you live where there is snow, have the children collect it in buckets and put it into the water table where they can play with it. They will see it melt in the warm room and observe changes in form and mass. They may also notice that melted snow results in dirty water. (This observation may help convince children not to eat snow even when it looks clean and white.)

Let the children make ice by pouring water into ice cube trays or containers of varying sizes. Depending on your circumstances and climate, you can place the containers outdoors or in a freezer. Children can observe how water freezes and how long it takes for water in the various containers to freeze. When the water is frozen solid, children can put the ice in the water table, play with it, and see how long it takes to melt. Adding hot water to the ice in the water table will add another dimension to this exploration, as will putting ice cubes in the children's juice.

WEATHER STATION

Materials you will need

Large calendar for the month
Outdoor thermometer
Plastic measuring cup to
    gauge amount of rainfall
Flag or banner to determine
    wind velocity

Pictures of people dressed for
    hot, warm, and cold weather
Symbols for rain, clouds, sun,
    snow, wind, and lightning
Glue stick

Choose two or three children each week (mix up the sexes) to record the weather for the week. This activity becomes boring if it is done by the whole group every day, but children look forward to occasional turns as weather monitors.

Ask the designated weather monitors to observe the temperature, the sky, and the weather conditions every day of the week and record their observations by gluing the appropriate symbols onto the calendar. This cooperative activity helps children develop observation and recording skills and is an easy way to arrange for girls and boys to work together.

DAY/NIGHT SKY PICTURES

Materials you will need

Blue and black poster paint
Easel brushes
White glue
Glue brushes
Containers for paint and glue
Paper plates

Sun, moon, cloud, rainbow,
    and star shapes or stickers
Paper punch
White and grey circles made
    with a paper punch

Before you initiate this activity, ask the children to observe day and night skies and discuss the differences. You can also show pictures of day and night and read books such as *Goodnight Moon* by Margaret Wise Brown, *It Looked Like Spilt Milk* by Charles Shaw, *Time for Bed* by Mem Fox, and *Archie, Follow Me* by Lynne Cherry.

Set up the materials for painting. Give the children paper plates and ask them to decide whether they want to make day or night sky pictures. Children who choose a day sky will paint their plates blue, and those who choose a night sky will paint their plates black. (Of course, some children will want to make both.)

When the paint has dried, the children can glue the appropriate night and day shapes and stickers onto their painted paper plates. They can add tiny grey and white circles to represent rain or snow or they might use a grey wash to represent a cloudy or foggy day if they wish. All the children will make choices and participate in discussion during this activity.

TOUCH AND FEEL BOX

Materials you will need

Sturdy square box (hat box size) with cover
Objects of various shapes and textures
Scarf or safety goggles with black paper inserts to cover lenses

Use this activity to explore with the children their sense of touch. First, prepare the box by cutting a circular hole the size of a child's fist in the cover. Fill the box with objects such as a small toy, a cotton ball, a bottle cap, a comb, a toothbrush, a rubber band, a paper clip, a spool, a dry sponge, a feather, a shell, and a stone. Cover each child's eyes in turn; then ask the child to grasp an object in the box, feel it carefully, and guess what it is before removing it. Both girls and boys will find that recognizing objects by touch alone is challenging and often funny.

TASTE AND SNIFF PARTY

Materials you will need

Small containers
3 trays
Sweet, salty, sour, and spicy things to taste
Pungent things to smell

Collect examples of things that have a distinct aroma and/or taste such as sugar, salt, vinegar, vanilla, cinnamon, honey, chocolate chips, cocoa powder, coffee beans, flowers, perfume, an onion, a garlic clove, a lemon, a pine needle cluster, a sachet, and a bar of scented soap. Talk with the children about the senses of smell and taste. (You will need to be certain that no children are allergic to these specimens. Also, you can use this activity to remind children that some substances are unsafe to smell or taste.)

Then ask the children to categorize the objects into three sets: things to taste, things to smell, and things to both smell and taste. The objects should then be placed on the appropriate trays. Let the children taste and/or smell the samples. If you call this activity a taste and sniff party and include chocolate chips to taste, you are sure to have representatives of each gender involved.

SOUND CYLINDERS

Materials you will need

Empty and clean frozen juice
  containers with lids
Masking tape
Construction or contact paper
  (one color only) cut to fit
  around the containers

Transparent tape
Objects and materials to make
  sounds

Use this activity to focus on the sense of hearing and children's auditory perception. Collect objects and materials such as beans, rice, marbles, sand, bells, nails or screws, buttons, bottle caps, toothpicks, and styrofoam pieces.

Ask the children to fill the juice containers about ⅓ full with each sound maker, and tape the lids on tightly with masking tape. Help the children cover the cans with construction or contact paper. Children of both sexes will like the challenge of trying to identify the various sounds as they shake the cylinders.

For an added challenge, fill two containers with the same sound makers. Mix up all the sound cylinders, and ask the children to make pairs of the ones that sound alike.

SPYGLASSES

Materials you will need

Toilet paper and paper towel rolls
Red, blue, and yellow cellophane
Black construction paper
Rubber bands
Pins

Use this activity to focus on each child's sense of sight. Cut cellophane into small squares (approximately 4" × 4"). Show the children how to place the cellophane square over the end of the tube and secure it with a rubber band. Children will be intrigued by seeing a red, blue, or yellow world through their spyglasses. To make more colors, the children can put two pieces of cellophane together on each tube. For another variation, let the children prick tiny holes in black construction paper, cover the tubes, and look for "stars."

ANIMAL ENVIRONMENTS GAME

Materials you will need

Trays with pictures representing earth, sky, and water
Small pictures of animals
Cardboard

Use pictures of animals from old matching games, magazines, and wildlife stickers, and mount them on cardboard. Have several pictures of the same animal.

Begin this game by asking children if they recognize any of the animals and know where they might be able to see these animals in the wild. Then have the children place the animal cards on the appropriate earth, sky, and water trays. The children will problem solve together as they decide where to find different animals. As they determine that many animals can be found in more than one place, they can put the animal cards on one or more trays.

LIFE CYCLES

Bring in a caterpillar, place it in a see-through container with air holes, and add the leaves it eats and a branch. Children will delight in seeing the caterpillar spin a cocoon and turn into a moth, or seeing a caterpillar form a chrysalis and become a butterfly. Record the events as they take place. Let the butterfly or moth fly away outdoors on a nice day. (If you cannot find your own caterpillars, you can order kits called Butterfly Gardens from catalogs of early childhood materials. See the resources listed at the end of Chapter 2.)

In the spring, collect polliwog eggs from a pond or swamp and bring them into your classroom. Children will be fascinated to watch the eggs become polliwogs and the polliwogs develop into tiny frogs. Chart the process with the children. At the end of the project, return the frogs to their original home.

If you have a humane way of providing for the offspring, consider incubating chicken or duck eggs. Children of both sexes will be intensely involved as they record the number of days the eggs must incubate and as they eventually see the chicks or ducklings crack open their shells. And, of course, they will be fascinated by the growth and development of these small birds.

ANIMAL STUDY

Consider having a classroom pet such as a guinea pig, a rabbit, or a hamster. If your situation makes it difficult to have a live-in pet, try to borrow pets from the children's families, the local humane society, or a pet shop. Help the children discover how much each animal weighs, what food it eats, and how to care for it. Children of both sexes will work together as they touch, describe, and observe the pets.

Read both fiction and nonfiction books about pets and discuss how make-believe and real animals differ. In addition, some children may want to write stories about pets.

PLANT STUDY

Children are fascinated by growing and changing plant life. What child, of either sex, can resist watching a tiny seed sprout and grow roots in a plastic bag or baby food jar, or watching a plant develop from a seed she or he has placed in soil? Children like to plant carrot tops and sprout potato plants and experiment with planting grapefruit, avocado, pumpkin, and bean seeds.

If your setting permits, consider planting an outdoor garden with the children and decorating the room with the flowers or eating the vegetables they grow. If this is impractical, seeds planted in a plastic dish pan or storage box can become an indoor mini-garden.

Both boys and girls will enjoy experimenting with plants. For example, to show how plants "drink" water, place white flowers (such as carnations) in water colored with food coloring and let the children see the flowers change color. Also, to show that plants need sun and water, set up a control experiment with plants receiving both sun and water, only water or sun, and no water and sun.

PEOPLE WATCHING

Use opportunities that arise spontaneously to help children observe how human beings feel, behave, grow, and change. For example, encourage the children to observe babies and siblings and other members of their families and others in their classroom to become aware of their own and others' attributes, similarities and differences, and feelings and behavior. Encourage observation and hypothesizing skills by asking a child how she decided that the baby Mahal's mother has in her arms is a girl, or asking a child how he thinks a friend feels about being excluded from play and what he thinks might solve the problem.

COOKING PROJECTS

Unfortunately, cooking continues to be thought of by many people as the province of females; however, both males and females make excellent cooks. To combat the stereotype that only females cook, provide frequent opportunities for gender-inclusive cooking activities in your classroom. You can help both girls and boys become interested in cooking and learn to cooperate as they prepare food and follow recipes. Children like to measure, pour, and mix ingredients and, of course, eat the results of their efforts.

Some of the simplest cooking projects are as much fun as the more elaborate ones and offer as many opportunities for observation, discussion, and cooperation. Washing, peeling, and slicing fruits and vegetables and serving them with a simple dip, or preparing jello and instant pudding with fruit can be as satisfying and instructive as making cookies or pizza.

With many cooking activities, you must have careful adult supervision. You and/or other adults will need to teach the children the proper hygiene for cooking and how to use kitchen tools, utensils, and equipment. This is a perfect opportunity to ask a father or male relative to assist with the cooking project. (One example can be worth a thousand words!)

For many cooking activities you can use an electric fry pan, an electric cooking pot, a hot plate, or a toaster oven instead of a stove. If possible, have a collection of measuring cups and spoons, hot pads and pot holders, mixing bowls, and basic utensils readily available in your setting.

As you plan cooking experiences for the children, keep in mind that children should be eating nutritious as well as delicious foods. Avoid overly fatty and sweet foods. However, we make an exception with birthdays; no boy or girl can resist helping create his or her own special birthday cupcakes.

You will undoubtedly have many favorite recipes to use with the children. In addition, you may wish to try some of ours that have been particularly popular with both genders. We recommend that you make a picture recipe of any cooking activity and include the names of the chefs. You may also wish to share recipes with parents through a bulletin board or newsletter.

FOOD PREPARATION AND COOKING ACTIVITIES

ANTS ON A LOG

Materials you will need

Paring knives
Popsicle sticks or butter knives
Cutting boards
Celery

Peanut butter
Raisins
Tray

You or another adult will help the children wash the celery and cut it into "logs" with a paring knife. Then the children will use popsicle sticks or butter knives to spread peanut butter into the crevices of their celery logs. They will add raisins to the peanut butter to represent the ants on the logs. Both boys and girls love the humor in this activity and get a big bang out of pretending to eat ants!

EGG BOATS

Materials you will need

Eggs
Mayonnaise
Paprika
Triangular pieces of paper
   approximately 3″ × 3″ × 4 ½″
Large toothpicks
Transparent tape

Pot with lid
Hot plate
Forks for mashing
Table or paring knives
Mixing bowl
Paper plates with children's
   names

First, ask the children to tape a triangular "sail" to each of their two toothpicks. Then, help each child gently place an egg in a cooking pot. Next, let the children pour cold water in the pot to cover the eggs. Put the lid on the pot, put the pot on the hot plate at medium heat, and bring the water to a boil. Turn off the heat and let the eggs sit in the hot water for 5 minutes or until hard. You will pour the hot water off the eggs, and let the children pour cold water over the eggs until the eggs are cool enough to handle.

Children will then peel their hard-boiled eggs, cut the eggs in half lengthwise and remove the yolks. Then they will place the yolks in a mixing bowl with a few dollops of mayonnaise. Both girls and boys will enjoy using forks to mash up the yokes with the mayonnaise. Each child will put a scoop of this mixture back into the egg halves, sprinkle with paprika if desired, and put a toothpick mast and sail in place. The "boats" can be eaten immediately or stored in the refrigerator for later.

PEAR BOATS

For a variation on the egg boats, make pear boats by slicing pears in half lengthwise, removing stems and cores, and filling the halves with flavored yogurt or cottage cheese sprinkled with cinnamon.

BUTTERFLIES

Materials you will need
Canned pineapple slices
Green peppers
Table knives
Cutting boards
Paper plates with children's names

Let the children cut pineapple slices into halves to represent butterfly wings. Then ask them to wash the peppers, remove the cores, and cut them into thin strips for "antennae." Each child then assembles a "butterfly" on a paper plate to make an appealing snack or desert.

BUTTER

Materials you will need
Plastic see-through jar with lid
Half-pint heavy cream
Popsicle sticks or butter knives
Bread
Toaster

Ask a child to pour the cream into the jar. Screw the lid on tightly. Next, let the children take turns shaking the jar until butter is formed.

When the butter is made, let the children make toast and use popsicle sticks or butter knives to spread their butter on the warm toast. Boys who avoid cooking activities find this one hard to resist!

OATMEAL PANCAKES

Materials you will need

I cup flour
1 cup quick-cooking oats
2 cups milk
2 Tbsp. vinegar
2 Tbsp. sugar
2 tsp. baking powder
I tsp. baking soda
2 eggs
Butter, syrup, honey, powdered
   sugar, and jelly

Mixing bowl
Measuring cups and spoons
Eggbeater or whisk
Electric griddle or electric
   fry pan
Pancake turner
Paper plates

Help the children measure all the dry ingredients into the mixing bowl. Next, have a child add vinegar to the milk to make sour milk. Let other children pour the milk and break the eggs into the bowl with the dry ingredients. All the children can mix the batter with the beater or whisk. You will heat the griddle or fry pan to the pancake setting and grease the pan lightly. Each child will then have a turn to pour ¼ cup of batter onto the griddle and to flip the pancake when it is bubbly and browning around the edges. When their pancakes are ready, let the children have their choice of toppings. Few children of either sex will want to miss out on this activity.

CARROT-RAISIN SALAD

Materials you will need

Carrots
Raisins
Mayonnaise
Pineapple
Mixing bowl

Mixing spoon
Vegetable peeler
Table knives
Grater

Let the children wash, peel, and grate the carrots. Supervise the peeling and grating carefully. (Try using fine, medium, and coarse graters so the children can see the differences.) The children will then cut up the pineapple into small pieces and take turns adding pineapple, raisins, and a few dollops of mayonnaise to the carrots. Mix until well blended. Eat immediately or store in the refrigerator for later.

WALDORF SALAD

Materials you will need

Apples	Paring knives
Celery	Cutting boards
Finely chopped walnuts (optional)	Apple corer (optional)
	Mixing bowl
Raisins (optional)	Spoons for mixing
Mayonnaise	

The children will wash, core, and cut the apples into small pieces. (If you have an apple corer, the children will enjoy using this tool.) When the apples are ready, have the children wash and cut the ends off the celery before cutting it crosswise into small pieces. As always, carefully supervise those children using knives. Finally, mix the apples, celery, walnuts, raisins, and a few dollops of mayonnaise together in a mixing bowl. Eat immediately or store in the refrigerator until later.

SOFT PRETZELS

Materials you will need

1 Tbsp. yeast	Mixing bowls
½ cup warm water	Measuring cups and spoons
1 tsp. honey	Whisk or fork
I tsp. salt	Cookie sheet(s)
1 ⅓ cups flour	Pastry brush
1 egg	Pot holders

You will need access to an oven for this activity. Preheat the oven to 425 degrees. Have the children dissolve the yeast in the water in a large mixing bowl and then add honey, salt, and flour. Ask a child to break the egg into a small bowl and beat it thoroughly with a whisk or fork and set it aside.

Let the children knead the pretzel dough. When the dough is ready, give each child a small piece to form into a snake, a shape, or a letter. The children then brush their pretzels with egg mixture, sprinkle them lightly with salt, and place them on a cookie sheet. You will place the cookie sheet(s) in the preheated oven and bake the pretzels for about 10 minutes.

Even children who do not often choose cooking activities will come to the table to make pretzels. Girls and boys will talk together about the letters or shapes they are making.

YOGURT DESSERT

Materials you will need

Bananas
Applesauce
Vanilla yogurt
Forks

Spoons
Dessert dishes
Measuring cups

Using a fork, each child will mash up half a banana in his or her dish and then add ¼ cup of applesauce and ¼ cup of yogurt to the banana and mix it up. The children can eat this snack immediately or store it in the refrigerator for later.

POPCORN BLIZZARD

Materials you will need

Popping corn
Air corn popper
Clean sheet (a plain, colored sheet works best)
Extension cord

We recommend this activity for children age 6 and over, since younger children can choke on popcorn. Pour the proper amount of popcorn kernels in the air popcorn maker. Have children help spread the clean sheet on the floor, being careful not to step on it. Ask the children to sit around the edges of the sheet. You will place the corn popper in the middle of the sheet and plug it into an outlet. (If necessary, use an extension cord.) Leave the top off the corn popper, and let the popcorn pop out of the machine onto the sheet. Children find this activity exciting and love to grab for the popcorn that falls near them. You can collect the extra popcorn that falls in the center to share with those children who would like more.

JUICE POPSICLES

Materials you will need

Frozen concentrated juice
Small (5-ounce) paper cups
Popsicle sticks
Cardboard circles to fit over
   cups

Plastic juice pitcher
Long slotted spoon
Tray

Let the children mix the frozen juice and water following instructions on the frozen juice container. Help each child put a popsicle stick through the middle of a cardboard circle. Pour the juice into the cup and tell each child to place the circle with the stick in it on top of the cup. Put all the cups on a tray to go into the freezer. If you are planning to eat these the next day, be sure to have children make extras for friends who are absent.

PIZZA

Materials you will need

Pizza dough mix or frozen pizza
   dough
Pizza sauce
Mozzarella cheese
Green and yellow peppers
Mushrooms
Broccoli florets
Mixing bowls

Pizza pan(s)
Pizza cutter
Cooking spoons
Paring knives
Grater
Pastry brush
Cutting boards
Pot holders

You will need an oven for this activity. Preheat the oven according to the instructions on the package of pizza dough. Let the children prepare the pizza dough following the recipe on the package, and then help them spread the dough into the pizza pan(s). The children then pour the sauce over the dough and spread it around evenly with a pastry brush. Other children can wash and prepare the vegetables and shred the cheese. Next, the children will spread the cheese evenly on top of the pizza and decorate the pizza with the vegetables. Bake the pizza according to the package directions. This activity is a sure winner with children and is particularly popular with the Ninja Turtle set.

MACARONI AND CHEESE

Materials you will need

Large kettle
Medium pot
Colander
Casserole dish(es)
Grater
Mixing spoons
2 hot plates
5 quarts water

1 ½ pounds macaroni
1 pound cheddar cheese
5 cups milk
8 Tbsp. flour
8 Tbsp. butter
Bread crumbs (optional)
Pot holders

You will need access to an oven for this activity. Preheat the oven to 375 degrees. Let the children fill a large kettle with warm water. You or another adult will put the water on a hot plate and keep a constant eye on the boiling water and any children who are nearby. Add the macaroni and cook according to the package instructions. Children like to watch the water come to a boil and compare the size and consistency of the macaroni at various stages in the cooking. Carefully drain the cooked macaroni into the colander.

While the water is boiling and the macaroni is cooking, help the children prepare the cheese sauce. Let some of the children grate the cheese, while others warm the butter in the medium pot on the hot plate. When the butter is melted, help the children measure, add, and stir in the flour. Then have them measure and slowly stir in the milk. Next, have the children gradually add the grated cheese and stir the mixture continually until it thickens.

Let the children grease the casserole dish(es) and spoon the macaroni into the casserole(s). You will pour the hot cheese sauce over the macaroni. Ask the children to stir the mixture. Add bread crumbs if desired. Put the casserole(s) in the preheated oven for about 30 minutes.

Preparing this recipe will involve young cooks in a sustained activity with many steps. Children will observe dramatic changes as the ingredients change form, color, texture, size, and consistency. When you help them write up this recipe, encourage both boys and girls to comment on these changes and to share their observations with other children in the group.

MASHED POTATOES

Materials you will need

Hot plate	12 medium potatoes
Vegetable peelers	1 cup milk
Paring knives	4 Tbsp. butter
Large kettle	Pot holders
Large bowl	Hot pad
Potato masher(s)	

Help the children peel and cut up the potatoes. When the potatoes are ready, have the children put them in the kettle and add water to cover. Boil until soft. (You will need an adult next to the kettle to supervise the children carefully as they observe the water change from warm to boiling and the potatoes become softer.)

Put the cooked potatoes into a large bowl. Let the children take turns mashing the potatoes and adding the milk and butter as they work. Children relish this activity as an outlet for their abundant energy.

Additional Ideas to Attract Both Sexes to Cooking Activities

FRESH ORANGE JUICE

Children love to cut and squeeze oranges to make delicious juice. You can use a variety of juice makers, from a simple hand juicer to an electric machine.

MILKSHAKES

Both boys and girls will love to make and drink milkshakes they blend themselves. Using an electric blender, let the children blend milk and bananas or strawberries, milk and dollops of frozen orange juice, or milk and ice cream.

CINNAMON TOAST

Let the children make toast, butter it, and sprinkle cinnamon sugar on the top. The children can mix their own cinnamon sugar.

TRAIL MIX

Have the children mix several varieties of cereal (such as, Chex, Cheerios, and Kix) with raisins, broken pretzels, cut-up dried apricots, dried banana pieces, and so on, for a tasty snack.

SCRAMBLED EGGS

Set up an electric fry pan. Invite each child to break an egg or two into a bowl, add a bit of milk, and beat the mixture. Then let each child scramble his or her eggs in the frying pan. Children who cook their own eggs are likely to eat them!

FRUIT OR VEGETABLE SALADS

Let the children cut up fruits or vegetables to make salads, choosing which fruits or vegetables to put in their own dishes. Some children will like yogurt or salad dressing toppings.

APPLESAUCE

This standard favorite is still worth doing! If you have an apple corer/peeler machine, boys and girls will come to this activity in droves. Children also like using a food mill to make cooked apples into sauce. As an alternative to cooked applesauce, put cut-up pieces of apple (skins on) into the blender. The red from the skins makes this a colorful treat.

PACKAGED FOODS

For a simple, but enjoyable, cooking activity, try making packaged foods such as puddings, jellos, cornbread, muffins, or biscuits with children.

HOLIDAY THOUGHTS

You can provide children with opportunities to gain a broader understanding and acceptance of other cultures and customs through observing different holidays. As children are introduced to other cultures through friendships, stories, music, and holiday celebrations, they will begin to appreciate diversity and to develop respect for people of different beliefs and backgrounds.

At the same time, we realize that for religious reasons some families oppose celebrating all holidays, and others are troubled by holiday celebrations that are outgrowths of a religious tradition different from their own. In addition, many schools have established policies regarding holidays. You will need to tailor your holiday activities to fit your particular program.

If your situation allows for some choice, we suggest you start by talking with the parents in your program about what holidays their families celebrate, their feelings regarding holiday celebrations and activities, and their ideas about how you and other staff members might help counteract myths and stereotypes about their cultures. Check with parents and staff members of a given culture to be sure that information you share with children about their holidays is accurate and free of cultural bias.

We like to ask parents (or other staff members) to share a special holiday tradition with the group. An activity a parent shares—playing a game with dreidels, singing a Solstice chant, sharing a Kwanzaa story, telling about the Chinese New Year, or coloring Easter eggs—can have special meaning for children who share the custom and can introduce other children to the rituals of different cultures.

Holiday activities can be enriching and fun for both girls and boys, and, with careful planning, you can enhance the enjoyment of these special days. We urge restraint, however, since children often become too excited and overstimulated by holiday activities and diverted from their own spontaneous and self-directed play.

Furthermore, it is important that, whatever holiday activities you plan, the children can decide whether or not to participate. We have seen too many reluctant children (more often boys) being pressured into making a pumpkin picture, a Valentine card, or a present for their parents at holiday time.

Remember that children can not be coerced to be generous. In your parent meetings, you may be able to help parents understand that a spontaneous gift of a painting or a clay figure proudly presented on an ordinary day contains the real spirit of giving. (If you feel you must mark a holiday with a gift, you can save earlier art work or take snapshots of the children participating in various activities throughout the year to use for holiday presents.)

In the event that you decide *not* to celebrate holidays, you can use virtually any holiday activity we include by featuring it as either a seasonal activity, a friendship activity, or a history lesson. As always, we have chosen activities that are popular with both genders.

HALLOWEEN/FALL ACTIVITIES

Halloween can be frightening for some young children, and some families object to celebrating Halloween. We urge you to think carefully before donning a witch costume or bringing in scary Halloween pictures. In this section, we have included some activities that are fun, but not frightening, and could easily be fall activities rather than ones associated directly with Halloween.

A TRIP TO A PUMPKIN PATCH (OR A FARM MARKET)

Materials you will need

Bags with handles (optional)
Permanent marker
Scales
Measuring tape(s)

This can be a successful trip if you have a pumpkin patch or a farm market nearby and enough adults to help. Each child can pick a pumpkin from the vine at the farm or choose one to buy from a vendor at the market. Help the children choose pumpkins they can carry. To avoid later mix-ups, write the children's names on the bottoms of their pumpkins using a permanent marker.

When you return to your classroom, the children will wash their pumpkins in the water table or sink and dry and polish them. Then let the children weigh and measure their pumpkins and record the weights and measurements on a class chart.

COOKING WITH PUMPKIN

Materials you will need

Pumpkins
Hot plate
Cooking pot
Steamer

Potato mashers
Paring knives
Fork

The children will wash the pumpkins and weigh and measure them. Next, you will peel and cut up the pumpkins. Have the children place the pieces of pumpkin in the steamer and pot, add a small amount of water, and cook the pumpkin on the hot plate until the pieces are soft. Let the children poke the pumpkin with a fork at various stages of the cooking to determine how soft the pumpkin is. When the pumpkin meat is cool, allow the children to mash it up. Some children will like sampling the cooked pumpkin as a vegetable. Others will enjoy using the mashed pumpkin to help make pumpkin bread, pumpkin cookies, or pumpkin pie.

Make a picture chart of the project from start to finish, including the recipe and the names of the "chefs." Share the finished product with all the children.

MAKING A SCARECROW

Materials you will need

Old jeans
Flannel shirt
Straw hat
Work boots
Small pillow with a plain white
  or skin-colored pillow case

Rags, towels, straw, and
  newspapers for stuffing
Paper, paste, and tape

Talk with the children about the growing season and explain the role of the scarecrow in protecting crops and in helping to ensure a bountiful harvest. Then let the children work together stuffing the clothing with rags, towels, straw, and paper and assembling the parts to create a scarecrow. The children can tape or paste paper features on the pillow case to make a face. (This activity can also take place in the spring during planting season.)

CATCHING APPLES

Materials you will need

Apples (a variety of colors if possible)
Water table or tubs
Clothesline and string

Put apples in clean water in the water table or in tubs, and/or hang apples on strings from a clothesline. Children of both sexes will find trying to catch an apple using only their teeth (no hands, please!) an irresistible challenge. (If you can, try to combine this activity with a trip to an apple orchard or a farm market.)

APPLESAUCE

Fall is also a good time to make applesauce. (See our applesauce suggestions on page 81 in the Cooking Projects section of this chapter.)

THANKSGIVING/HARVEST TIME ACTIVITIES

Thanksgiving often has little meaning for children. We like to stress that it is a time for families to get together to share a good time and special foods in a loving atmosphere. To help children understand the idea of being thankful, you can talk with them about what they need to live and who makes them feel special and loved. Then try asking them to finish the sentence, "I'm glad I have . . . " and see what they come up with.

Avoid engaging in the inaccurate and stereotypical Pilgrim and Indian activities (for example, making Pilgrim hats and Indian head-dresses) all too common in early childhood settings. If you choose to teach the story of the first Thanksgiving, be sure you have an accurate account of the event and make children aware of the differences between past and present Native American cultures. We urge you to read the several articles in *Young Children, 47*(6) (1992) that suggest new ways to help children learn about Native Americans.

We have included two activities for girls and boys that relate to the season as well as to the Thanksgiving holiday.

CRANBERRY SAUCE

Materials you will need

1 pound fresh cranberries	Cooking spoon
2 cups sugar	Baby food jars
2 cups water	Teaspoons
Hot plate	Butter knives or popsicle sticks
Large saucepan	Crackers

If your group is larger than 12 children, you may need to double this recipe. After the children have washed the cranberries, let each child have one to examine. Then help the children measure the water and pour it into the saucepan. Next, have them add the sugar and cranberries. Bring the mixture to a boil, change the setting to simmer, stir occasionally, and wait for the cranberries to pop!

Cool the sauce and then let each child fill a baby food jar with the sauce to take home. The remaining cranberry sauce can be spread on crackers for a snack.

DRIED WEED ARRANGEMENTS

Materials you will need

Dried weeds (such as Queen Anne's Lace, empty milkweed pods, thistles, and various grasses)
Clay or playdough
Sturdy paper plates (approximately 5-inch diameter)
Scissors

You will collect the weeds and cut them into manageable lengths. Let each child form a ball of clay or playdough and press it down onto a paper plate. Then ask each child to choose dried weeds to stick into the base to form an arrangement. Let the clay or dough dry. Both boys and girls are impressed with these attractive decorations or centerpieces.

HANUKKAH/SOLSTICE/CHRISTMAS/KWANZAA/WINTER ACTIVITIES

We like to preserve a relaxed atmosphere and avoid overstimulation during these particular holidays. Both genders become overexcited when there is too much emphasis on a holiday that involves gifts, parties, and related activities. Have some activities available if you like, but be sure that children can choose to build with blocks or play with clay rather than making Hanukkah or Solstice presents, Christmas decorations, or Kwanzaa foods.

However low-key you decide to be, do remember that these holidays are times of celebrating special traditions and can broaden children's understanding of cultural commonalties and differences. Often, parents will share something special from their family traditions, and you can read books, sing songs, and play games related to each holiday.

You will not have trouble finding activities for these holidays, but you may have trouble deciding which few to choose. We have included a few of our favorites that engage both genders and that can stand on their own without reference to a specific holiday.

FINGERPAINTING PRINTS

Materials you will need

Red or green fingerpaint for Christmas and Kwanzaa
Blue and white fingerpaint for Hanukkah
Green fingerpaint for Solstice
Large sheets of white, red, green, and blue construction paper

If you wish to relate this activity to specific holidays, you may use the colors that represent these holidays. Let the children select a color of fingerpaint, then invite them to fingerpaint on large surfaces such as table tops, cookie sheets, or cafeteria trays.

When the children have finished their paintings, tell them to wash and dry their hands. Then place large sheets of construction paper of contrasting colors on the paintings, and let the children rub their papers with their hands. Lift the papers to show the children prints of their work. The prints—dried, mounted, and/or laminated—make attractive gifts.

PINE CONE DECORATIONS

Materials you will need

Pine cones
Pine branches
White glue
White poster paint
Containers for paint mixture

Table salt
Paintbrushes
Salt shakers (optional)
Newspaper or styrofoam trays

You will mix equal parts of white glue and white paint, and thin the mixture with water. Spread out newspaper or give each child a styrofoam tray. Let the children paint their pine cones with the sticky paint and sprinkle the painted cones with salt. When dry, the pine cones will glitter. Lay the pine cones on pine branches for an attractive winter decoration.

PINE BRANCH PAINTING

Materials you will need

Small pine branches
Poster paints of holiday colors
Cookie trays or styrofoam trays
Construction paper
Newspaper

Begin by covering the tables with newspaper for easy clean-up. After you pour the paint into the trays, invite the children to paint with the pine branches on construction paper. Both boys and girls enjoy using an unusual brush and seeing the resulting designs.

COOKIE CUTTER DECORATIONS

Materials you will need

Seasonal and/or holiday cutters
2 cups baking soda (1-pound box)
1¼ cups water
1 cup cornstarch
Flour
Hot plate
Saucepan

Cooking spoon
Plate
Dish towel
Wax paper
Rolling pins (cylinder blocks can substitute)
Toothpicks
Poster paints
String or yarn

Have the children combine and mix the baking soda, water, and cornstarch in the saucepan. Set the pan on the hot plate at medium heat. Children will take turns stirring until the mixture comes to a low boil, and continue stirring until a dough-like consistency is reached. Turn the dough out onto a plate, cover with a damp dish towel, and refrigerate for about 30 minutes.

When the dough is cool, flour the rolling pins and the wax paper. Give each child a piece of dough to knead and roll out to a ¼-inch thickness on a piece of wax paper. Let the children choose which cutters to flour and use to cut out their ornaments. They will make a hole in the top of each of their ornaments.

Leave the ornaments on the wax paper to dry for three or more days, and then let the children paint them. When the paint is dry, help the children thread string or yarn through the holes for hangers.

MACARONI NECKLACES

Materials you will need

Macaroni of different shapes
Food coloring
Spoons (slotted spoons work well)

Paper towels
Yarn
Masking tape

Let the children color the macaroni by dipping it in the food coloring, using holiday colors if they wish. Remove the macaroni using spoons, and dry it thoroughly before having the children string it on colored yarn. Make a "needle" by taping one end of the yarn, and tie a knot around a piece of macaroni at the other end. When the necklace is finished, tie a final knot. Make sure the necklace is long enough to go over the child's head!

MARTIN LUTHER KING, JR.'S BIRTHDAY/ HISTORY LESSON ACTIVITIES

We like to introduce the children to Martin Luther King, Jr.—his life and message—early in the school year when the issues of friendship, cooperation, and inclusion first emerge. If you read and discuss books such as *Martin Luther King, Jr.: A Biography for Young Children* by Carol Hilgartner Schlank and Barbara Metzger, *Happy Birthday, Martin Luther King* by Jean Marzollo, and *My Dream of Martin Luther King* by Faith Ringgold with the children early in the year, then you can refer to Dr. King's beliefs whenever children say things such as, "No girls/boys allowed" or "You can't play." A simple question from you, such as, "How would Martin Luther King feel about that?" can help children think about and change their behavior.

Martin Luther King's struggles for equality, freedom, and nonviolence are important for all children to learn about. In January, you may wish to try the following activities to highlight this great man's ideas.

ONE-WORLD MURAL

Materials you will need

Pictures of people's faces   Glue brushes
  representing both sexes,   Containers for the glue
  different ages, and cultures   Butcher paper
White glue

Select and cut out pictures of interesting faces representing the wide variety of people in the world. Search for pictures of real-life people, not models. And be sure to use as many pictures of girls and women as you do of boys and men.

Spread out the face pictures and discuss and appreciate individual differences with the children. Then let the children choose some face pictures to glue on the butcher paper. Hang the resulting mural in a prominent spot to highlight its one-world message.

Additional Suggestions

MARTIN LUTHER KING BIRTHDAY PARTY

Have a birthday party in Dr. King's memory. Make cupcakes and sing *Happy Birthday* to him. Have the children talk about Dr. King's life and his beliefs.

FREEDOM MARCH

Explain how people marched to show their support of Martin Luther King's ideas. Teach the children the song *We Shall Overcome* and let them reenact a freedom march.

THE ROSA PARKS STORY

Tell the children the story of Rosa Parks, using pictures and books about this woman activist. We like the book she wrote, entitled *Rosa Parks: Mother to a Movement*. Suggest that the children make a "bus" using chairs and/or hollow blocks and help them act out the story.

MLK FOOD

Involve African American parents in helping children make different foods Martin Luther King might have eaten when he was their age: cornbread, collard greens, black-eyed peas, fried okra, and sweet potato pie.

VALENTINE'S DAY/LOVE AND FRIENDSHIP ACTIVITIES

This holiday provides an opportunity for children and adults to express love and friendship in a tangible way. You may wish to celebrate this holiday by letting children make cards for family members or by having a few activities and a simple party. If you do not celebrate Valentine's Day, you can let children send "love letters" home, joining the activity with a trip to the mailbox or post office.

If you decide to have a valentine box and/or exchange, we suggest that you tell the parents how many children are in your group and/or provide a class list for the children to take home. You will want to make sure that every child receives cards and has a turn to act as the mail carrier. Older "mail carriers" can practice reading as they deliver cards.

We have included several activities that children of both genders enjoy as either Valentine or love and friendship activities.

SPONGE DESIGN CARDS

Materials you will need

Sponges
Scissors
Poster paints
Styrofoam trays
Red, pink, and white construction paper

In advance, you will cut heart-shaped sponges of different sizes for this activity. (Wet sponges are much easier to cut.) You will fill the trays with poster paints of different colors, such as red, white, lavender, and pink. Let the children put the sponges in the paint and print with them on the paper. When the pictures are dry, ask the children to fold their papers and either dictate or write a message for their cards.

SURPRISE CARDS

Materials you will need

Poster paints
Red, pink, and white construction paper
Child-sized scissors
Styrofoam trays
Teaspoons

Fold the construction paper in half and draw a line to make half a heart. Children who want to cut out their own cards can follow your lines. Ask the children to unfold their paper hearts and place dollops of paint inside. Then instruct them to close the hearts and rub their hands over their folded papers. Children enjoy opening the cards and seeing the different designs. When the paintings are dry, some children may wish to dictate or write messages and sign their names on their cards.

Additional Activities

TRADITIONAL VALENTINES

Gather lace, silk, satin, ribbons, and doilies for children to glue onto heart shapes. If you bring in some Valentine stickers to add to the collection, boys will often join this activity.

HEART-SHAPED TREATS

Using the recipes on the box, help the children make red jello to put in a heart-shaped mold or make finger jello to cut into heart shapes with cookie cutters. You can also make and decorate heart-shaped cookies with the children.

FRIENDSHIP PLAYDOUGH

Make red or pink playdough with the children, then let them loose with rolling pins and heart-shaped cookie cutters.

WOMEN'S HISTORY MONTH/HISTORY LESSONS

Although we like to emphasize the achievements of women throughout the school year, we urge you to take advantage of Women's History Month to educate children and parents about great women in history who challenged gender stereotypes to accomplish their aims. Display pictures and books about courageous and strong women such as Susan B. Anthony, Clara Barton, Elizabeth Blackwell, Mary McLeod Bethune, Rachel Carson, Emily Dickinson, Juliette Low, Elizabeth Cady Stanton, Sojourner Truth, Harriet Tubman, and Ida B. Wells. Consider activities to highlight women's accomplishments that are appropriate for the developmental level of the children you teach. For example, you might help older children dramatize the Harriet Tubman story, reenact the struggle of women's suffrage, or make a mural using pictures of women who have made or are currently making a difference.

EASTER/PASSOVER/SPRING ACTIVITIES

Give children opportunities to talk about their special holidays and/or invite parents in to share family traditions with the children. One parent might dye Easter eggs with the children, another might prepare a Seder platter, and another might share a spring ritual.

We like to focus on activities that celebrate the return of spring. The activities we include are particularly interesting to both boys and girls.

GROW AND CUT GRASS

Materials you will need

Grass seed
Potting soil and earth
Paper cups, small milk cartons, or small starter pots
Spoons
Child-sized scissors

Have the children mix the potting soil and earth. Then let each child fill a pot with the mixture, sprinkle grass seed on top, and add a thin layer of soil before watering the seeds and placing the pot in the sun. Both girls and boys will love watching their grass grow and trimming it with scissors when it gets long. With enough water and sunlight, the grass will continue to grow and need "mowing" for a long time!

BULB PLANTING

Materials you will need

Tulip, narcissus, hyacinth, amaryllis, and/or other bulbs
Containers
Small stones or pebbles or soil

Before spring arrives, you will show the children how to plant bulbs in containers by surrounding each bulb (pointed end up and uncovered) with pebbles or soil to hold it in place. The children will pour water over the pebbles to keep the roots watered. You and the children will observe and record changes in the growth of the flowers. Both boys and girls feel rewarded when the flowers finally bloom.

MUSIC AND MOVEMENT

To interest children of both genders in music and movement, prominently display your audiotapes and records (or, if you are concerned about damage to the actual tapes or records, use pictures of the inserts and jackets). Children will often ask to hear a recording that has an attractive or familiar cover.

We like to use earphones so that one or more children can listen to a recording without being interrupted or intrusive. It is also important to play music in response to a request or as an enhancement to an activity, such as fingerpainting to waltz music or dancing at a pretend party. But we urge you to avoid having music on at all times for several reasons: (1) music as background creates more "noise" in the room and causes children and adults to raise their voices to be heard above the music; (2) children may need to "tune out" the music in order to concentrate on something else; and (3) to really appreciate music, children should give it their full attention at specific times.

Of course, you will sing and move spontaneously with girls and boys throughout the day. For example, when the children are getting dressed to go outside in winter, you might sing, "Thumb goes in the thumb's hole, fingers all together . . . " or you might invent a clean-up time song such as "Pick up the scissors and put them in the holder, . . . and soon our room will be completely cleaned up," to the tune of *Way Down Yonder in the Paw Paw Patch*. As you walk to the playground, you might march with the children singing, "Oh the children in our class, they are an active group; They all march out to the playground now and will soon march back again," to the tune of *The Royal Duke of York*.

Our ideas for planned music and movement activities are presented in Chapter 4. In that chapter, you will find ideas for revising sexist songs, rhymes, and fingerplays; for changing musical and other games to promote our goals for gender equity and cooperation; and for planning specific activities for movement and dance and for using musical instruments to foster cross-gender interaction.

INDOOR/OUTDOOR ACTIVE PLAY

Active physical play is an integral part of any good early childhood program. Children need opportunities for indoor/outdoor active play in order to release their abundant energy, to develop their strength and coordination, to gain awareness of their bodies in space, and to challenge and test themselves physically.

Of course, indoor/outdoor play must be well supervised to make it safe and comfortable for both girls and boys. You will want to plan ways to help a child who is hesitant to join in active play gain confidence and dare to try, and one who becomes too wild and reckless during active play gain self-control and direction. You will also want to plan for some quieter activities in your indoor/outdoor active play space in order to give children a chance to move in and out of strenuous play.

By providing some activities for indoor/outdoor play, you can help cautious, physically inactive children get involved in active play and those whose play is unruly and aimless become more focused. Through careful planning and frequent changes of equipment and materials, you can help maintain the interest of both sexes in constructive indoor/ outdoor active play and decrease the tendency of boys and girls to divide themselves by gender when playing active games.

In the following pages, we include some activities we have found helpful for encouraging cross-gender and cooperative active play. Many of them require little or no special preparation or materials.

ACTIVITIES FOR INDOOR/OUTDOOR ACTIVE PLAY

HOUSE PAINTING

Materials you will need

Painter's brushes
Buckets
Water
Painter's hats (optional)

The children will fill their buckets with water (pretend paint) and paint on outside walls or structures. As the sun dries the "paint," the children will start all over again. Both girls and boys love this activity.

OBSTACLE COURSE

Materials you will need

Hollow blocks	Tunnel
Boards for bridges	Rocking boat
Walking beam	Stair steps

Using whatever equipment you have, build an obstacle course with the children. Have them begin at a designated starting point and follow the course, up and down, over and under, around and through the obstacles. Keep the course simple until the children become familiar with the activity. Then use your imagination and additional equipment to help children add length and complexity to the course. Both girls and boys find this activity compelling. For a special obstacle course, read *Berenstain Bears in the Dark* by Stan and Jan Berenstain and replicate the young bears' adventure.

FOLLOW THE TAPES

Materials you will need

Colored tape
Duct tape
Masking tape

Using a variety of tapes, outline a course for children to follow along (walking, hopping, or crawling). Make zigzags, straight lines, loops, triangles, and squares. Leave occasional breaks in the taped lines so that the children have to jump to connect with the next line. Both girls and boys find taking turns following the different colored lines intriguing and will often have ideas for additions to the course.

RULES OF THE ROAD

Materials you will need

Wooden or plastic riding toys	Markers
	Cardboard
Tricycles	Masking tape
Hot wheels	

You will help children make signs to post along the "road." Some popular signs are STOP, GO, ONE WAY, CURVE, SLOW, WORK ZONE, and PARKING. While some children drive vehicles following the instructions on the signs, others will take turns being police officers and direct traffic to prevent traffic jams or accidents. Girls and boys learn to problem solve and cooperate during this play.

PARACHUTE PLAY

Materials you will need

Parachute (a king-sized sheet will work too)
Balls

The children will grasp the sides of the parachute. You will place a ball in the middle of the parachute, telling the children to lift the parachute and roll the ball from side to side. Boys and girls will have to cooperate to get the parachute in the air and keep the ball from rolling over the edge. Add more balls for complexity. (To order parachutes and books/recordings of parachute games, see the resources listed at the end of Chapter 2.)

BOX STRUCTURES

Materials you will need

Cardboard cartons of all sizes
Poster paint
Containers
Painter's brushes
Utility knife
Paper tubes

Corrugated cardboard
Fabric
White glue
Glue brushes
Drop cloth (an old shower
    curtain works well)

Girls and boys will work together to plan, construct, paint, and decorate their structures (houses, cars, castles, airplanes, space ships, trains, etc.). You will use the utility knife to cut the windows and doors suggested by the children. When the paint has dried, children can climb into their creations and use them in pretend play.

BEAN BAG GAMES

Materials you will need

Beanbags
Buckets
Basketball ring (one made from a coat hanger works well)

Children will have a good time playing catch and tossing beanbags into buckets or through a hoop. In addition, you can play games, such as Follow the Leader, in which one child performs different motions for the other children to copy.

For more ideas, we suggest recordings of *Bean Bag Activities and Coordination Skills* and *Me and My Bean Bag*. (See the resources listed at the end of Chapter 2.)

Additional Ideas for Indoor/Outdoor Play

GYM MAT TRICKS

Put out gym mats and let children experiment with different movements and tricks, such as rolling and doing somersaults. Children of both sexes feel a sense of accomplishment when they master new skills.

RED LIGHT, GREEN LIGHT

Designate a starting line and a finish line. Girls and boys will alternate as leaders. When the leader says, "Green light," the group moves forward; when she or he says, "Red light," everyone must stop. When every child has reached the finish line, the game starts again with a new leader.

GIANT STEPS

Designate a starting line and a finish line and choose a leader. Be sure to have boys and girls alternate as leaders. Each player will take turns asking the leader, "May I take x number of giant (or baby) steps?" The leader will respond either, "Yes, you may" or "No, you may take $x + y$ (or $x - y$) number of giant (or baby) steps." When every child has reached the finish line, the game starts again with a new leader.

SWIMMING PARTY

On a hot day, set up sprinklers and a wading pool. Children can bring swimsuits and towels from home. Invite parents to help with the changing and life guarding.

SANDBOX PLAY

Vary your sand toys, and when the sand is dry, add water to make it easier for children to make molds, build sand castles, or construct highways. Girls and boys will often cooperate in sandbox projects.

STORIES UNDER A TREE

To give children a chance to take a rest during active play, bring a blanket and books to a shady spot and invite boys and girls over to listen to a story.

OUTDOOR CAFE

For a change of pace, set up a cafe with juice and snacks for thirsty and hungry children. Boys and girls will enjoy the roles of servers and customers.

SNOW FUN

If you live where there is snow, help the children make snow people (not just snowmen!), ride on sleds or saucers, make angels, and shovel snow with child-sized shovels.

SIDEWALK ART

Artists of both sexes will like to draw with colored chalks on the sidewalk. It is also fun to make crayon rubbings (use light-weight white paper) of textured outdoor surfaces such as metal access covers, signs with raised or indented letters, and brick walls.

TO SUM UP . . .

In this chapter, we shared many ideas for activities you can incorporate in your curriculum planning. Of course, you can adapt any of these activities to fit your classroom situation. As you plan your curriculum and activities, however, be sure to consider whether a given activity will be attractive to both sexes, will promote gender equity and self-esteem, and will encourage girl/boy cooperation.

CHAPTER FOUR
UPDATING CIRCLE TIME

Activities to Develop Understanding of and Respect for Both Genders

At some time in your day, you will undoubtedly bring the whole group (or a smaller group) together to sing songs, play games, listen to stories, and have group discussions. You may find that you have unwittingly overlooked the fact that Simon, not Sarah, says, "Touch your toes," that Polly, not Paul, puts the kettle on, that the five little monkeys who jump on the bed are all male, and that the Royal Duke of York is a leader of men. But once you have become sensitive to the stereotypes and the preponderance of male characters in simple songs, rhymes, and fingerplays, you will be able to make changes that show both genders in a positive light and include more female characters. You can eliminate or change games in which some children are losers and in which only males take the leadership roles, and you can initiate music and movement activities that help both girls and boys feel good about themselves and each other.

In this chapter, we suggest ways to deal with bias and stereotyping in the songs, rhymes, fingerplays, and games you select to use with children. We introduce win-win games and musical activities you can use to promote positive cross-gender interaction. We also propose ways to use discussion as a means for helping the children become sensitized to bias and issues of fairness. In addition, we provide a bibliography for circle-time activities. (A discussion of storytime and children's books will be found in Chapter 5.)

SONGS, RHYMES, AND FINGERPLAYS

Think carefully about the subtle or not so subtle messages about gender that may be conveyed in the songs, rhymes, and fingerplays you teach. Of course, there are many songs, rhymes, and fingerplays that do not require editing for gender equity and that are popular with children. But as you gather your favorites together, scrutinize them for gender bias and make needed changes, or use them as opportunities for discussion with the children.

In the following pages, we show how we have adapted some familiar circle-time verses. You can use our suggestions or come up with your own versions. The children can help with this too.

FIVE LITTLE DUCKS

The following song is often sung with the father duck giving the strong command in the last verse. We made the change from *father* to *mother* because we believe it is important that mothers not be seen as weak and ineffectual while fathers are seen as authoritative and effective. It is equally important to get away from the habit of placing males in the position of having to act as the "heavies" or the disciplinarians. (In addition, our version of the song is scientifically more accurate, since father ducks typically abandon the mothers before the eggs are hatched.)

Five little ducks went out to play
Over the fields and far away.
Mother Duck said, "Quack, quack, quack!"
And four little ducks came waddling back.

Four little ducks went out to play
Over the fields and far away.
Mother Duck said, "Quack, quack, quack!"
And three little ducks came waddling back.

Three little ducks went out to play
Over the fields and far away.
Mother Duck said, "Quack, quack, quack!"
And two little ducks came waddling back.

Two little ducks went out to play
Over the fields and far away.
Mother Duck said, "Quack, quack, quack!"
And one little duck came waddling back.

One little duck went out to play
Over the fields and far away.
Mother Duck said, "Quack, quack, quack!"
But no little ducks came waddling back.

No little ducks went out to play
Over the fields and far away.
***Mother** Duck said, "QUACK, QUACK, QUACK!"*
And five little ducks came waddling back.

FIVE LITTLE MONKEYS

For a more equitable way to say this fingerplay, alternate *her* for *his* and *Papa* for *Mama*.

> *Five little monkeys jumping on the bed.*
> *One fell off and bumped **her** head.*
> ***Papa** called the doctor and the doctor said,*
> *"NO MORE MONKEYS JUMPING ON THE BED!"*
>
> *Four little monkeys jumping on the bed.*
> *One fell off and bumped his head.*
> *Mama called the doctor and the doctor said,*
> *"NO MORE MONKEYS JUMPING ON THE BED!"*

Continue alternating *Mama* and *Papa* and *her* and *him* in the verses with three little monkeys, two little monkeys, and one little monkey.

Children like to act out the parts of the monkeys, the parents, and the doctor. Both boys and girls should have opportunities to try out different roles. If any child challenges the choice of a girl for the role of doctor, use the opportunity to teach that both women and men can be doctors.

FIVE LITTLE MONKEYS AND THE ALLIGATOR

In this fingerplay, the alligator is called *Mr. Alligator* throughout. Rather than assuming the clever alligator has to be male, change the name so the alligator can be either gender. (We suggest *Hungry Alligator, Clever Alligator,* or *Sneaky Alligator.*)

> *Five little monkeys swinging in a tree*
> *Teasing **Hungry Alligator,***
> *"You can't catch me! You can't catch me!"*
> *Along came **Hungry Alligator,***
> *Quiet as can be, quiet as can be,*
> *And snap!*

Continue with four little monkeys, three little monkeys, and so on.

In addition to using this verse as a fingerplay, children will enjoy acting it out. Be sure to give girls equal opportunities to play the part of the alligator.

POLLY PUT THE KETTLE ON

If you use this familiar song, alternate male and female names to show that both sexes can and do make and serve tea, and that kitchen duties are not relegated to females alone. You can use the names of the children in your class, and let them act out the song using a teapot as a prop.

*Polly (**Willy**) put the kettle on, kettle on, kettle on,*
*Polly (**Willy**) put the kettle on,*
We'll all have tea.

*Sukey (**Timmy**) take it off again, off again, off again,*
*Sukey (**Timmy**) take it off again,*
We'll all go home.

THE WHEELS ON THE BUS

If you act this song out with a driver at the wheel, make sure that girls have as many chances to be the driver as boys do. For the *Mommies* on the bus, substitute the *parents* on the bus.

The wheels on the bus go round and round,
Round and round, round and round.
The wheels on the bus go round and round,
All through the town.

The driver on the bus says, "Move on back," . . .

The children on the bus go up and down, . . .

The horn on the bus goes beep, beep, beep, . . .

The babies on the bus go wah, wah, wah, . . .

*The **parents** on the bus go shh, shh, shh, . . .*

Add gender-neutral verses about the money, lights, wipers, buzzer, and so on.

THE MUFFIN MAN

In this popular song, substitute *baker* or *maker* for *man*, or alternate *muffin man* with *muffin woman*.

> *Oh, do you know the muffin **maker**, the muffin **maker**, the muffin* **maker***;*
>
> *Oh, do you know the muffin **maker**, who lives in Drury Lane?*
>
> *Oh, yes we know the muffin **maker**, . . .*
>
> *Our **mothers and our fathers** buy their muffins from the muffin* **maker***, . . .*
>
> *Our **sisters and our brothers** buy their muffins from the muffin* **maker***, . . .*
>
> *Our **grandmas and our grandpas**, . . .*
>
> *Our **aunts and our uncles**, . . .*
>
> **We all** *buy our muffins from the muffin* **maker***, . . .*

MARY HAD A LITTLE LAMB

Both genders like to sing and act out this song. Substitute the names of the children in your class for the name *Mary* to let both genders have a chance to be leaders and loving pet owners. Let both boys and girls experience being the lamb who follows and the teacher who explains why the lamb loves its owner.

> *Mary (**Omar**) had a little lamb, little lamb, little lamb;*
> *Mary (**Omar**) had a little lamb,*
> *Its fleece was white as snow.*
>
> *And everywhere that Mary (**Omar**) went, . . .*
> *The lamb was sure to go.*
>
> *It followed her (**him**) to school one day, . . .*
> *Which was against the rule.*
>
> *It made the children laugh and play, . . .*
> *To see a lamb at school.*

*What makes the lamb love Mary (**Omar**) so, . . .*
The eager children cry.

*Why Mary (**Omar**) loves the lamb you know, . . .*
The teacher did reply.

JOHNNY POUNDS WITH ONE HAMMER

Be sure to give equal time to female carpenters if you sing this song. Alternate *Jenny* with *Johnny*, or use the names of the children in your class in place of the name *Johnny*.

*Johnny (**Jenny**) pounds with one hammer, one hammer, one hammer,*
*Johnny (**Jenny**) pounds with one hammer,*
*Now he (**she**) pounds with two.*

Continue the song, as above, up to five hammers. Each child acts out the song using one fist for one hammer; two fists for two; two fists and one foot for three; two fists and two feet for four; and two fists, two feet, and head for five.

WHERE IS THUMBKIN?

To promote gender equity in this fingerplay, we like to substitute *Friend* for *Sir*, *tall finger* for *tall man*, and *ring finger* for *ringman*.

Where is Thumbkin? Where is Thumbkin?
Here I am. Here I am.
*How are you today, **Friend**?*
*How are you today, **Friend**?*
Very well, I thank you.
Very well, I thank you.
Run away. Run away.

Where is pointer? . . .

*Where is tall **finger**? . . .*
*Where is ring **finger**? . . .*
Where is pinkie? . . .
Where's the whole family? . . .

FRÈRE JACQUES (BROTHER JOHN)

Substitute the children's names for *Frère Jacques* or *Brother John*. Or alternate *Soeur Marie* with *Frère Jacques* or *Sister Sue* with *Brother John*.

A relaxing and fun way to act out this song is to ask the children to lie down and pretend to sleep. Sing to the "sleeping" children to wake them up. The children who are "awake" can help sing to other "sleepers." You can also choose a child to ring a bell along with the *ding ding dongs* in the song.

> *Are you sleeping, are you sleeping,* **Angela, Angela**?
> *Morning bells are ringing,*
> *Morning bells are ringing:*
> *DING, DING, DONG!*
> *DING, DING, DONG!*

JOHN BROWN'S BABY

Alternate *Jane Brown* with *John Brown* or use the children's names when you sing this song.

> *John (**Jane**) Brown's baby had a cold upon its chest,*
> *John (**Jane**) Brown's baby had a cold upon its chest,*
> *John (**Jane**) Brown's baby had a cold upon its chest,*
> *And he (**she**) rubbed it with camphorated oil.*

Sing the first verse through in its entirety. Then sing it again and in place of singing the word *baby,* have the children pretend to rock their babies. This motion will be repeated instead of the word in the subsequent verses. Next time through the song and thereafter, substitute a sneeze sound for the word *cold*. Next, leave out the word *chest* and have the children pat their chests with their hands, repeating this substitution from then on. The next time through the song, have the children leave out the word *rubbed* and rub their chests instead. In the final verse, the children will also leave out *camphorated oil* and hold their noses and make faces. The inevitable mistakes that children make as they try to omit all of the designated words and substitute the right motions for these words add to the fun in this challenging song.

OLD MACDONALD HAD A FARM

This song implies that only men are farmers and owners of farms. Discuss this fallacy with the children. Try substituting *the MacDonalds* for *Old MacDonald* to show coownership and partnership, or substitute a woman's name or the names of the children in your group for *Old MacDonald*.

> ***The MacDonalds*** *had a farm,*
> *Eeigh, eeigh, oh!*
> *And on **their** farm,*
> ***They*** *had some chicks,*
> *Eeigh, eeigh, oh!*
> *With a chick, chick here,*
> *And a chick, chick there;*
> *Here a chick, there a chick,*
> *Everywhere a chick, chick.*
> ***The MacDonalds*** *had a farm,*
> *Eeigh, eeigh, oh!*
>
> *And on **their** farm,*
> ***They*** *had some ducks . . . cows . . . pigs . . .*

MISS POLLY HAD A DOLLY

This rhyme is a favorite with children, but it reinforces the idea that boys do not play with dolls and are not caregivers. We like to substitute the children's names or use the names *Paul* and *Polly*. Substitute *her* for *his* often to remind children that both females and males are doctors.

> *Polly (**Paul**) had a dolly (**doll**),*
> *Who was sick, sick, sick.*
> *So she (**he**) called up the doctor*
> *To come quick, quick, quick.*
> *The doctor came with his (**her**) bag and hat,*
> *And took care of the dolly (**doll**) just like that!*
> *He (**She**) gave the dolly (**doll**) a pill, pill, pill,*
> *And came back in the morning with the bill, bill, bill.*

MISS LUCY

Another favorite rhyme can be adapted to have both sexes take turns saying the lines of the doctor and the nurse. This verse provides an opportunity to demonstrate that males can be nurses and females can be doctors. We like to interchange the sexes of the main characters and use *woman* in place of *lady*.

> *Lucy (**Luke**) had a baby,*
> *She named him Tiny Tim. (**He named her Tiny Kim**.)*
> *She (**he**) put him (**her**) in the bathtub*
> *To see if he (**she**) could swim.*
>
> *He (**she**) drank all the water,*
> *And ate up all the soap,*
> *And tried to eat the bathtub,*
> *But it wouldn't go down his (**her**) throat.*
>
> *Lucy (**Luke**) called the doctor,*
> *Lucy (**Luke**) called the nurse,*
> *Lucy (**Luke**) called the lady (**woman**)*
> *With the alligator purse.*
>
> *In came the doctor,*
> *In came the nurse,*
> *In came the lady (**woman**)*
> *With the alligator purse.*
>
> *"Measles," said the doctor.*
> *"Mumps," said the nurse.*
> *"Flu," said the lady (**woman**)*
> *With the alligator purse.*
>
> *"Ten dollars," said the doctor.*
> *"Ten dollars," said the nurse.*
> *"Ten dollars," said the lady (**woman**)*
> *With the alligator purse.*
>
> *Out went the doctor,*
> *Out went the nurse,*
> *Out went the lady (**woman**)*
> *With the alligator purse.*
>
> *"Goodbye," said the doctor.*
> *"Goodbye," said the nurse.*
> *"Goodbye," said the lady (**woman**)*
> *With the alligator purse.*

Other Quick Fixes

Many songs that children love are easily adapted by simply alternating the gender of the main character of the song. *This Old Man* can become *This Old **Woman**, I Know an Old Woman Who Swallowed a Fly* can become a song about an old **man**, *She'll Be Comin' 'Round the Mountain* can be changed to ***He'll** Be Comin' 'Round the Mountain*, and *Aunt Rhody* can become ***Uncle Albert***. Sometimes you can substitute the names of children in your class for the main characters. In the song *This Old Man*, change the words *this old man* to various children's names. For example, "**Sharrod Jones**, he played one, he played knick knack on his drum . . . **Inez Torres**, she played two, she played knick knack on her shoe . . ." and so on.

Friendship Songs

There are songs, rhymes, and fingerplays that encourage cooperation, inclusion, friendship, and girl/boy interaction. We have included some of our favorites.

The More We Get Together
The more we get together, together, together,
The more we get together,
The happier we'll be.
For your friend is my friend,
And my friend is your friend,
The more we get together,
The happier we'll be.

Use the names of children in your group for this chant that we made up.

I Have a Friend
I have a friend
And you do too.
Her (his) name is Janet (James).
What can she (he) do?
Will she (he) stand up?
Will she (he) sit down?
Will she (he) say, "Hi!"
To friends all around?

Two Little Blackbirds
Two little blackbirds sitting on a hill,
*One named Jack (**Beth**) and the other named Jill (**Bill**).*
*Fly away Jack (**Beth**). Fly away Jill (**Bill**).*
*Come back Jack (**Beth**). Come back Jill (**Bill**).*

We have made up the following verses to the tune of *You'll Sing a Song and I'll Sing a Song* by Ella Jenkins. It emphasizes our point about girls and boys being friends.

The Friendship Song
You'll be my friend, and I'll be your friend,
And we'll be friends together,
You'll be my friend, and I'll be your friend,
In every kind of weather.

Girls can be friends, and boys can be friends,
And both can be friends together,
Girls can be friends, and boys can be friends,
In every kind of weather.

Additional Suggestions

Girls and boys love silly songs. Try songs such as *On Top of Spaghetti, Supercalifragilisticexpialidocious, Shake Your Sillies Out, Put Your Finger in the Air, Skinnamarink,* and *Ten in the Bed* for some good cross-gender fun. If the children become interested in certain themes, try to find songs to support those interests. For instance, if girls and boys are involved in building train stations and tracks, introduce songs such as *Down By the Station, Little Red Caboose,* and *Train Is a Comin'.*

You may also introduce picture books that use the lyrics and verses of songs, rhymes, and fingerplays as text. For example, you might choose a song picture book such as *Go Tell Aunt Rhody* by Aliki and/or popular rhyme and fingerplay books such as *Five Little Monkeys Jumping on the Bed* and *Five Little Monkeys Sitting in a Tree* by Eileen Christelow. (The two Christelow books are delightfully amusing, but be aware that the doctor is male and the mother is shown as somewhat helpless and ineffective.)

WIN-WIN GAMES

Games provide children with opportunities to learn social skills, cooperation, rules and strategies. Young children love games but hate to lose or be left out. When playing games with girls and boys, arrange the games so there are no losers, only winners, and use rules and strategies that ensure inclusion of all children. Select games that give both genders opportunities to lead and follow and that show both girls and boys as strong, capable, and caring.

We have chosen some examples of nonsexist win-win games to share with you. As you search for more win-win games, you will, of course, want to adapt or eliminate any games that contain gender stereotypes.

DUCK, DUCK, GOOSE

Ask the children to sit in a circle and select a child (one who is less likely to be chosen by peers) to be IT. This child goes behind the children sitting in the circle and gently touches their heads in sequence, saying with each touch, "Duck, duck, duck . . . " and then "Goose!!" to one child. That child then stands up and chases the child who is IT around the circle. The child who is IT runs to and sits in the empty spot left by the Goose. (If the child who is IT is caught, she or he rejoins the game, rather than being put inside the circle and labeled a "loser.")

The Goose is then IT, and the game continues. You may wish to use the rule that leads to inclusion: No child gets a second turn until everyone has had one turn. To help the child who is IT identify who has not yet had a turn, ask those children to raise their hands.

ATISKIT, ATASKET

Materials you will need

Basket with a handle
Green and yellow crepe paper, yarn, or ribbon to trim the basket
Envelope with the words *MY FRIEND* written on it

Ask the children to sit in a circle and select a child (one who is less likely to be chosen by peers) to be IT. The child who is IT walks around the circle behind the other children as everyone sings,

> *ATISKET, ATASKET,*
> *A green and yellow basket,*
> *I wrote a letter to my friend*
> *And on the way I dropped it, I dropped it,*
> *And on the way, I dropped it.*

The child who is IT drops the letter behind another child, who then chases the child with the basket. The child who is IT runs around the circle and sits in the empty spot left by the child who has been doing the chasing. (If the child who is IT is caught, he or she goes to the empty spot in the circle, rather than being put inside the circle as a "loser.")

The second child is then IT, and the game continues. You may want to make sure that no child gets a second turn to be IT until everyone has had one turn.

THE FARMER IN THE DELL

When you play this singing game, remember that farmers can be both male and female and that both parents participate in child care. Instead of a *nurse(maid)* taking the child, try substituting a *sitter*, who can be either male or female.

Ask the children to form a circle and then select a farmer. (Choose a girl as often as a boy, or, if the group is large, start the game with two farmers, a girl and a boy.) The farmer stands in the center of the circle as everyone sings,

> *The farmer in the dell,*
> *The farmer in the dell,*
> *Heigh-ho the derry-o,*
> *The farmer in the dell.*
>
> *The farmer takes a **mate**,*
> *The farmer takes a **mate**, . . .*
>
> *The **parents** take a child, . . .*
>
> *The child takes a **sitter**, . . .*
>
> *The **sitter** takes a dog, . . .*

and so on until the cheese stands alone.

LITTLE SALLY WATERS

This game has Sally wiping her weeping eyes. Since it is important for boys to be able to cry too, we suggest that you substitute *Sammy* for

Sally at least 50 percent of the time. Or you can use the names of the children in your group in place of *Sally*.

> *Little Sally (**Sammy**) Waters*
> *Sitting in a saucer,*
> *Rise, Sally (**Sammy**), Rise!*
> *Wipe your weeping eyes.*
> *Put your hands on your hips,*
> *And let your back bone slip,*
> *Shake it to the east,*
> *And shake it to the west,*
> *And shake it to the one*
> *Who you like the best.*

The children will hold hands and form a circle. The child who is IT ("Sally" or "Sammy") will sit in the center of the circle and act out the words of the song as the children sing and circle around her or him. At the end of the song, the child who is IT stands and shakes her or his hips while walking toward a friend. The two will then trade places. Again, if necessary, invoke the rule that no child can be chosen twice until all children have had a turn.

LONDON BRIDGE

We like to substitute *my good friend* for *my fair lady* in this game. Select a boy and a girl to clasp hands and raise them to form a bridge. Everyone walks, in turn, under the bridge, round and round, singing,

> *London Bridge is falling down,*
> *Falling down, falling down,*
> *London Bridge is falling down,*
> ***My good friend***.

As the bridge falls at the word *friend*, the captured child is then rocked back and forth as everyone sings,

> *Take the key and lock him (her) up, . . .*
> ***my good friend***.

The captured child is released at the end of the verse and rejoins the children going under the bridge.

HOKEY POKEY

This traditional favorite still plays well with the younger set. You and the children will form a circle and sing together,

> *You put your right hand in;*
> *You put your right hand out;*
> *You put your right hand in,*
> *And you shake it all about;*
> *You do the Hokey Pokey (shake hips),*
> *And you turn yourself around;*
> *And that's what it's all about.*
> *HOKEY POKEY!*

Continue using the left hand, the right foot, the left foot, the head, and other body parts. End the game with the whole self.

GO IN AND OUT THE WINDOWS

This game gives you a chance to choose the leader each time the song repeats, and in this way, you can select girls as leaders as often as boys. You can also choose a child who needs a turn to be IT. The children will form a circle, hold hands, and raise them up to make spaces for "windows." Then everyone sings to the leader,

> *Go in and out the windows,*
> *Go in and out the windows,*
> *Go in and out the windows,*
> *As we have done before.*
>
> *Now stand and face your partner,*
> *Now stand and face your partner,*
> *Now stand and face your partner,*
> *As we have done before.*

Holding hands, the partners weave in and out the "windows" made by the circle of children as everyone sings the first verse again. The partners return to the circle when they have been through the windows. You then select another leader, and the game continues. You can add verses such as "Now skip and turn your partner," but we like to leave out any verses about kneeling and bowing before a partner as those actions imply inequality.

BLUEBIRD, BLUEBIRD

In this game, choose children to act as the birds according to the colors they are wearing. The children will form a circle, hold hands, and raise them up to make spaces for "windows." You select a child (or several children wearing the same color) to act the part of the flying bird(s), weaving in and out of the "windows." Then everyone sings,

Bluebird, bluebird, fly through my window,
Bluebird, bluebird, fly through my window,
Bluebird, bluebird, fly through my window,
And find molasses candy.

Redbird, redbird, . . .

Yellowbird, yellowbird, . . .

Greenbird, greenbird, . . .

Purplebird, purplebird, . . . etc.

HERE WE GO LOOBY LOO

This game offers children a chance to play together acting out a variety of motions. First, the children will walk or skip in a circle to the following:

Here we go looby loo,
Here we go looby lie,
Here we go looby loo,
All on a Saturday night.

The children will stop and act out the motion before repeating the first verse.

I put my right hand in,
I put my right hand out,
I give my right hand a shake, shake, shake,
And turn myself about.

I put my left hand in, . . .

I put my right foot in, . . .

I put my left foot in, . . .

I put my whole self in, . . .

Of course, you can be creative, and put right and left hips, knees, and elbows in the circle.

ALICE THE CAMEL

Both girls and boys get caught up in the hilarity of this game. You can have a male camel, as well as a female one, by substituting a male name for *Alice*.

The children form a tight circle with their hips almost touching. They hold out their fingers into the circle to indicate the number they are singing, and on the words, "Boom, boom, boom," they bump hips together.

> *Alice (**Archie**) the camel has ten humps,*
> *Alice (**Archie**) the camel has ten humps,*
> *Alice (**Archie**) the camel has ten humps,*
> *So go, Alice (**Archie**), go.*
> *Boom, boom, boom!*
>
> *Alice (**Archie**) the camel has nine humps, . . .*
> *Alice (**Archie**) the camel has eight humps, . . . etc.*

And end with:

> *Alice (**Archie**) the camel has no humps,*
> *Alice (**Archie**) the camel has no humps,*
> *Alice (**Archie**) the camel has no humps,*
> *'CAUSE ALICE (**ARCHIE**) IS A **HORSE**!*

THE BAKERY SHOP GAME

The children form a circle. One child, acting as the shopkeeper, goes to the middle of the circle and calls out the names of children in the circle. The child whose name is called goes to the "shop," takes an imaginary cookie, and runs around the outside of the circle before returning to his or her original place. Then another child is called, and the game continues in this way. Everyone chants,

> *Ten yummy cookies in the bakery shop,*
> *Shining so brightly with the sugar on top.*
> *Along comes **Tawanda** with a nickel to pay.*
> *Takes **her** cookie and runs away.*
>
> *Nine yummy cookies in the bakery shop, . . .*
>
> *Eight yummy cookies in the bakery shop, . . . etc.*

And end with:

> *No yummy cookies in the bakery shop,*
> *Shining so brightly with the sugar on top.*
> *No children come with nickels to pay.*
> *The bakery shop is closed for the day.*

As a variation, choose half the children to act as imaginary cookies in the center of the circle. Then you call the name of the cookie buyer. That child then selects one of the "cookies" in the center, and the two children return to the outside circle.

This rhyme can be adapted to use different goods and different shops. For example, during Hanukkah, you could have a holiday shop with pretty dreidels whirling so briskly with handles on top.

WHO STOLE THE COOKIE?

Both girls and boys love this "who dunnit" chant game. Be sure everyone gets a chance to be a suspect.

> *Group:*   "*Who stole the cookie from the cookie jar?*"
> *Teacher:*   "***Yolanda*** *stole the cookie from the cookie jar.*"
> ***Yolanda:***   "*Who me?*"
> *Group:*   "*Yes, you!*"
> ***Yolanda:***   "*Not me!*"
> *Group:*   "*Then, who stole the cookie from the cookie jar?*"
> *Yolanda points to Robb:* "***Robb*** *stole the cookie from the cookie jar.*"
> ***Robb:***   "*Who me?*"
> *Group:*   "*Yes, you!*"
> ***Robb:***   "*Not me!*"

After all have said, "Not me!," you can either add our solution ("The **mouse** stole the cookie from the cookie jar!") or make up an ending with the children.

PUNCHINELLA

This is a good game to give girls and boys equal opportunities to be leaders and followers. Repeat *Punchinella* rather than using the usual funny fellow. Encourage each child to invent original motions or movements for others to follow. Everyone sings or chants,

> *Look who's here, Punchinella, **Punchinella**,*
> *Look who's here, Punchinella, funny you.*
>
> *What can you do, Punchinella, **Punchinella**,*
> *What can you do, Punchinella, funny you?*
>
> *We can do it too, Punchinella, **Punchinella**,*
> *We can do it too, Punchinella, funny you.*
>
> *Who do you choose, Punchinella, **Punchinella**,*
> *Who do you choose, Punchinella, funny you?*

Continue the game until all have had a turn to be Punchinella.

THE ELEPHANT GAME

After the children form a circle, select a child to be the first "elephant." As the whole group sings the first verse, the elephant begins swinging his or her trunk and singing and walking around the outside of the circle. At the end of the first verse, the elephant selects a friend to be the second elephant. The second elephant follows the first, and the game continues in this way.

> *One elephant went out to play*
> *On a spider's web one day.*
> *She (**He**) had such enormous fun,*
> *That she (**he**) asked another elephant to come.*
>
> *Two elephants went out to play, . . .*
>
> *Three elephants went out to play, . . . etc.*

Continue in this fashion until all the children are in the elephant line. We then like to end the game with:

> *All the elephants went out to play*
> *On a spider's web one day.*
> *They had such enormous fun,*
> *That they played and played 'til day was done.*

At this point, the children like to fall down in their tracks and pretend to sleep.

ROLL THE BALL

Girls and boys both like this ball game, and no one "fails" to catch the ball. The children sit in a circle with their feet out and apart. You will give the ball to a child to start the game; the child will roll it to another child calling out that child's name as the ball rolls. If the ball rolls off course, the child whose name was called gets up to get it, and the game continues. The children chant,

> *Roll the ball to **Ricardo's** door.*
> ***Ricardo** will catch it and roll it once more.*

> *Roll the ball to **Wanda's** door.*
> ***Wanda** will catch it and roll it once more.*

MUFFIN MAKER GAME

Ask the children to hold hands and form a large circle. Choose one child to walk around the outside of the circle while the others sing the first verse. The child then chooses a partner, takes the partner's hand, and the two walk around the outside of the circle as the second verse is sung. Next, the two children each choose a child to form the next pair. The two pairs now walk around the circle to the same verse. The game continues until all the children have been chosen. Then the children will sing the final verse.

> *(First verse)*
> *Oh, do you know the muffin **maker**, the muffin **maker**, the muffin*
> ***maker**;*
> *Oh, do you know the muffin **maker**, who lives in Drury Lane?*

> *(Second verse)*
> *Oh, yes we know the muffin **maker**, . . .*

> *(Final verse)*
> *We all have seen the muffin **maker**, . . .*

MULBERRY BUSH

When the children play this game, you should choose work that is often considered primarily female or male work to reinforce the idea that all work can be done by both genders. Here is our version, but you can adapt it, of course. The children form a circle and walk around in one direction singing,

> *Here we go 'round the mulberry bush,*
> *The mulberry bush, the mulberry bush;*
> *Here we go 'round the mulberry bush,*
> *So early in the morning.*

The children now stand still in the circle and act out the motions in each verse.

> *This is the way we wash our clothes, . . .*
> *So early Monday morning.*
>
> *This is the way we mow the lawn, . . .*
> *So early Tuesday morning.*
>
> *This is the way we vacuum the house, . . .*
> *So early Wednesday morning.*
>
> *This is the way we do the dishes, . . .*
> *So early Thursday morning.*
>
> *This is the way we bake the bread, . . .*
> *So early Friday morning.*
>
> *This is the way we rock the baby, . . .*
> *So early Saturday morning.*
>
> *This is the way we drive the car, . . .*
> *So early Sunday morning.*

Talk with the children about the work they see their parents and other males and females doing. Then incorporate their ideas into the song, reinforcing the point that both sexes can do all kinds of work.

SIMON SAYS

You can substitute the names of the children in your class for *Simon*, and give each child a turn to be the leader. As followers, boys and girls will have to listen carefully to avoid being caught.

Choose a child to start the game. This child will say, "**Terry** says, 'Put your hands on your head'; Terry says, 'Rub your stomach' " and so on. Eventually, Terry will omit the words, "Terry says," but will give a direction. To make this a win-win game, the children who are caught are not asked to leave the game. They continue to play and listen even more carefully.

After several minutes, ask the leader to choose a replacement. Make sure that all children get a turn to lead by having those children who have not yet been chosen raise their hands when it is time to choose a new leader.

MOVEMENT AND DANCE

Children need to move their bodies and feel them in relation to the world around them. Through movement and dance, children learn how to work cooperatively and as individuals in a group.

Circle time can serve as a logical time for planned movement activities. At circle time, too many teachers expect children to sit still and listen, rather than move and make noise. Or teachers rely too heavily on a song, an action rhyme, or a fingerplay to provide an outlet for children who need to move. Although these and musical games are fine activities, it is important that you give children many opportunities to express themselves through creative movement and dance.

When you begin movement and dance activities, it is helpful to use musical warm-ups with specific movements in order to help children become used to moving to music. Ella Jenkins and Hap Palmer recordings are among those filled with good songs that have directions that tell children how and when to move. (For example, Ella Jenkins sings, "And you walk, and you walk, and you walk, and you STOP; and you walk, and you walk, and you walk, and you STOP; . . . " on one recording.) Once children are comfortable with moving to music, you can go on to more creative movement and dance activities, thereby giving children opportunities to discover their own ways to move in space.

Before you start a movement activity, make sure to clear a large enough space and assemble any materials you plan to use. To avoid confusion and chaos, give the children simple instructions about the activity. Be sure to remind them to respect each other's space and to avoid bumping into one another.

Above all, when children create their own motions and movements, accept their interpretations and refrain from making comments. Of course, belittling or negative comments are damaging, but even positive comments are not necessarily constructive. If you praise or make a positive comment about a child's interpretation, you may interrupt that child's involvement in the activity, make that child self-conscious, and/or make other children feel that their motions and movements are not valued. You also may get imitation instead of originality as children strive to be singled out for your attention. If you feel you must comment, use descriptive rather than evaluative words (for example, "Miguel's leaf is twisting and turning; SuYun's is drifting down slowly").

You may be one of a large number of teachers who feel self-conscious with movement and dance. Perhaps as a child you were made to feel that dancing was for sissies or show-offs and not for the clumsy and awkward. But since you know that movement is an essential component of a good early childhood program, it is important for you to persevere in planning and implementing these activities. As you encourage children to interpret ideas and feelings through movement and accept their creations, make a special effort to accept your own attempts as valid rather than seeing them as ungainly and inadequate. You may surprise yourself by beginning to relax and have fun.

As you consider what creative movement activities to introduce at circle time, keep in mind your goal of fostering cooperation between children of both genders. For example, children need to cooperate to perform a line dance. Also be sure that any movement activity you choose is free of gender bias. For example, you would not ask children to march like toy soldiers or waltz like princesses, but rather to march like musicians in a parade or waltz like dancing bears.

As you plan for interpretive dance and movement activities, you will want to try various kinds of music: classical, jazz, rock and roll, and music of other cultures. (Parents are often good resources for ideas of recordings that relate to their particular cultures.) Children of the same culture often respond eagerly to music that is familiar and will feel a sense of commonality with others (male and female) of their culture. Of course, all children profit from a chance to more fully explore and appreciate global diversity.

Remember that creative movement need not be planned to take place only at circle time. Be alert to opportunities to enjoy spontaneous dance and movement with girls and boys throughout the day.

In the activities we have chosen to share with you, we focus on strategies to encourage children to express their ideas and feelings through movement and dance, starting with the somewhat structured and moving to the expressive. We also feature activities that foster cooperation between the genders and are free of gender bias.

Movement and Stories

Both girls and boys need to move after sitting still. Here are some simple, nonthreatening activities to give children a chance to deepen their understanding and enjoyment of a story through movement.

- A book such as *Where the Wild Things Are* by Maurice Sendak cries out for children to roll their terrible eyes, show their terrible claws, gnash their terrible teeth, roar their terrible roars, and go to sleep. *Caps for Sale* by Esphyr Slobodkina is another story with dramatic movements children love to copy. After listening to *We're Going On a Bear Hunt* by Michael Rosen, the children will go through the motions of the bear hunt as you retell the story.

- When you read stories about animals, be alert to the possibilities for movement related to the animals. For example, after hearing *The Elephant and the Bad Baby* by Elfrida Vipont, most children will love imitating elephants going "rumpeta, rumpeta" all down the road, stopping suddenly and sitting down.

- When you read a story about a rainy day—for example, *Rain Talk* by Mary Serfozo—talk with the children about the story and the weather portrayed. Then ask them to pretend it is a rainy day, that they are walking in a heavy rainstorm, carrying umbrellas, splashing in puddles, squishing in mud, feeling raindrops, getting soaked, and finally drying off.

- After reading a story about a day at the beach, such as *Beach Ball* by Peter Sis, talk with the children about the story and any of their experiences at a beach. Then ask the children to pretend to swim in the water, walk and lie on the sand, make sandcastles, get covered with sand, walk along some rocks, and bask in the sun.

- Read and discuss winter stories such as *Geraldine's Big Snow* by Holly Keller and *The Snowy Day* by Ezra Jack Keats. Then ask the children to pretend to walk in deep snow, climb a snow mountain, roll or slide down the mountain, make angels in the snow, make snowpeople and snowballs, slip and fall on ice, be pushed along by a strong wind, feel chilled, and come into a warm house.

- If you read *The Hungry Caterpillar* by Eric Carle, discuss real caterpillars and the changes they go through to become butterflies or moths. Children of both sexes will want to move like voracious caterpillars, curl up and make cocoons, emerge to test their wings, and fly and dance around the room.

- After reading *The Carrot Seed* by Ruth Kraus, suggest that children demonstrate the growth of seeds. Tell the children they can be any kind of seed they want to be: a flower seed, a tree seed, or a bean seed. They will move from being tight little seeds to seedlings pushing through the earth and putting down roots, to sprouts growing slowly to maturity.

- After reading and listening to recordings of *The Teddy Bears' Picnic* (we like the book by Jimmy Kennedy and the recordings by Anne Murray and the King's Singers), ask the children to bring in their teddy bears from home. (You can bring in extras for children who might not have bears.) Then spread a blanket or two out, play a recording of the song, and have the children walk, dance, and skip to the music with their bears. When they tire, they can settle down for a pretend picnic on the blanket. Of course, you can have a real picnic by helping the children make sandwiches, pack baskets with napkins, cups, and juice, and regale themselves in dress-up clothes.

Movement from Nature

Before trying some of these activities, you will want to have the children observe real nature in action when possible. For example, if you want the children to sway like trees in the wind, first point out trees in motion outdoors, or if you want them to dance like falling leaves, show them how real leaves fall from trees to the ground. Ask the children to pretend to be the following:

Icicles melting into puddles

Trees swaying in a gentle breeze, a light wind, a stronger wind, and a hurricane

Leaves falling from trees

Polliwogs becoming frogs

Birds hatching from eggs, eating worms or insects, and learning to fly

Hibernating bears waking up in the spring

Clouds floating in the sky

Moving and Dancing to Music

SKELETON DANCE

Materials you will need

Picture or model of a skeleton
Anatomical drawing showing bones inside the body
Recording of *Night on Bald Mountain* by Mussorgsky or *Mack the Knife* by Kurt Weil

Show the children the pictures and have them feel their own bones. Suggest words such as *rattle, shake,* and *click.* Then ask the children to pretend they are skeletons dancing on a dark spooky night while the music plays. Tell the children that when the music stops, the skeletons will fall to the ground and lie still. Both sexes respond enthusiastically to this musical experience.

SCARF DANCING

Materials you will need

Brightly colored chiffon scarves (one or two per child)
Recording of *Bolero* by Ravel (or any music that will suggest fluid movement)

Read *Color Dance* by Ann Jonas to the children and then give each child a colored scarf. Tell the children to move their scarves and their bodies to the music. Let the children explore waving their scarves over, under, behind, and to the sides of their bodies. Some children may wish to let their scarves touch or entwine as they dance. Tell the children that when the music stops, they will put their scarves away and sit down.

Most children love this activity. Even a child who is shy about dancing will often find making the scarf float and ripple to the music irresistible. Before long, he or she may be dancing around the room with the others. For a variation on this activity, use crepe paper streamers instead of scarves.

CARNIVAL OF THE ANIMALS

Materials you will need

Recording of Saint-Saen's *Carnival of the Animals*

Play the parts of this piece that represent different animals, and have the children move to the music as if they were lions, elephants, kangaroos, swans, and so on. Both genders like moving to this evocative music.

PETER AND THE WOLF

Materials you will need

Recording of Prokofieff's *Peter and the Wolf*

Assign the children the parts of the characters in this story and let them move to their musical parts. To share the parts in an equitable way, you can have *Peter* and *Grandfather* become *Patricia* and *Grandmother* (or use the names of the children themselves). And you can assign both boys and girls to play the parts of the animal characters. For example, a girl might enjoy being the wolf, and a boy might like to fly around like the bird.

DANCE AND FREEZE

Materials you will need

Recording of music to fit the mood needs of your group

If your group is keyed up, try calm, restful music. If they need to let off steam, try lively, energetic music. Start the music and ask the children to move and dance to it. Tell them that when you stop the music, they must "freeze" like statues in whatever positions they are in. Both sexes find this activity entertaining and often comical.

AEROBICS/JAZZ DANCE

Materials you will need

Recording of any jazzy, invigorating music with a strong beat

As you play the music, demonstrate some simple aerobic dancing and exercises. As the children become involved and confident, let them take turns being the "aerobics instructor." They will enjoy inventing dance/ exercise routines for the others to follow.

BALLOON DANCE

Materials you will need

Balloons (one for every three children)
Recording of slow waltz music (for example, Johann Strauss)

Instruct the children to work together to try to keep the balloons afloat as they dance to the music. Be sure the children understand that they tap only those balloons that float into their space, and that they do not compete to get a chance to touch the balloon. Explain that the idea is to have children and balloons both dancing: children on the ground and balloons in the air. As children learn to cooperate in this dance activity, you may wish to experiment with faster, more rhythmic dance music such as polkas, flamenco music, Irish jigs, and African drum music. (*Caution*: Immediately dispose of broken balloons to avoid the possibility of children choking on the pieces.)

STUCK-ON-YOU DANCING

Materials you will need
Recording of lively dance music

Start the music and ask the children to dance separately until the music stops. Now ask each child to touch the child nearest her or him and pretend to be glued to her or his friend at that spot. Now start the music and let the glued-together children dance. When you stop the music next, each group will touch (and stick to) the group nearest them. Start the music again, and continue the dance until everyone is stuck together and trying to dance without coming unglued! This cooperative dance can lead to lots of levity and laughter.

LULLABY

Materials you will need
Sheet or blanket
Recording of *Brahms' Lullaby* or other restful music

Choose a child to be rocked and ask this child to lie in the middle of the spread-out sheet or blanket. Explain to the other children that they will rock the child in the sheet gently back and forth in time to the music. Then ask the children and the adults to hold on to the edge of the sheet. Lift the child up a few inches off the ground, spacing the adults strategically to guarantee safe rocking.

At an appropriate interval, have the child who has been rocked get off the sheet, choose a friend to be rocked next, and join the circle of rockers. Continue this music activity until each child who wishes to have a turn has been rocked.

Movement Riddles

Since all children find it hard to resist a riddle, this is a good way to get reluctant boys and girls moving. Ask the children how they might clap if they could not use their hands. They will come up with clapping feet, knees, thighs, elbows, wrists, and even lips together to make different clapping sounds.

Ask the children to move around a circle in one direction using any method that does not rely on their being upright. They may try creeping, crawling, kneeling, swimming, scooting, rolling, walking on all fours, or crab walking.

Describe some features of an animal and ask the children to move like that animal. For example, say, "I'm thinking of an animal with a shell, four feet, and a head that can move in and out of the shell. Can you guess who I am, and move the way I would move?" The children can solve your riddle and become turtles crawling along the ground. As you continue with new riddles, you will see your room fill with galloping horses, slithering snakes, and hopping rabbits. After they learn the game, some children may enjoy making up animal riddles.

Partnership Movement

MIRRORING

Help the children form pairs. (This is a good time to pair girls with boys.) The first child does a motion and the second one mimics it as if she or he is a mirror image. Tell the children when to switch places as leader and mirror.

SCULPTURING

Help the children form pairs. (Again, this is a good opportunity to pair boys with girls.) The child who is the sculptor moves the arms, legs, head, and torso of the child who is "clay." The only rule is that the sculptor cannot move the "clay" in any hurtful way. The "clay" remains malleable until you say that it is time to finish up. At this point, the "sculptures" hold their poses for all to see. Then help the children exchange roles. Both girls and boys become absorbed in this engaging movement activity.

BACK TO BACK

Help the children form pairs of roughly equal heights. (When possible, pair a boy and a girl.) Tell the pairs of children to sit down back to back. Help the children lock arms together and ask them to stand up. This cooperative activity is a challenge that both girls and boys will rise to!

Relaxing and Stretching

RAG DOLLS

Play restful music and ask the children to pretend they are rag dolls dancing, flopping, drooping, sagging, and finally falling down in a heap. Then see if they can remain totally loose and relaxed while you lift up arms and legs and put them down again.

SPAGHETTI

Ask the children to pretend they are uncooked spaghetti sticks. Then ask them to pretend they are being cooked, getting more and more limp as they "cook." Eventually, they will droop to the floor. Then you can see if the strings of "spaghetti" stay limp when you move their arms, legs, hands, or feet.

STRETCH LIKE CATS

Ask children to pretend they are sleeping cats who are just waking up. Suggest that they take deep breaths and stretch all the parts of their bodies.

BALLOONS

Request that the children lie curled up on the floor like empty balloons. Then ask them to pretend they are filling up with air. When they have taken in all the air they can and have grown big and round, tell them to pretend they have developed small leaks. The "balloons" will let their air out slowly and sink to the floor as they deflate. You can also ask the "balloons" to pretend someone has pricked them with a pin. Then they will explode with loud pops and fall to the floor.

MUSICAL INSTRUMENTS

Both genders like to experiment with the sounds they can make with musical instruments. (It is fascinating to discover that a triangle sounds musical if it is held properly, but goes clunk if the child's hand is on the metal.) Children also like to use musical instruments to enhance their dramatic play. (A child may ring a bell to announce the arrival of the guests at the house or of the ice cream truck in the neighborhood.)

Children who feel shy about singing or movement are usually comfortable playing an instrument. Children may simply enjoy experimenting with the different instruments, or they may want to join with other children to form a band or orchestra.

Playing in a group requires cooperation, as the children follow directions and pay close attention to sequence, melody, tempo, dynamics, and rhythm. When children play musical instruments together, they have an opportunity to experience how following a leader can result in a cohesive group "performance."

As you work with the children, remember that no child needs special musical talent to experience pleasure and success with musical instruments. Through group interaction with their peers as they play musical instruments together, children will learn to listen to one another, respect individual contributions, and experience the rewards of cooperation.

On the following pages, we include some group activities with musical instruments that are sure to capture the interest of both boys and girls.

INSTRUMENTAL BAND OR ORCHESTRA

Materials you will need

Rhythm instruments: drums, triangles, bells, maracas, jingle clogs, rhythm sticks, tone blocks, sand blocks, and castanets
Recordings of musical accompaniments

Be sure to have enough instruments for each child to have one—or, if possible—several of each type of instrument. Introduce the instruments and teach the children the movements you will use to indicate when to start, stop, play in unison, play by section, play loudly or softly, and play rapidly or slowly. Encourage the children to listen to the beat, melody, and dynamics of the accompanying music.

To avoid problems over who plays what instrument, hold an instrument up, and ask, "Who would like to play the tone blocks?" If you do not have enough of a particular instrument to satisfy the demand, be careful not to favor one sex over the other when you choose who will play the coveted instruments. Reassure children that they will have a chance to switch instruments later.

You may wish to use a song such as Ella Jenkins's *Play Your Instruments and Make a Pretty Sound* from her recording *You'll Sing a Song and I'll Sing a Song*, or you can use any rhythmic music for accompaniment. (Make sure the accompaniment serves as background to the rhythm instruments.)

When the children are familiar with the conductor's signals, let them take turns leading the band or orchestra. Use this as an opportunity to teach that both women and men are conductors, and that girls, as well as boys, can aspire to that career.

MARCHING BAND

Materials you will need

Rhythm instruments
Recording of marching music (Sousa is a good choice)

Show the children the route for the march and select a band leader. (Make sure girls are leaders as often as boys are.) If you wish to add complexity, you can explain how the band leader can stop, turn around to face the musicians, and direct the players of the various instruments to play by section. Distribute the instruments and start the accompaniment.

Consider taking your rhythm instruments outside on a nice day. Children may form an outdoor marching band or simply experiment with the instruments and their sounds in outdoor space.

BLOCK RHYTHMS

Materials you will need

Sand blocks, and pairs of any plastic, wooden, or cardboard
    blocks you have
Recording of rhythmic music

Explain to the children that the instruments in this band are different kinds of blocks. Distribute the blocks so that each child has a pair of identical blocks. Let the children listen to how each set of blocks sounds when they are clapped, tapped, rubbed, or brushed together or against the floor. Then start the music and invite the children to accompany the music with their block instruments. Children of both genders are intrigued by the subtle differences in sound these pairs of instruments produce. For a variation on this theme, use sticks and rhythm sticks instead of blocks.

RAG TAG BAND

Materials you will need

Household objects: wooden and plastic spoons, wooden and
    plastic bowls of varying sizes, pots and pans, clay pots, strainers,
    pot lids, wooden scrub board, buckets, and so on
Recording of lively music with a pronounced beat

Introduce and distribute the household objects and let the children
experiment with different combinations to produce a medley of sounds.
Then form a ragtag band. Put on your recording and let the group
accompany the music. You may decide to conduct the first sessions, but
later you can let children take turns as the conductor. What child could
forego being part of this outlandish band?

MUSICAL CHAIRS

Materials you will need

Rhythm instruments (enough for each child)
Recording of catchy music

Ask the children to place their chairs in two lines back to back and to sit
on their chairs. Tell the children they are to walk around the outside of
all the chairs while the music plays and to sit down in any empty chair
when the music stops.

   Start the music and, as the children march, remove one chair. Then
when the timing feels right, stop the music. Each child will then scramble to find a chair to sit on. The child who finds no chair will choose a
rhythm instrument and play along with the music as the game continues. At the game's end, you will have a band playing a concert instead
of a group of unhappy losers and one triumphant winner! Both sexes
have fun playing this win-win game, especially since no children end up
on the sidelines with nothing to do.

Drum Beat Games

NAME RHYTHMS

As the children sit in a circle and listen, you will beat on a drum the
cadence of the name of a child in the group. For example, if the child's
name is Jamal Jefferson, you will beat two equal beats accenting the
second beat, skip a beat, and then beat three equal beats accenting the

first beat. The children will try to guess the name you are playing. When they have succeeded, continue with more names.

FOLLOW THE DRUM BEAT

The children will listen as you beat the drum at different tempos and volumes. Show the group the various drumming patterns you will use to represent ways to move around the room. For example, the children will tiptoe to a light tap, walk slowly stomping their feet to a slow heavy beat, and walk quickly or skip to a fast light beat. As children become adept at following the drum beats, you can increase the complexity of the patterns. Once they are accustomed to the game, children can take turns being the drummer.

Multicultural Instruments

Both girls and boys are fascinated by new and unusual instruments and sounds. If you can borrow or collect multicultural instruments such as rainsticks, talking drums, Tibetan gongs, Native American and African drums, children will love to play them and learn about their origins. Try to get recordings of music that are representative of the kind of music the instrument would accompany. Children will be interested in the variety of music from around the world.

Mini-Concerts

Tap into the resources in your immediate community. If the parents or older siblings of the children in your class play instruments, invite them in to give demonstrations and short "concerts" for your group. The children you work with will come together to hear and learn about a violin, a flute, an accordion, or a mandolin that a classroom guest plays.

In addition, you may be able to take the children in your group to a performance for young children, a band or an orchestra rehearsal, or a school concert. You will want to be sure ahead of time that the content and length of the performance is age appropriate.

CIRCLE-TIME DISCUSSIONS

As you interact with the children in your group, be alert to the "teachable moment" that occurs when a child behaves in a sexist way and/or makes a statement that reflects gender bias. You will also need to address any instances of conflict or divisiveness that have a negative impact on a particular child or on cooperation and friendship within your group.

For instance, if you were to hear a girl tell a boy who is dressing a doll, "Boys shouldn't play with dolls," you would, of course, address the situation right then. However, you might decide to use the incident as a springboard for sharing ideas and attitudes at circle time. Perhaps you would read the book *William's Doll* by Charlotte Zolotow, play the selection about William's doll from the Marlo Thomas recording *Free to Be . . . You and Me*, and follow up with a discussion about the issue. You would not embarrass the children involved by bringing up the incident you witnessed. Instead you would ask the group to share their ideas about William's feelings and their own feelings about "boy toys" and "girl toys." You would listen carefully to their comments and try to understand what assumptions the children were making and what experiences they were bringing to the discussion before posing questions to extend their thinking or sharing your own ideas and beliefs.

If you notice that the children in your group are dividing into single-gender groups or are excluding children from play, plan ways to promote friendship and cross-gender interaction at circle time. Read and discuss some books about friendship and introduce some of our circle-time activities that encourage togetherness. For example, you might read and discuss *George and Martha One Fine Day* by James Marshall, sing and talk about the song *The More We Get Together*, and play the *Elephant Game* in which all the "elephants" end up having tremendous fun together. Of course, you can decide to use circle time to discuss a classroom problem that emerges around these issues without using a song or a book as a lead-in. You might begin a discussion with a comment such as, "I've been noticing that only boys are using the block area" or "Some girls are telling the boys they can't play in the house corner."

If children seem to be making assumptions such as women are not police officers and men are not nurses, try to invite a female police officer and a male nurse to your circle time. Concrete examples are worth a plethora of words.

When you use a song, rhyme, fingerplay, or game and change some of the words to achieve gender equity or eliminate gender bias, you may need to discuss the changes with the group. You may be pleased to discover that although some children may begin by saying, "That's not the way it goes!" they will gradually understand the reasons for the changes.

After many discussions and sharing opportunities, you may be rewarded with a group of children who are often able to recognize instances of gender bias and unfairness and to speak up for themselves and each other in the event of inequity. You may stand back one day and observe that the children you teach are developing the ability to interact as equals and to function cooperatively within and as a group.

TO SUM UP . . .

Circle time is a perfect time to help counteract any sexist messages you find being perpetrated in popular songs, rhymes, fingerplays, and games; to plan group movement and musical activities and games in which all children are winners and both girls and boys can experience leading, following, and cooperating; and to discuss issues of gender equity and cooperation with the children. Your ongoing efforts to update your circle time will help children gain respect for their own and the other gender, develop the ability to question established attitudes and beliefs, and feel comfortable to be themselves.

BIBLIOGRAPHY FOR CIRCLE-TIME ACTIVITIES

The following bibliography contains many fine articles and books about music, movement, rhymes, fingerplays, and games. In addition, we have created a bibliography of songbooks, picture books of songs, and recordings with many popular songs and movement activities. But you should be aware that not every one of these selections is totally free of gender bias. When you read these articles and books or choose which songs or activities to include in your program, be sure to use your judgment as to whether the material meets your goals for gender equity and fostering cooperative play. Be creative in adapting materials to meet your needs.

General References

Barclay, Kathy Dulaney, and Walwer, Lynn. "Linking Lyrics and Literacy Through Song Picture Books." *Young Children* 47(4) (1992):76–85.

Bayless, Kathleen M., and Ramsey, Marjorie E. *Music: A Way of Life for the Young Child*. St. Louis, MO: C. V. Mosby, 1982.

Brand, Manny, and Fernie, David E. "Music in the Early Childhood Curriculum." *Childhood Education* 59(5) (1983):321–326.

Buchoff, Rita. "Joyful Voices: Facilitating Language Growth Through the Response to Chants." *Young Children* 49(4) (1994): 26–30.

Haines, Beatrice J. E., and Gerber, Linda L. *Leading Young Children to Music*. Columbus, OH: Merrill, 1988.

McDonald, Dorothy T. *Music in Our Lives: The Early Years*. Washington, DC: National Association for the Education of Young Children, 1979.

Reid, Rob. *Children's Juke Box: A Subject Guide to Musical Recordings and Programming Ideas for Songsters Ages 1 to 12*. Chicago, IL: American Library Association, 1995.

Sale, Laurie. *Growing Up with Music: A Guide to the Best Recorded Music for Children*. New York: Avon Books, 1992.

Sullivan, Molly. *Feeling Strong, Feeling Free: Movement Exploration for Young Children*. Washington, DC: National Association for the Education of Young Children, 1982.

Wolfe, Jan. "Singing with Children Is a Cinch!" *Young Children* 49(4) (1994):20–25.

_____. "Let's Sing It Again: Creating Music with Young Children." *Young Children* 47(2) (1992):56–61.

Books with Songs, Rhymes, Chants, Fingerplays, and Musical Games

Cole, Joanna. *Anna Banana: 101 Jump Rope Rhymes*. New York: Morrow, 1989.

_____. *A New Treasury of Children's Poetry: Old Favorites and New Discoveries*. Garden City, NY: Doubleday, 1984.

Cromwell, Liz, and Hibner, Dixie. *Finger Frolics: Finger Plays for Young Children*. Beltsville, MD: Gryphon House, 1993.

Dowell, Ruth I. *Move Over, Mother Goose! Finger Plays, Action Verses, and Funny Rhymes*. Beltsville, MD: Gryphon House, 1994.

Dunn, Sonja. *Crackers and Crumbs*. Portsmouth, NH: Heinemann, 1990.

_____. *Butterscotch Dreams: Chants for Fun and Learning*. Portsmouth, NH: Heinemann, 1987.

Fulton, Eleanor, and Smith, Pat. *Let's Slice the Ice: A Collection of Black Children's Ring Games and Chants*. St. Louis, MO: Magnamusic-Baton, 1978.

Graham, Terry Lynne. *Fingerplays and Rhymes*. Atlanta, GA: Humanics Learning, 1994.

Hastings, Scott E., Jr. *Miss Mary Mac All Dressed in Black*. Little Rock, AR: August House Publishers, 1990.

Mattox, Cheryl Warren. *Shake It to the One That You Love the Best: Play Songs and Lullabies from Black Musical Traditions*. El Sobrante, CA: Warren-Mattox Productions, 1989.

Schiller, Pam, and Moore, Thomas. *Where Is Thumbkin? 500 Activities to Use with Songs You Already Know*. Beltsville, MD: Gryphon House, 1994.

Weissman, Jackie. *My Toes Are Starting to Wiggle!* Overland Park, KS: Miss Jackie Publishing, 1989.

Winn, Marie. *The Fireside Book of Children's Songs*. New York: Simon and Schuster, 1974.

_____. The *Fireside Book of Fun and Game Songs*. New York: Simon and Schuster, 1974.

Wirth, Marian, Stassevitch, Verna, Shotwell, Rita, and Stemmler, Patricia. *Musical Games, Fingerplays and Rhythmic Activities for Early Childhood*. West Nyack, NY: Parker Publishing, 1983.

Yolen, Jane (Ed.). *Old MacDonald Song Book*. Honesdale, PA: Boyds Mills Press, 1994.

_____. *The Lap-Time Song and Play Book*. New York: Harcourt Brace Jovanovich, 1989.

Books with Movement Activities

Thompson, Myra K. *Jump for Joy*. West Nyack, NY: Parker Publishing, 1993.

Torbert, Marianne, and Schneider, Lynne B. *Follow Me Too: A Handbook of Movement Activities for Three to Five-Year-Olds*. Menlo Park, CA: Addison-Wesley, 1993.

Books with Win-Win Games

Gregson, Bob. *The Incredible Indoor Games Book*. Belmont, CA: Pitman Learning, 1982.

Luvmour, Sambhava, and Luvmour, Josette. *Everyone Wins!* Philadelphia, PA: New Society Publishers, 1990.

Sobel, Jeffrey. *Everybody Wins*. New York: Walker and Co., 1983.

Wilmes, Liz, and Wilmes, Dick. *Parachute Play*. Elgin, IL: Building Blocks, 1994.

Picture Books of Songs

Adams, Pam. *This Old Man*. New York: Child's Play International, 1975.

_____. *There Was an Old Lady*. New York: Child's Play International, 1972.

Aliki. *Go Tell Aunt Rhody*. New York: Macmillan, 1974.

_____. *Hush Little Baby*. New York: Prentice Hall, 1968.

Bullock, Kathleen. *She'll Be Comin' 'Round the Mountain*. New York: Simon & Schuster, 1993.

Carle, Eric. *Today Is Monday*. New York: Scholastic, 1992.

Conover, Chris. *Six Little Ducks*. New York: Thomas Y. Crowell, 1976.

Glazer, Tom. *On Top of Spaghetti*. New York: Good Year Books, 1995.

Hale, Sarah J. B. *Mary Had a Little Lamb*. New York: Scholastic, 1990.

Kennedy, Jimmy. *The Teddy Bears' Picnic*. San Diego, CA: Green Tiger Press, 1983.

Kovalski, Maryann. *The Wheels on the Bus*. Boston: Joy Street Books, 1987.

Peek, Merle. *Mary Wore Her Red Dress and Henry Wore His Green Sneakers*. New York: Houghton Mifflin, 1993.

Raffi. *Baby Beluga*. New York: Crown, 1988.

————. *One Light, One Sun*. New York: Crown, 1988.

————. *Shake My Sillies Out*. New York: Crown, 1987.

Rosen, Michael. *We're Going on a Bear Hunt*. New York: Margaret K. McElderry Books, 1989.

Spier, Peter. *London Bridge Is Falling Down*. New York: Doubleday, 1967.

Westcott, Nadine Brown. *The Lady with the Alligator Purse*. Boston: Little, Brown, 1989.

————. *I Know an Old Lady Who Swallowed a Fly*. Boston: Little, Brown, 1980.

Recordings

Arnold, Linda. *Happiness Cake*. A&M Records.

Beall, Pamela Conn, and Nipp, Susan Hagen. *Wee Sing and Play*—Musical Games and Rhymes for Children. Price, Stern, Sloan.

————. *Wee Sing Silly Songs*. Price, Stern, Sloan.

Berman, Marcia, and Zeitlin, Patty. *Won't You Be My Friend?*—*Songs for Social and Emotional Growth*. Educational Activities.

Brown, Linda Saxton. *Steppin' to the Music*. Linda Saxton Brown.

Chapin, Tom. *Family Tree*. Sony Kids' Music.

Collins, Mitzie. *Sounds Like Fun: Folksongs, Games, and Poems for Children*. Sampler Records.

Greg and Steve. *On the Move with Greg and Steve*. CTP/Youngheart Records.

————. *Playing Favorites*. CTP/Youngheart Records.

————. *We All Live Together—Volumes 1–4*. CTP/Youngheart Records.

Jenkins, Ella. *And One and Two*. Folkways/Smithsonian.

_____. *Play Your Instruments and Make a Pretty Sound*. Folkways/Smithsonian.

_____. *You'll Sing a Song and I'll Sing a Song*. Folkways/Smithsonian.

The King's Singers. *Kids' Stuff*. EMI Records Limited.

Mattox, Cheryl Warren. *Shake It to the One That You Love the Best: Play Songs and Lullabies from Black Musical Traditions*. Warren-Mattox Productions.

Murray, Anne. *There's a Hippo in My Tub*. Capitol Records.

Palmer, Hap. *Backwards Land*. Hap-Pal Music.

_____. *Getting to Know Myself*. Educational Activities.

_____. *Rhythms on Parade*. Hap-Pal Music.

Paxton, Tom. *Suzy Is a Rocker*. Sony Kids' Music.

Raffi. *Baby Beluga*. Shoreline/MCA.

_____. *One Light, One Sun*. Shoreline/MCA.

_____. *Singable Songs for the Very Young* and *More Singable Songs*. Shoreline/MCA.

Ronno. *"Yes, I Can!" Songs*. Kimbo.

Rosen, Gary, and Shontz, Bill. *Uh-Oh!* Rosenshontz Records.

Seeger, Pete. *Song and Play Time*. Folkways/Smithsonian.

Sharon, Lois, and Bram. *In the Schoolyard*. Elephant Records/A&M.

_____. *Smorgasbord*. Elephant Records/A&M.

Thomas, Marlo, and Friends. *Free to Be . . . a Family*. A&M Records.

_____. *Free to Be . . . You and Me*. A&M Records.

Various Artists. *Kids in Motion*. CTP/Youngheart Records.

RESOURCES

The following catalogs are good sources for early childhood recordings, rhythm band instruments, multicultural instruments, and music for movement activities. Recordings can also be ordered through your local music and book stores that carry music for children. Many of the recordings we have named can be found in these early childhood catalogs.

CHILDCRAFT
250 College Park
P.O. Box 1811
Peoria, IL 61656-1811
1-800-638-1504

CONSTRUCTIVE PLAYTHINGS
1227 E. 119th St.
Grandview, MO 64030
1-800-448-4115

KAPLAN SCHOOL SUPPLY
CORP.
1310 Lewisville-Clemmons Rd.
P.O. Box 609
Lewisville, NC 27023-0609
1-800-334-2014

KIMBO EDUCATIONAL
Dept. W
P.O. Box 477V
Long Branch, NJ 07740
1-800-631-2187

LAKESHORE LEARNING
MATERIALS
2695 E. Dominquez St.
P.O. Box 6261
Carson, CA 90749
1-800-421-5354

MUSIC FOR LITTLE PEOPLE
P.O. Box 1720
Lawndale, CA 90260
1-800-727-2233

SAMPLER RECORDS
P.O. Box 19270
Rochester, NY 14619
1-800-537-2755

Choosing Books That Are Free of Gender Stereotypes and That Promote Friendship between the Sexes

You may have already screened your early childhood book collection in order to remove books and stories that have obvious gender stereotypes or that show either sex in an unfavorable light. But as you look more closely at the books and stories you currently share with the children you teach, you may be surprised to discover other subtle yet insidious sexism.

In this chapter, we offer ways to cope with the problems related to gender that are reflected in children's literature. We examine what makes a good book about girls and/or women and how to identify books that treat female and male characters as individuals, not only as traditional representatives of their gender. We suggest ways to counteract sexist messages in folktales, fairy tales, and nursery rhymes and discuss the importance of books that show females and males in friendly, cooperative relationships. And finally, we present an annotated bibliography that emphasizes books that are generally free of gender stereotypes, books with girls and/or women as protagonists, and books that promote friendship and cross-gender cooperation.

A BALANCED BOOKSHELF

When we refer to a balanced bookshelf, we are not talking about one that is stable and without a wobble! In this instance, we are speaking of the number of books with male protagonists compared to the number of books with female protagonists. Check your shelves and count how many books you have in which boys and men are the main characters. Then do the same for girls and women. (Be sure to count male and female animal characters as well. Note that in a book such as *Little Blue and Little Yellow* by Leo Lionni the main characters are male, even though they are not people or animals.)

If you have as many books with female protagonists as you do books with male protagonists, yours is an unusual collection. Since many more books about boys are published, your bookshelves are more likely to reflect that reality. This imbalance sends a message to both genders: boys and men are more important than girls and women.

To address this imbalance, add books with female main characters to your shelves. In addition to purchasing new books, use the public library to borrow books about girls and women for your classroom. Of course, it is important to assess the attributes of any female protagonist, since having a female as the main character does not guarantee that the book is nonsexist and free of stereotypes.

When glaring stereotypes are present (particularly in mediocre books), remove these books from your bookshelf. But be careful not to throw the baby out with the bath water. There are some books in which stereotyping may occur that are worth reading for their literary merit. Or you may have overriding reasons for wishing to include a less than perfect book in your program. Perhaps a book is particularly good at clarifying a value or reaching children through humor. In Donald Hall's prize-winning book, *Ox-Cart Man*, the male protagonist goes out into the world, while the women characters stay home and do house-work. If you read this book to children, you can discuss with them what life was like in the days of ox-carts and how times have changed since. In the case of a classic, such as *Peter Rabbit* by Beatrix Potter, where Peter is shown as curious and naughty, and his sisters as quiet and obedient, you can use the stereotypes as a basis for discussion. If you feel compelled to use a book such as *Amelia Bedelia* by Peggy Parish, in which Amelia is portrayed as comically obtuse, be sure to discuss the fact that anyone, male or female, can, like Amelia, take instructions too literally.

When choosing books for your shelves, *always* keep in mind the general characteristics of a good book for children. Even a nonsexist book should meet the criteria for quality children's literature! Look for books that are written clearly, use language in interesting ways, are relevant to children, and have believable characters, strong plots, and fine illustrations. Good books should stimulate children's thinking, arouse their feelings, awaken their senses, and help them deepen and extend their understanding of their world.

GIRLS CAN BE STRONG AND BOYS GENTLE

In recent years, more books have been published that are free of rigid sex roles and that include a wider range of possible careers, activities, and behaviors for both sexes. There are more smart and active female characters and sensitive and nurturing male characters than ever before. More books show females and males as multidimensional human beings with a wide range of interests, feelings, desires, strengths, and foibles. More books reflect the diversity of people in the world and deal with real-life situations faced by children and adults, such as death and divorce. More books acknowledge different lifestyles: mothers working outside the home, fathers taking care of children, parents sharing family responsibilities, children living with one parent, and women remaining happily single. But since these books are hidden among the many that continue to center around nuclear families and traditional roles and behaviors, you will need to look carefully to find them.

Once you have found appropriate books, read them to the children and use them to contradict stereotypes and open up discussions that illustrate that differences and similarities are more pronounced between individuals than between genders. Read a book such as Vera B. William's *A Chair for My Mother*, in which the female protagonists are all proactive, or *Ten, Nine, Eight* by Molly Bang in which a nurturing father puts his daughter to bed. Share books such as *Come to the Meadow* by Anna Grossnickle Hines, in which a girl is an initiator, and *My Mama Says There Aren't Any Zombies, Ghosts, Vampires, Creatures, Demons, Monsters, Fiends, Goblins, or Things* by Judith Viorst, in which a boy is afraid. As children share their responses to these books and listen to each other's similar and different feelings and experiences, they will be moving toward accepting other points of view and recognizing commonalities they share with the other gender.

ENCOURAGING FRIENDSHIP AND COOPERATION BETWEEN THE SEXES

Most children's books about friendship show same-sex friendships. Of course, it is fine when two girls or two boys are friends, but too often children's literature suggests that the *best* friends are those of the same gender or, as in the case of many fairy tales, that male/female friendships have a romantic component. Children should be helped to feel free to choose their friends without regard to gender. For that reason, it is especially important to have as many books as possible that show cross-gender friendships. These books will demonstrate to children that it is appropriate to have friends of the other sex and, more importantly, that such friendships can be rewarding.

In your search for books about cross-gender friendship, be sure to look for books in which children of both sexes are shown playing together, cooperating, and working together to solve problems. (Try to find books that show girls or women as able to provide solutions to problems, not just books that show their male counterparts as the problem solvers.) Look for books that show the sexes intermingling rather than dividing into separate camps.

Plan to use picture books about friendship and cooperation as a basis for discussions with children about these issues. To lead into a discussion of friendship and harmony in your group, read a book about friendship between males and females, such as *Everett Anderson's Friend* by Lucille Clifton. Get children to think and talk about why Everett and Maria become friends and what makes people like each other. If your agenda is to encourage group togetherness and cooperation, try *Swimmy* by Leo Lionni, in which the fish cooperate to hide Swimmy and protect themselves. If you want to address the problem of conflict, you can choose one of the many books that deal with conflict and show children solving interpersonal problems. Books such as *The Hating Book* by Charlotte Zolotow and *Let's Be Enemies* by Janice Udry could be followed by a discussion of how two friends can be furious with one another but still remain friends. *Benjamin and Tulip* by Rosemary Wells and *Oliver Button Is a Sissy* by Tomie dePaola can open a discussion of bullying and gender bias. Since Tulip is the bully in *Benjamin and Tulip*, you will have an opportunity to point out that bullying is not based on gender.

WHAT TO LOOK FOR IN BOOKS

As you search for books of merit for your early childhood program, pay attention to the subtle and not so subtle messages in every book you consider. Keeping in mind that not every statement will apply to every book, use the following list as a guide for selecting a particular book for your collection or for reading to children.

> Boys, as well as girls, are allowed to cry, to express fear and anxiety, to show caring and compassion.
>
> Girls, as well as boys, are problem solvers.
>
> Girls, as well as boys, are leaders and have adventures.
>
> Girls and boys are shown as intelligent, courageous, and curious.
>
> Girls, as well as boys, are allowed to express anger.
>
> Fathers and mothers are equally caring.
>
> Women and men are seen in nontraditional, as well as traditional, roles.
>
> Men and women in traditional roles are seen as liberated in other ways. (For example, a mother may do the dishes but also solve a family problem.)
>
> Women and men are seen as working in nontraditional, as well as traditional, careers and jobs.
>
> Secondary characters are free of obvious stereotypes.
>
> There is a reasonable balance between the numbers of female and male protagonists and secondary characters.

Females and males are friends.

Males and females cooperate to accomplish a goal or solve a problem. Females have equal input.

Characters are respectful of members of the other sex.

Remember that these criteria serve as guidelines, not as absolutes. Few books will send all the messages considered in this list. One book may have one message, a second book another. And, as we have said earlier, a book that fails these standards may be worth including in your program for its literary merit and its potential for enlightening discussion. On the other hand, books that meet these standards but fail to meet general standards for quality children's books (those that are poorly written or have mediocre illustrations, for example) should be eliminated.

Our annotated bibliography of books that are nonsexist and that promote cooperation and friendship between the sexes can be found at the end of this chapter.

MESSAGES IN FOLKTALES, FAIRY TALES, AND NURSERY RHYMES

Folktales and fairy tales are rife with stereotypes and absolutes. The females in these stories are usually either young and beautiful or aging and vicious, and the majority of female characters are negatively portrayed in some way. Many of the lovely heroines are submissive and ineffective, the women in powerful positions are wicked and vitriolic, and virtually all stepmothers and stepsisters are mean and ugly. Nurturing and compliant females such as Snow White and Cinderella are frequently victims, and more adventurous females such as Red Riding Hood and Goldilocks get into serious trouble. It is the rare girl in a fairy tale or folktale who saves the day by using her brain.

On the other hand, males have to be clever and industrious to succeed (witness what happens to the three little pigs), whereas females need only be beautiful (Rapunzel and Sleeping Beauty) and lucky (Cinderella and Snow White) to attract husbands who will rescue and take care of them. Men are usually shown as handsome and brave (Prince Charming), or as ugly and evil (Rumplestiltskin and all those ogres and giants). Male wolves and foxes, while cunning and wily, are up to no good. Males who are stupid and lazy either change dramatically and overcome these liabilities through cleverness and diligence, or they end up vanquished or dead. Kings are shown as patriarchal rulers with the power to pass on their lands and daughters to males of their choice. (The queens are rarely consulted.) The males, who are chosen by the kings to inherit their kingdoms and marry their daughters, are nearly always young, clever, and handsome.

Nursery rhymes, too, perpetrate stereotypes. The old woman who did not know what to do with her many children is not only old and unattractive, she is incompetent as well. Little Miss Muffet is afraid of a spider, Little Bo Peep is inept, and Mistress Mary is quite contrary. Peter, Peter Pumpkin Eater abuses his wife, Georgie Porgy bullies and teases girls, Little Boy Blue sleeps on the job, and the Royal Duke of York seems to have nothing better to do than to charge up and down hills leading his 10,000 men.

So what to do? Since folktales, fairy tales, and nursery rhymes are very much a part of the culture, it is hard to avoid them. And children love them for many reasons. But when fictional females are characterized as vicious, shrewish, ineffective, and needy and when males are rendered as domineering, devious, covetous, and lazy, children are bound to absorb these negative messages about their own and the other gender. Children who hear in these tales that females must be beautiful and submissive in order to be chosen by a successful male, or that females must not aspire to leadership roles, will be influenced by these damaging and limiting stereotypes. Children who hear stories that say males must be smart and hardworking to rise to the top and that only handsome men deserve beautiful wives, cannot avoid being affected by these moralistic and constraining lessons. For children who live in blended families, the stereotypes about wicked and ugly stepmothers and stepsisters can be particularly distressing.

In spite of the problems involved in using folktales, fairy tales, and nursery rhymes in your program, we urge you not to ban them categorically. Instead, use them to sensitize children to the problems of stereotyping and absolutes. Through discussions with the children you teach, you can help them begin to understand that no one is totally good or bad and that everybody makes mistakes. In your discussions with the children, ask questions that will help them recognize that most older women are not ugly, jealous, and vengeful, and that most males are not mean, scheming, and greedy. Talk with children about the fact that beauty is not necessarily paired with goodness, that ugliness is not necessarily joined to evil, and that comeliness is not essential to success. Using examples from their own experience, remind children that both girls and boys can be brave and capable, and that both boys and girls can be frightened and need help.

In addition, be sure to provide frequent antidotes to the stereotypes in folktales and fairy tales you use with children. For instance, in the Chinese folktale *Lon Po Po*, retold by Ed Young, three girls outwit the hungry wolf, and in the modern fairy tale *The Paper Bag Princess* by Robert Munsch, the smart and courageous princess lets the prince know that behavior is more important than appearance. Children will enjoy the contrast between these stories and the usual tales! Of course, you will also want to read a majority of nonsexist books about real people: stories that depict everyday characters with human motives and with both strengths and weaknesses.

In *Father Gander Nursery Rhymes* by Doug Larche, you will find nonsexist and nonviolent revisions of popular nursery rhymes. After reading the original and rewritten version of a rhyme to the children, encourage them to discuss the differences in the two. Ask the children which version they like better and why, and explore with them which one they think describes people more accurately. Remember—there are no right or wrong answers!

You will also want to read poems, such as those found in Shel Silverstein's *Where the Sidewalk Ends* and Joanna Cole's *A New Treasury of Children's Poetry: Old Favorites and New Discoveries*, as alternatives to traditional nursery rhymes. If any poems contain gender stereotypes, either avoid them or use them as a basis for discussion.

Dramatizing stories or rhymes with the children acting the various parts can be a particularly good way to develop children's awareness of what is or is not biased in folktales, fairy tales, and nursery rhymes. As you work with the children to help them act out different tales and nursery rhymes, you can involve them in figuring out nonstereotypic ways to "perform" the stories. Use their ideas (and your own, as needed) to alter or alternate roles and reverse or change some of the actions.

On the following pages, we include a few examples of popular tales and nursery rhymes children like to dramatize and that can be easily adapted to eliminate gender stereotyping.

ACTING OUT FOLKTALES AND FAIRY TALES

You may wish to use several versions of any traditional folktale or fairy tale you decide to share and act out with the children in your group. Children are often fascinated by the variations in tales and the different interpretations by illustrators. You can talk with the children about any gender stereotypes in the tales and ask them to think about ways to adapt the stories to remedy the problem.

THE GINGERBREAD BOY

Materials you will need

Copy of the book *The Gingerbread Boy* (Use more than one version of this story if possible; we like Paul Galdone's interpretation.)
Gingerbread mix

After reading the story of the gingerbread boy, discuss whether the gingerbread boy could have been a **gingerbread girl** and whether the clever fox could have been a female. Then suggest that the children can make both a gingerbread girl and a gingerbread boy.

Following the recipe on the box of mix, make gingerbread dough with the children. Then help them shape two large gingerbread figures—one a girl and one a boy. This is a good time to discuss what makes boys and girls different (anatomy) and what helps people guess what sex a person is (clothes, hairstyles).

After children put the gingerbread boy and girl into the oven, it can be fun to have a parent or another staff member remove the cooked figures and hide them in a prearranged place. When the children return with you to take the gingerbread cookies out of the oven, they will find the oven is empty! Then you will help the children go on a hunt for the "runaways." When the two gingerbread children are found (with your help), everyone can have a good time eating pieces of the gingerbread figures. All the children in your group will like pretending they are hungry foxes!

THE THREE BILLY GOATS GRUFF

Materials you will need

Copy of the book *The Three Billy Goats Gruff* (Use several versions of this tale; we like the one by P. C. Asbjornsen.)
Climber with a bridge locked in place at a safe height

Discuss the fact that there are female goats as well as male goats. Choose children to be the first, second, and third billy/**nanny** goats. Then choose a girl or a boy to be the troll. Often, quiet girls or boys will be surprisingly effective in this role! (Of course, no children should be made to act out parts they do not want. For example, a child who is sensitive about being small may refuse the part of the tiniest goat, an overweight child may not want to be the biggest goat, and some children may not want to take the part of the unpleasant troll.)

Children say the lines as the three goats cross the bridge.

> *Goat:* "*Trip, trap, trip, trap.*"
> *Troll:* *Who's that tripping over my bridge?*
> *Goat:* *It is I, the little Billy / Nanny Goat Gruff. And I'm going over to the hillside to eat the green grass.*
> *Troll:* *Oh, no you're not, for I'm going to gobble you up! . . . etc.*

In the end, the largest Billy/**Nanny** Goat jumps off the bridge and the troll runs away.

LITTLE RED RIDING HOOD

Materials you will need

Copy of the book *Little Red Riding Hood* (Try more than one version of this tale to share with the children; we like Trina Schart Hyman's illustrations in her retelling of this tale by Grimm.)

Basket and pretend goodies
Red cape or shawl (A red sweatshirt with a hood works well for a gender-equitable version of this story.)
Blanket and "bed"

Choose children for the roles of Red Riding Hood, the grandmother, the mother, the woodcutter, and the wolf. Let them act out the story in the traditional way, and then reverse the roles. Try having a boy take the role of Red Riding Hood, girls act out the roles of the woodcutter and the wolf, and change the grandmother to grandfather and the mother to father. Children will love repeating the lines, "Grandmother/grandfather, what big eyes you have . . ." and "The better to see you with, my dear . . . ." Of course, no children should be made to take parts they do not want, but by alternating roles you can demonstrate dramatically that the victim need not be female, that the villain can be either sex, that the rescuer is not always male, and that both genders can participate in parenting and nurturing.

If a child refuses a role based on gender bias, use this as an opportunity for later discussion. Of course, you will not single out any individual child as biased, but will open a discussion with a statement such as, "I have noticed that sometimes boys don't want to act out the part of Red Riding Hood."

Two variants of the Red Riding Hood story that children of both sexes like to hear and act out are *The Gunniwolf* by Wilhelmina Harper and *Lon Po Po: A Red Riding Hood Story from China* by Ed Young.

GOLDILOCKS AND THE THREE BEARS

Materials you will need

Copy of the book *The Three Bears* (A collection of different versions of the book will provide a richer experience for the children; Jan Brett's interpretation is beautiful.)

Cooking pot

Large cooking spoon

Measuring cup

Hot plate

Oatmeal, cornmeal, grits, or other grains to make porridge

Three cereal bowls (one large, one medium, one small)

Three spoons of the three different sizes

Three chairs of the three different sizes (You can use hollow blocks or real chairs.)

Three beds of the three different sizes (You can make these using whatever you have: blankets, hollow blocks, a cot, a mat, or a child-sized doll bed.)

Curly blond wig (optional)

After reading and talking about the story, set the stage with the props listed here. Then make porridge (either the old-fashioned kind or instant oatmeal works well) with a group of children. Place some porridge in each of the three different-sized bowls. Next, tell all the children that they are going to pretend to be the bears and go for a "walk in the forest" outside of the room while the porridge cools.

In advance of this activity, plan for a parent or colleague to act the part of Goldilocks while you and the children are out walking. Unbeknownst to the "bears," "Goldilocks" will slip into your room, put the right-sized spoons into the bowls, stir up the two bigger bowls of porridge, ladle the porridge from the smallest bowl back into the cooking pot, and return the smallest spoon and bowl to the table; then "Goldilocks" will turn the smallest chair on its side and climb into the smallest bed and pretend to sleep. When you return with your "bears," lead them to the porridge table and the chairs, and let them discover what has happened in their absence. Then have them look at the three beds. When they find "Goldilocks," she or he will wake up, cry out in fear, and run from the room. Children of both genders are excited and delighted by this reenactment of the story. At snack time, you can let each child eat the reheated porridge.

Children will use the props you have gathered for this play to make up their own dramatizations of the story. As children act out the tale, you can suggest that the baby bear could be a girl, that Goldilocks could be a boy, and that papa bear could be the parent who cooks the porridge.

THE LITTLE RED HEN

Materials you will need

Copy of the book *The Little Red Hen* (Two you might use are the versions by Janina Domanska and Paul Galdone.)
Child-sized rake

Container for pretend seeds
Watering can
Basket for harvesting
Bread pan
Plate

Select children to play the parts of the little red hen and her barnyard friends. The little red hen will ask her friends if they wish to help plant, sow, or harvest the wheat, and they will answer, "Not I!" She will reply, "I will then." In the end, the little red hen will mime eating the bread she has made without the help of her friends. Each time the children act out this story, they will get the message that a female can be self-reliant, capable, and persevering. They will also have a good time acting out the story together. (Remember that you can switch the lead role of the little red hen to that of the little red rooster to give boys a chance to be independent, competent, and determined too.)

STONE SOUP

Materials you will need

Copy of the book *Stone Soup* (We like the Marcia Brown and Ann McGovern versions, but there are others. They all vary somewhat, so decide which one to act out with your group, or act out all of them.)
Large pot
Clean stone

Hot plate or stove
Large cooking spoon
Soup ladle
Paring knives
Cutting boards
Vegetables such as potatoes, tomatoes, onions, carrots, peas, celery, corn, and beans
Container of water

Choose a child or children to be the hungry traveler(s). The other children will be the villagers who bring the water and vegetables for the soup pot. The traveler(s) will put the stone in the pot, and the villagers will cut up and add the vegetables. You will supervise the preparation of the vegetables and the cooking of this "stone soup." When the soup is finished, all the players will enjoy sampling it together. Be sure to give girls and boys equal opportunities to be the clever traveler(s).

ACTING OUT NURSERY RHYMES

You may wish to collect some books of traditional nursery rhymes for children to examine and compare. A few to try are Tomie dePaola's *Mother Goose*, Arnold Lobel's *The Random House Book of Mother Goose*, Anne Rockwell's *Grey Goose and Gander: And Other Mother Goose Rhymes*, and Charlotte Voake's *Over the Moon: A Book of Nursery Rhymes*. These collections are not free of stereotypes, but they will provide you with the original verses and a variety of illustrations to go with them. You can use the books to talk with the children about ways to change and update the rhymes. (We also like to include Douglas Larche's *Father Gander Nursery Rhymes* in any collection, since he rewrites many traditional rhymes to eliminate sexism and violence.)

LITTLE MISS MUFFET

Materials you will need

Pillow to represent a tuffet
Plastic bowl and spoon

Change *Little Miss Muffet* to *Little Friend Muffet*. Give both girls and boys turns acting the parts of Little Friend Muffet and the spider. Substitute a child's name if you wish.

> *Little **Tyrone** Muffet*
> *Sat on a tuffet*
> *Eating **his** curds and whey.*
> *Along came a spider,*
> *And sat down beside **him**,*
> *And frightened **Tyrone** away.*

Before you begin this dramatization, show the children where the frightened Little Friend Muffet can run. Let a child act the part of the spider and creep up next to the tuffet and frighten Friend Muffet. Little Friend Muffet will enjoy feigning fear, dropping the bowl and spoon, and running away along the designated route before rejoining the group. (If you have a large group, you can include more children by having two or more spiders and friends. Add pillows, bowls, and spoons for each new set of players.)

Both girls and boys are interested to learn that curds and whey is another way of identifying cottage cheese. Some of them will enjoy getting together to make and sample curds and whey.

> **Curds and Whey Recipe**
> 1 quart milk
> ¼ cup vinegar
> Measuring cup
> Saucepan
> Cooking spoon
> Hot plate (or stove)

Combine the vinegar and milk. Simmer the mixture in a pan on a hot plate until curds form. Drain the whey. Cool the curds and add salt to taste. This cottage cheese can be eaten on crackers for a snack.

JACK BE NIMBLE

Materials you will need
Candle holder
Candle

Use the names of the children in your group instead of *Jack*. Have the children stand in a circle around the candlestick. One at a time, in order, let the children jump over the candlestick while you and the other children say the rhyme using the name of the child who is jumping. This game gives everyone an equal chance to be agile and active.

> *Jack (**Ramona**) be nimble,*
> *Jack (**Ramona**) be quick.*
> *Jack (**Ramona**) jump over*
> *The candlestick!*

JACK AND JILL

Materials you will need
Pail
Ramp for the hill
Pillows
Strip of gauze

Choose two children, a boy and a girl, and have them walk up the "hill" holding the pail between them. On cue, "Jack" and "Jill" will fall down the hill into the soft pillows. "Jack" will rub the crown of his head, and "Jill" will wrap it in a bandage. With the next pair of children, reverse the rhyme and have "Jill" fall down and break her crown and "Jack" tend to her injured head.

If you like, you can play this using the original verse and adding our verse, which mentions Jill before Jack.

Jack and Jill went up the hill
To fetch a pail of water.
Jack fell down and broke his crown,
And Jill came tumbling after.

Jill and Jack went right on back
To fetch a pail of water.
Jill fell down and broke her crown,
And Jack came tumbling after.

This is a good rhyme to stage outdoors, particularly if you have a small hill. In hot weather, put water in the pail. The actors will be eager for a chance to get splashed!

HEY DIDDLE DIDDLE

Materials you will need

Fiddle and bow made from cardboard

Name boards with pictures for each of the players

Paper punch

Sturdy cord

White or yellow paper plate

Cut out a cardboard fiddle and bow and enlist the children's help in decorating them. The children can also help make the name boards for the cat, the dog, the cow, the dish, and the spoon. Use cut-out pictures to represent the characters or have the children draw the pictures. If the children are able, have them print the names on the name boards. Cut cords long enough to go over the children's heads with room to spare. Punch two holes in each name board, string a cord through the holes, and tie it. Use the paper plate to represent the moon and place it on a hollow block or a small cardboard carton.

Name a child for each of the parts: the cat, the cow, the dog, the dish, and the spoon. Give them the appropriate name cards to wear around their necks. The players will act out the rhyme, while the children in the audience chant the following verse. In order not to lose your "dish" and "spoon," be sure to tell these children where they should run and when to return to the group.

Hey diddle diddle,
The cat and the fiddle,
The cow jumped over the moon.
The little dog laughed
To see such sport,
And the dish ran away
With the spoon!

Repeat with a new cast of characters.

THE THREE LITTLE KITTENS

Materials you will need

Three pairs of mittens
Wash basin
Drying rack
Pie pan

Copy of the book *The Three Little Kittens* (We like the version by Lorinda Bryan Cauley.)

Read the book and familiarize the children with the rhyme. When you are ready to act out the rhyme, choose three children to be the kittens (mix up the sexes) and one child to be the mother or father cat. The players will act out the rhyme while you and the children in the audience chant the following verses. When the children know the rhyme well, they can stop the chant to let the three kittens and the parent cat say their own lines as they act out their parts. Give the "kittens" some ideas as to where they can lose their mittens, how to pretend to wash them, and so on.

The three little kittens,
They lost their mittens,
And they began to cry,
*"Oh, Mama (**Papa**) dear,*
We sadly fear,
Our mittens we have lost."

"What! Lost your mittens,
You naughty kittens!
Then you shall have no pie."

"Meow, meow, meow, meow,
We shall have no pie."

The three little kittens,
They found their mittens,
And they began to sigh,

*"Oh, Mama (**Papa**) dear,*
See here, see here,
Our mittens we have found."

"What! Found your mittens,
You good little kittens!
Then you shall have some pie."

"Purr, purr, purr, purr,
We shall have some pie."

The three little kittens
Put on their mittens,
And soon ate up the pie.

*"Oh, Mama (**Papa**) dear,*
We sadly fear,
Our mittens we have soiled."

"What! Soiled your mittens,
You naughty kittens!"
Then they began to cry,
"Meow, meow, meow, meow,"
They began to cry.

The three little kittens,
They washed their mittens,
And hung them up to dry.
*"Oh, Mama (**Papa**) dear,*
Look here, look here,
Our mittens, we have washed."

"What! Washed your mittens,
You good little kittens!
But I smell a rat close by!
Hush, hush, hush, hush,
I smell a rat close by!"

TO SUM UP . . .

As you can see from the material presented in this chapter, there are many ways to counteract sexism and divisiveness through literature and related activities. Use your growing knowledge of gender issues to judge the merits of any books, folktales, or fairy tales you include in your repertoire. Although you will read mainly nonsexist books and act out folk and fairy tales and nursery rhymes in new ways, you may choose to read and use as a basis for discussion some literature that contains gender bias and dissension between the sexes. Through your ongoing efforts to "revisit storytime," you will heighten the awareness of the children you teach to the benefits of gender equity and friendship and cooperation between girls and boys.

ANNOTATED BIBLIOGRAPHY OF CHILDREN'S BOOKS THAT ENCOURAGE GENDER EQUITY AND FOSTER COOPERATION AND FRIENDSHIP BETWEEN THE SEXES

Our annotated bibliography includes a variety of books to help children feel free to be themselves and to be aware of a wider range of possibilities in their lives. To address the unbalanced bookshelf, we decided to include a majority of books in which females are the protagonists. Although we looked for books about females who are adventurous, resourceful, curious, assertive, and intelligent, we did not omit books about females who are nurturing and kind or have faults. We made an effort to find books that show males as nurturing, caring, friendly, and cooperative, as well as some that show males as vulnerable, fearful, and sad. We selected books in which both males and females are shown in nontraditional roles and/or taking part in nontraditional activities. We sought out books about friendship and cooperation, particularly those about strong cross-gender friendships and cooperation between girls and boys. We also found books in which characters accept differences and solve conflicts.

We left out some fine books from this bibliography because they do not apply to the issues of gender equity and cross-gender cooperation or because they have a preponderance of male characters. Of course, you will share with the children you work with many excellent books with male protagonists. But to address the imbalance between the numbers of books about males and the numbers of books about females that exist in literature for children, we urge you to read at least as many good books about females as about males.

Here, we share books we have found to be suitable and we give our reasons for selecting these books. Our list, though comprehensive, is by no means all inclusive. You are sure to discover books that we missed. And, of course, more books that meet our criteria for good nonsexist literature for children continue to be published. Keep this in mind as you use our list and continue your own search for nonsexist children's literature.

Since children develop at different rates and have different interests at different times, the age designations in the following annotations are intended to be used as guidelines, not as absolutes.

Abercrombie, Barbara. Illustrated by Mark Graham. *Charlie Anderson*. New York: Margaret K. McElderry Books, 1990. (3–7)
Two sisters, whose parents are divorced, find a cat who, like them, spends time in two homes. The sensitive pastel illustrations capture the emotions of the two young girls and the fat and happy cat.

Aliki. *Overnight at Mary Bloom's*. New York: Greenwillow Books, 1987. (3–5)
An energetic little girl spends the night with her extraordinary friend, Mary Bloom, and has a rollicking good time with this delightful woman. The brightly colored drawings have as much energy as the characters. For more fun with these friends, read At Mary Bloom's.

_____. *Feelings*. New York: Greenwillow Books, 1984. (3–7)

Children will learn words to describe such feelings as boredom, jealousy, grief, and frustration as they read about the emotions of the characters in this engaging book. The text informs without lecturing, and the cartoonlike illustrations show a whole range of feelings.

_____. *We Are Best Friends*. New York: Greenwillow Books, 1982. (4–8)

The boys in this book must deal with their feelings when one of them moves away. They each make new friends but remain best friends. The clear, colorful illustrations reflect the boys' feelings and show girls and boys interacting in school activities and outdoor play. In Annie Bananie, *by Leah Komaiko, two girls face the same problem.*

Andrews, Jan. Illustrated by Ian Wallace. *Very Last First Time*. New York: Margaret K. McElderry Books, 1985. (5–8)
An Inuit girl goes alone under the ice to collect mussels for the first time. Radiant illustrations depict the world of the Inuit culture, and the pictures that show the sea bed under the ice seem as real to the reader as to the brave protagonist.

Angelou, Maya. Photographed by Margaret Courtney-Clarke. *My Painted House, My Friendly Chicken and Me*. New York: Clarkson N. Potter Publishers, 1994. (5–8)
Thandi, an 8-year old African girl, describes Ndebele culture in poetic language. Lovely photographs depict this girl's daily life experiences.

————. Illustrated by Jean-Michel Basquiat. *Life Doesn't Frighten Me.* New York: Stewart, Tabori & Chang, 1993. (5–8)

This poem by Maya Angelou speaks of the many fears children experience in the process of growing up. The bold, contemporary art of the illustrations and the words of the poem unite to express determination and courage in the face of fear.

Anholt, Catherine, and Anholt, Lawrence. *All about You.* New York: Viking Press, 1992. (2–4)

This book invites children to talk about themselves and their likes and dislikes. The colorful and engaging illustrations show equal numbers of girls and boys.

————. *Kids.* Cambridge, MA: Candlewick Press, 1992. (2–5)

Delightful and detailed illustrations show girls and boys involved together and separately in everyday life. Many cross-gender friendships are shown in the pages of this lively rhyming book. One cautionary note: Two of the three large pictures are of boys; the one of a girl shows her sleeping. However, overall there are more pictures of girls than of boys, and the parents are shown as equally involved in chores and childcare. A charming book by the same authors, Here Come the Babies, *has a similar format.*

Baer, Edith. Illustrated by Steve Bjorkman. *This Is the Way We Go to School: A Book about Children around the World.* New York: Scholastic, 1990. (3–8)

Boys and girls from all over the world go to school by conventional and not-so-conventional means. Girls and boys are shown traveling together, in same-sex groups, and by themselves. The rhyming text and the light-hearted illustrations add interest to this multicultural geography lesson.

Bang, Molly. *Delphine.* New York: William Morrow, 1988. (4–8)

In this fantastical book, a young girl, unaware of her bravery and skills, feels unsure she can conquer her fear and master riding her new bike. Children will return to the dramatic, full-page illustrations that reveal Delphine's struggle and success.

————. *Ten, Nine, Eight.* New York: Greenwillow Books, 1983. (2–5)

A nurturing African American father counts with his little daughter as she gets ready to fall asleep. The colorful illustrations in this Caldecott Honor Book reflect the warmth of this father/daughter relationship.

Barber, Barbara E. Illustrated by Anna Rich. *Saturday at The New You.* New York: Lee & Low, 1994. (5–8)

Saturdays are special days for Shauna, an African American girl, who likes to help out at her mother's beauty parlor. Everyone is happy when Shauna finds a hairstyle to please a truculent young customer. The vivid paintings capture the feelings of Shauna, her mother, and the clients at The New You.

Barbour, Karen. *Nancy*. New York: Harcourt Brace Jovanovich, 1989. (4–8)
> *Four best friends (all girls), who engage in active and imaginative ventures, shun and tease the new girl in the neighborhood. When the new girl invites them to her extraordinary birthday party, everything changes. The bold, energetic, brilliantly colored illustrations perfectly capture this unusual assemblage.*

Bate, Lucy. Illustrated by Tamar Taylor. *How Georgina Drove the Car Very Carefully from Boston to New York*. New York: Crown Publishers, 1989. (3–7)
> *Georgina is in the driver's seat as she takes her family on an imaginary ride to her grandparents' house. The simple, bright illustrations enhance the charming text.*

Bauer, Caroline Feller. Illustrated by Diane Patterson. *Too Many Books*. New York: Frederick Warne, 1984. (3–7)
> *The female protagonist in this story loves books from infancy on. The whole town becomes involved with Marilou's passion for reading. Fanciful illustrations enliven the pages of this delightful book.*

_____. Illustrated by Nancy Winslow Parker. *My Mom Travels a Lot*. New York: Frederick Warne, 1981. (3–6)
> *A little girl and her father cope admirably when her working mother needs to be away on business. The humorous illustrations embellish the simple story.*

Bedard, Michael. Illustrated by Barbara Cooney. *Emily*. New York: Delacorte Press, 1992. (4–8)
> *A little girl of the nineteenth century meets the reclusive poet, Emily Dickinson. The paintings of the characters and their New England homes beautifully capture the time and place.*

Bemelmans, Ludwig. *Madeline*. New York: Viking Press, 1939. (4–8)
> *A brave and spirited heroine, who lives in a boarding school in Paris, has an adventure that both boys and girls will find compelling. The bold line drawings of Madeline's life in Paris and the rhythmic verses are wonderfully complementary in this Caldecott Honor Book.*

Berry, Holly. *Busy Lizzie*. New York: North-South Books, 1994. (2–4)
> *In an easy-to-take lesson, very young children will learn about parts of the body as busy Lizzie goes through a typically active day. Lizzie is featured in each full-page, brightly colored illustration. Fortunately, her traditional parents are very much in the background.*

Birdseye, Tom, and Birdseye, Debbie Holsclaw. Illustrated by Andrew Glass. *She'll Be Comin' 'Round the Mountain*. New York: Holiday House, 1994. (4–8)
> *This rollicking and funny story and song adaptation of the familiar ballad is filled with ebullient illustrations. The surprise ending will delight both girls and boys.*

Blegvad, Lenore. Illustrated by Erik Blegvad. *Rainy Day Kate*. New York: Margaret K. McElderry Books, 1987. (3–7)

A little boy imagines all the fun he and his friend Kate will have when she comes to play. But when Kate can't come over, he comes up with an ingenious plan. The rhymed text and the colorful pictures are a winning combination in this book about a strong cross-gender friendship.

————. Illustrated by Erik Blegvad. *Anna Banana and Me*. New York: Margaret K. McElderry Books, 1985. (3–7)

A timid boy narrates this appealing story of his friendship with a daring and intrepid girl. Stereotypic gender roles are reversed in this book. The soft, muted watercolors capture the feelings of the characters and the city setting.

Bonsall, Crosby. *It's Mine!—A Greedy Book—*. New York: Harper & Row, 1964. (2–4)

A girl and a boy have trouble sharing, but, in the end, they resolve their differences and remain friends. Regrettably, this book about a cross-gender friendship shows the girl crying when she is angry. And on one page, the two friends wait together for the postman, not the mail carrier. Cartoon-like, black and white and orange illustrations capture the feelings of the two children.

Borden, Louise. Illustrated by Lillian Hoban. *Caps, Hats, Socks, and Mittens*. New York: Scholastic, 1989. (3–6)

This colorfully illustrated book shows girls and boys involved in a variety of activities that correspond to the four seasons. Girls are shown in active play, and boys and girls are shown playing together.

Bradbury, Ray. Illustrated by Leo and Diane Dillon. *Switch on the Night*. New York: Alfred A. Knopf, 1993. (4–8)

The main character of this dramatically illustrated and poetic book is a young boy who is afraid of the dark. But when a girl introduces him to the wonders of the night, he is finally able to join the girls and boys playing "on the summer-night lawns."

Brandenberg, Franz. Illustrated by Aliki. *Aunt Nina and Her Nephews and Nieces*. New York: Greenwillow Books, 1983. (3–8)

Aunt Nina, a single woman with three lively nieces and three lively nephews, is full of life and energy. Her home is a child's paradise. Full-page, brightly colored, detailed illustrations enliven the text. Other books about this vivacious aunt and her spirited nieces and nephews include Aunt Nina's Visit *and* Aunt Nina, Goodnight.

Branley, Franklyn M. Illustrated by Holly Keller. *Air Is All Around You*. New York: Thomas Y. Crowell, 1986. (3–6)

The "scientist" who experiments with air in this book is a little girl. In the colorful and lighthearted illustrations, a girl and a boy are shown together exploring the properties of air.

Brett, Jan. *Trouble with Trolls*. New York: G. P. Putnam's Sons, 1992. (4–8)
Brett's lavish illustrations fill the pages of this book about a brave and feisty girl who outwits the trolls to save her dog.

_____. *Annie and the Wild Animals*. Boston: Houghton Mifflin, 1985. (3–6)
In another of Brett's luxuriously illustrated books, Annie sets out to tame some wild animals to replace her pet cat, Tabby, who has vanished. The resourceful Annie is finally rewarded in the spring when Tabby returns with kittens.

Bright, Robert. *My Red Umbrella*. New York: William Morrow, 1959. (2–4)
In this small book, with its simple black and white drawings and contrasting bright red umbrella, the female protagonist takes her umbrella on her walk. She meets a host of animals and offers them shelter under her expanding red umbrella.

Brown, Marc. *D. W. Thinks Big*. Boston: Little, Brown, 1993. (3–7)
D. W., an irrepressible aardvark, wants a part in her Aunt Lucy's wedding. She gets her wish and ends up a star. The story and illustrations are full of humor and insight. Other books about this spunky female are D. W. Rides Again, D. W. All Wet, *and* D. W. Flips.

Brown, Margaret Wise. Illustrated by Susan Jeffers. *Baby Animals*. New York: Random House, 1989. (2–5)
The main character, a young African American girl who lives on a farm, observes the different farm animals throughout the day. The book, a rerelease of the 1941 version, has new and impressive illustrations.

Browne, Anthony. *Gorilla*. New York: Alfred A. Knopf, 1985. (3–7)
Hannah, whose father is too busy to spend time with her, has an amazing nighttime adventure with a toy gorilla who comes to life. The next day on her birthday, her father invites her to go to the zoo. The bold illustrations are fantastic.

Buckley, Helen E. Illustrated by Evaline Ness. *Josie and the Snow*. New York: Lothrop, Lee & Shepard, 1964. (3–6)
Josie tries to get her pets interested in going out into the snow, but they can't be budged. However, her parents and her brother decide to join her, and they all have a "lovely, blowy, snowy day." The story is told in lively rhymes and illustrated in bold black, white, aqua, and red tones.

Bunting, Eve. Illustrated by Kathryn Hewitt. *Flower Garden*. Harcourt Brace, 1994. (3–6)
An African American girl goes with her father to buy a flat of flowers to make a window box for her mother's birthday gift. The father and daughter shop and work together, and the whole family is shown as a loving one. The text, in simple verse, accompanies the full-page luminous paintings, which are as bright and colorful as a garden in bloom.

Burden-Patmon, Denise. Illustrated by Floyd Cooper. *Imani's Gift at Kwanzaa.* Cleveland, OH: Modern Curriculum Press, 1992. (3–8)

In this book about Kwanzaa, a young African American girl and her grandmother prepare for the holiday. The colorful, sensitive illustrations reflect the warmth of the relationship between the child and her grandmother as they share the meaning of the holiday.

Burningham, John. *Granpa.* New York: Crown Publishers, 1985. (3–7)

This book beautifully captures the loving relationship between a girl and her grandfather as it explores their memories and life experiences. The illustrations are whimsical and engaging.

_____. *Time to Get Out of the Bath, Shirley.* New York: Thomas Y. Crowell, 1978. (4–7)

While she is taking a bath, Shirley uses her considerable imagination to go far afield on a flight of fantasy. Shirley's daydreams are captured in fanciful illustrations. Regrettably, her mother, who is unaware of her daughter's "adventures," is a complainer and martyr. For another book about this inventive girl, read Come Away from the Water, Shirley.

Bursik, Rose. *Amelia's Fantastic Flight.* New York: Henry Holt, 1992. (4–8)

Amelia, a creative and imaginative girl, flies her own plane on a fantasy trip around the world. The dramatic and brightly colored illustrations and world map insets imaginatively complement this story about an adventurous girl.

Burton, Marilee Robin. Illustrated by James E. Ransome. *My Best Shoes.* New York: Tambourine Books, 1994. (3–6)

Active girls and boys dance, prance, run, hop, and tiptoe in this rhyming book about different kinds of shoes. The children, who represent both sexes and different cultures, are beautifully portrayed in the luxuriant paintings.

Burton, Virginia Lee. *Katy and the Big Snow.* Boston: Houghton Mifflin, 1943. (3–7)

In this enduring story, a courageous, indefatigable, and persistent snowplow named Katy comes through to save the day. The illustrations convey Katy's power and determination.

_____. *The Little House.* Boston: Houghton Mifflin, 1942. (4–8)

The little house enjoys the passing seasons until the burgeoning city crowds around her. In the satisfying ending, the descendants of the family who first lived in the little house move her back to the country where she can again experience beauty and tranquillity. The appealing illustrations perfectly fit the story in this Caldecott Medal winner.

_____. *Mike Mulligan and His Steam Shovel.* Boston: Houghton Mifflin, 1939. (3–7)

In this classic story, Mary Anne, Mike's steam shovel, is an equal partner in their venture to dig the new town hall in Popperville in just one day. A little boy helps Mike and Mary Anne by bringing the whole town over to watch and cheer them on. The illustrations capture the energy and urgency of the race against time.

Butler, Dorothy. Illustrated by Elizabeth Fuller. *My Brown Bear Barney*. New York: Greenwillow Books, 1988. (2–5)
The little girl in this book takes her brown bear everywhere she goes. Charming and colorful illustrations capture the little girl's experiences, which include a cross-gender friendship.

Butterworth, Nick. *Busy People*. Cambridge, MA: Candlewick Press, 1986. (2–5)
This book includes questions for children to answer about various jobs. The women workers include a doctor, gardener, baker, store owner, and farmer. Unfortunately, the number of male workers is almost double the number of female workers, and they are shown in traditional male jobs. The simple text and colorful illustrations are appealing.

Caines, Jeannette. Illustrated by Pat Cummings. *Just Us Women*. New York: Harper & Row, 1982. (4–8)
A young African American girl and her aunt take a car trip to North Carolina. Their shared activities and the warmth of their relationship are revealed in the two-color illustrations.

_____. Illustrated by Ronald Himler. *Daddy*. New York: Harper & Row, 1977. (3–7)

A young African American girl spends a happy Saturday with her father and his woman friend. Both adults are warm and loving toward the protagonist. Realistic black and white drawings enhance this sensitive story of a little girl whose parents live apart. For another girl's experience with parents who are separated, read At Daddy's on Saturdays *by Linda Walvoord Girard.*

_____. Illustrated by Steven Kellogg. *Abby*. New York: HarperCollins, 1973. (3–8)

Abby, an exuberant and curious African American girl who has been adopted, is devastated when her brother says he doesn't like girls. The mother, who is loving, intelligent, and perceptive, helps the children understand and appreciate each other. The black and white illustrations are warm and expressive.

Calmenson, Stephanie. Photographed by Justin Sutcliffe. *Rosie: A Visiting Dog's Story*. New York: Clarion Books, 1994. (4–8)
The author tells the true story of her partnership with her dog, Rosie, whom she has trained to comfort people in hospitals, schools, and nursing homes. The photographs capture the delight the dog and her trainer bring to the lives they touch.

Cannon, Janell. *Stellaluna*. New York: Harcourt Brace, 1993. (4–8)
In this celebration of diversity, Stellaluna, a baby fruit bat, is separated from her mother and the other bats. She makes friends with a family of

birds and rescues them from danger. In the satisfying end, she is reunited with and finds her own family. Every spread features luminous illustrations of the spunky bat and her bird friends.

Carle, Eric. *The Very Busy Spider*. New York: Philomel, 1984. (2–6)
As a spider spins her web, all the barnyard animals try to interest her in other activities. But she is too busy even to answer. The final result of her diligence and persistence is a beautiful web that captures the fly that has buzzed through every page of the book. The illustrations are a visual treat, and the embossed web, which grows bigger on every page, is a tactile delight as well.

Carlson, Nancy. *How to Lose All of Your Friends*. New York: Viking Press, 1994. (3–8)
This hilarious tongue-in-cheek book tells children exactly what to do if they want to end up with no friends. The illustrations are as funny as the words in this easy-to-take lesson about friendship.

_____. *I Like Me!* New York: Viking Kestrel, 1988. (3–7)

A female pig tells the reader that she is her own best friend. She tells how she is special, how she takes good care of herself, and how, if she fails at something, she tries again. The amusing and colorful illustrations support the important theme.

Carlstrom, Nancy White. Illustrated by Bruce Degan. *Happy Birthday, Jesse Bear!* New York: Macmillan, 1994. (2–6)
Children love the Jesse Bear books, and this charmingly illustrated one shows a party with girl and boy bears having a good time together. It would be easy to substitute the name of any birthday child for Jesse's name when reading this book.

_____. Illustrated by Diane Worfolk Allison. *Wishing at Dawn in Summer*. Boston: Little, Brown, 1993. (4–7)

The competent older sister in this story has taught her brother how to fish. The warm relationship between the siblings as they fish and wish together is captured by the softly colored illustrations.

_____. Illustrated by Jerry Pinkney. *Wild Wild Sunflower Child Anna*. New York: Macmillan, 1987. (3–6)

Anna, a young African American girl, is thrilled with the many changes she sees occurring in late spring. The lovely illustrations reflect the colors and warmth of the season.

Caseley, Judith. *Mama, Coming and Going*. New York: Greenwillow Books, 1994. (4–8)
When a new baby discombobulates her mother, Jenna comes to the rescue. The mother and daughter share love and laughter over the mistakes and mishaps of everyday life. Bright, expressive illustrations add to the humor in the story.

_____. *Dear Annie*. New York: Greenwillow Books, 1991. (4–8)

With the help and encouragement of her mother, Annie corresponds with her grandfather from the time she is born. Annie's collection of letters stimulates her classmates to start their own letter-writing exchanges. Bold, bright pictures imaginatively complement the story of a girl's loving, though long-distance, relationship with her grandfather.

_____. *Grandpa's Garden Lunch*. New York: Greenwillow Books, 1990. (3–6)

Sarah and her grandparents eat a lunch made from the vegetables grown in the garden she and her grandfather have tended. Grandpa puts on an apron and prepares the lunch with Grandma. Bright illustrations enliven the text.

Casteneda, Omar S. Illustrated by Enrique O. Sanchez. *Abuela's Weave*. New York: Lee & Low Books, 1993. (5–8)

Esperanza and her grandmother create exquisite weavings to sell at the marketplace. Esperanza, who must set up and sell the wares on her own, shows courage and determination. The vivid paintings which illustrate the story magnificently depict the Guatemalan culture and the relationship of the two characters.

Celsi, Teresa. Illustrated by Doug Cushman. *The Fourth Little Pig*. Madison, NJ: Steck Vaughn, 1992. (3–8)

In an extension of the well-known folk tale, the sister of the three little pigs comes to visit and persuades her brothers, who have been hermits since an episode with a wolf, to overcome their fears. The colorful and funny illustrations add to the story of the undaunted female pig.

Chall, Marsha Wilson. Illustrated by Steve Johnson. *Up North at the Cabin*. New York: Lothrop, Lee & Shepard, 1992. (5–8)

In poetic language, an imaginative and active girl describes her experiences in the north woods. Vibrant paintings embellish every page.

Chandra, Deborah. Illustrated by Max Grover. *Miss Mabel's Table*. New York: Browndeer Press, 1994. (4–7)

In the tradition of The House That Jack Built, *this repetitive rhyme shows an energetic woman traveling across the city to her restaurant. Once there, she prepares breakfast for 10 customers—who are the workers she has seen on her commute. Mabel is shown as an independent and capable entrepreneur, and the five women workers are shown in active, nontraditional roles. Bold, brightly colored illustrations of city life enhance the story.*

Cherry, Lynne. *Archie, Follow Me*. New York: E. P. Dutton, 1990. (4–7)

A little girl and her cat share adventures in the woods. The marvelous illustrations of the characters in the daytime and nighttime woodland setting are an integral part of this book.

Choi, Sook Nyul. Illustrated by Karen M. Dugan. *Halmoni and the Picnic*. Boston: Houghton Mifflin, 1994. (4–8)

A Korean girl, Yunmi, and her grandmother have immigrated to New York City. In this predictable but warm and engaging book, Yunmi and her school friends help the grandmother feel accepted. The graceful illustrations echo the words of the story.

Clifton, Lucille. Illustrated by Ann Grifalconi. *Everett Anderson's Friend*. New York: Holt, Rinehart & Winston, 1976. (5–8)

An African American boy, Everett Anderson, is initially disappointed to learn that the new child who has moved into his apartment building is a girl. Worse yet, she is better at baseball and running than he is. But when Everett Anderson needs her, Maria proves to be an empathic friend. The poetic verse form and the black and white drawings reveal the growth of this cross-gender friendship.

Cohen, Miriam. Illustrated by Lillian Hoban. *Will I Have a Friend?* New York: Macmillan, 1967. (3–6)

A reassuring and gentle father takes his son, Jim, to his first day of nursery school. Jim is anxious about this new experience, but before the day is over, he has made friends with another boy. The engaging illustrations show girls and boys involved together in active and quiet play. For female versions of this predicament, try Judy Delton's The New Girl at School *and Kevin Henkes's* Jessica. *And for more about Jim and his friends, read Cohen's* Best Friends *and* The New Teacher.

Coles, Robert. Illustrated by George Ford. *The Story of Ruby Bridges*. New York: Scholastic, 1995. (6–8)

This book tells the moving and true story of the African American girl who, at age 6, braved the mobs to go to an all-white school. The soft pastel illustrations that adorn each page highlight this powerful narrative of a young girl's faith and fortitude.

Cooney, Barbara. *Miss Rumphius*. New York: Viking Penguin, 1982. (4 –8)

The reader follows Miss Rumphius through her long, adventurous, life, as she looks for a way to make the world more beautiful. Lovely paintings, filled with intriguing details, illustrate this story of a resolute single woman.

Dabcovich, Lydia. *Mrs. Huggins and Her Hen Hannah*. New York: E. P. Dutton, 1985. (3–6)

Mrs. Huggins and her hen Hannah live and work happily together until Hannah dies. Mrs. Huggins is heartbroken until she hears a sound from Hannah's nest and discovers Hannah's legacy. The illustrations humorously portray the friendship of these two resourceful females.

Davol, Marguerite W. Illustrated by Irene Trivas. *Black, White, Just Right*. Morton Grove, IL: Albert Whitman, 1993. (3–6)

The girl who narrates this story is aware of and comfortable with the differences between people. The members of this loving, interracial family have an abundance of self-esteem. The book is realistically illustrated in warm colors.

Day, Nancy Raines. Illustrated by Ann Grifalconi. *The Lion's Whiskers: An Ethiopian Folktale.* New York: Scholastic, 1995. (5–8)

A good and loving stepmother, Fanaye repeatedly fails in her attempts to gain her stepson's love. After she fulfills the awesome task imposed by the wise medicine man, Fanaye learns how to realize her desire. Her unfailing love for her stepson and her determination to find a way to reach him are chronicled beautifully in both words and striking collages. Stepparents and stepchildren who struggle with the complexities of relationships in blended families are bound to identify with Fanaye and her stepson.

Delton, Judy. Illustrated by Lillian Hoban. *The New Girl at School.* New York: E. P. Dutton, 1979. (4–8)

Marcia shares her feelings of loneliness at her new school with her working mother, who urges her daughter to "give it time." Before long, Marcia begins to find a place in the group. Girls and boys are shown interacting together in the school setting, but, unfortunately, Marcia and another girl are shown having trouble understanding subtraction. Expressive illustrations support the text.

dePaolo, Tomie. *The Legend of the Poinsettia.* New York: G. P. Putnam Sons, 1994. (5–8)

This retold legend may be too religious for some settings, but the protagonist is a resilient and generous little girl who lives in Mexico. Mexican village life at Christmas time is lovingly portrayed in full-page color illustrations. For a story about a clever and charitable man who saves Hanukkah for an entire village, read Hershel and the Hanukkah Goblins *by Eric A. Kimmel.*

_____. *The Legend of the Bluebonnet.* New York: G. P. Putnam Sons, 1984. (5–8)

In this retold legend, a Comanche Indian orphan girl makes a great sacrifice to save her people from a drought. The illustrations convey both the sadness and the spirit of this Native American girl. Another strong Native American protagonist can be found in Paul Goble's The Girl Who Loved Wild Horses.

_____. *Oliver Button Is a Sissy.* New York: Harcourt Brace Jovanovich, 1979. (4–8)

Oliver doesn't "like to do things that boys are supposed to do." And because he is different, the boys tease him and call him a sissy. Even his father calls him a sissy. Only his mother and the girls stand up for him. In the end, Oliver works hard at his dancing and gains everyone's respect. The light-hearted illustrations complement the text.

Dorros, Arthur. Illustrated by Elisa Kleven. *Abuela*. New York: E. P. Dutton, 1991. (3–8)
Rosalba and her grandmother, who speaks only Spanish, go on a fantasy flight over New York City. Spanish phrases are neatly intermingled with the English text. Imaginative and brilliantly colored illustrations enliven every page of this heartwarming story.

Egger, Bettina. Illustrated by Sita Jucker. *Marianne's Grandmother*. New York: E. P. Dutton, 1987. (5–8)
In this warm, thoughtful book, a young girl comes to accept her beloved grandmother's death. Beautiful muted watercolors reflect Marianne's sadness and illustrate her memories of the good times she shared with her grandmother.

English, Betty Lou. *Women at Their Work*. New York: Dial Press, 1977. (5–8)
The informative photographs and the personal stories of the 21 women in this book will convince readers that women can become firefighters, judges, jockeys, carpenters, dentists, telephone installers, rabbis, and so on.

Flournoy, Valerie. Illustrated by Jerry Pinkney. *The Patchwork Quilt*. New York: Dial Books, 1985. (5–8)
Tanya and her grandmother start working together on a quilt made of scraps from the family's old clothes, but the quilt becomes a family project when the grandmother becomes ill. The warm, rich paintings reveal the strong ties that bind this African American family together.

Fox, Mem. Illustrated by Patricia Mullins. *Hattie and the Fox*. New York: Bradbury Press, 1987. (2–5)
Hattie, an alert chicken, thwarts the fox in this delightful barnyard tale. Children will love the repetitive language and the brightly colored and simple illustrations.

Freeman, Don. *Corduroy*. New York: Viking Press, 1968. (3–7)
Even though he has lost a button, Lisa wants Corduroy for her very own bear. Corduroy's adventures and his happiness at finding a home with Lisa are captured in delightful text and illustrations. In the sequel, A Pocket for Corduroy, *Lisa sews a pocket on her bear's overalls.*

Galdone, Paul. *The Little Red Hen*. Boston: Clarion Books, 1968. (3–6)
A self-reliant and determined female character does a job from start to finish without the help of any of her friends. She then enjoys the fruits of her labors by herself. The colorful illustrations imaginatively complement the text. For two more delightful interpretations of this story, try the versions by Janina Domanska and Byron Barton.

Gardner, Sally. *The Little Nut Tree*. New York: Tambourine Books, 1993. (4–8)
The author/artist of this book takes a new look at a traditional nursery rhyme. When the little nut tree miraculously grows a silver nutmeg and a golden pear, the girl who planted the tree has to give it to the King of Spain's bratty daughter. Fortunately, her generosity is rewarded. The

delightful illustrations depict nineteenth-century London and show the spunky heroine on every page.

Gauch, Patricia Lee. Illustrated by Satomi Ichikawa. *Tanya and Emily in a Dance for Two*. New York: Philomel Books, 1994. (5–8)
Two girls become friends through their experiences with dance. The book includes lovely sequences of the girls using ballet movements to imitate animals at the zoo. Delicate pastel paintings grace each page. Dance Tanya *and* Bravo Tanya *are earlier books about Tanya's dancing.*

————. Illustrated by Elise Primavera. *Christina Katerina and the Great Bear Train*. New York: G. P. Putnam's Sons, 1990. (3–6)

An adventurous, feisty little girl takes her bears and leaves home rather than waiting to meet her new baby sister. Nothing fazes Christina Katerina for long, and she returns from her journey ready to acknowledge the new baby. The father is shown as nurturing, and the grandmother is dressed in jeans. The colorful illustrations are full of life and action. For another delightful story about a big sister's jealousy, read Julius, the Baby of the World *by Kevin Henkes.*

————. Illustrated by Doris Burn. *Christina Katerina and the Box*. New York: Coward, 1971. (3–6)

The spirited and imaginative Christina Katerina uses a simple box to create a clubhouse, a racing car, a castle, and a dance floor. The illustrations are as colorful and buoyant as the heroine.

Goffstein, M. B. *Goldie the Dollmaker*. New York: Farrar, Straus, and Giroux, 1969. (4–8)
Goldie, a single woman and an independent craftsperson, loves creating and living with beauty. Simple black and white illustrations reflect the mood and straightforward storytelling in this small but profound book.

Goldreich, Gloria, and Goldreich, Esther. Photographed by Robert Ipcar. *What Can She Be? A Farmer*. New York: Lothrop, Lee & Shepard, 1976. (5–8)
The informative text and photographs in this book illustrate the lives of two women farmers at work. The book is one of a series showing that girls can become lawyers, veterinarians, newscasters, geologists, musicians, police officers, or architects, just as boys can.

Graham, Thomas. *Mr. Bear's Chair*. New York: E. P. Dutton, 1987. (3–6)
This amusing story shows how a chair is made from a tree. The relationship of Mr. and Mrs. Bear is a caring, sharing one, and Mr. Bear not only makes a chair but he also prepares the breakfast. The simple text and illustrations work well together.

Gray, Libba Moore. Illustrated by Jada Rowland. *Miss Tizzy*. New York: Simon & Schuster, 1993.
Miss Tizzy, an African American original with an unusual home and clothes, welcomes the neighborhood children into her world. The mixed-gender, multiethnic children make puppets, play music, roller skate, and

watch the stars. When Miss Tizzy becomes ill, the children plan splendid surprises for her. The full-page, colorful illustrations capture the caring and the cross-gender cooperation.

Griffith, Helen V. Illustrated by James Stevenson. *Grandaddy's Place*. New York: Greenwillow Books, 1987. (5–8)
Janetta goes with her mother to visit her grandfather in the country. Over time, she learns about country ways and becomes increasingly close to her grandfather. The full-page illustrations convey country life and the relationships of the characters.

Gwynne, Fred. *Easy to See Why*. New York: Simon & Schuster, 1993. (5–8)
In a surprise and hilarious ending to this humorous book, the little girl protagonist and her pet mutt win first prize at the dog show. The illustrations are comical.

Hall, Zoe. Illustrated by Shari Halpern. *It's Pumpkin Time*. New York: Scholastic, 1994. (3–6)
A sister and brother work together to raise pumpkins for Halloween. The huge colorful collages that illustrate the simple informative text are bold, attractive, and scientifically accurate.

Hallinam, P. K. *A Rainbow of Friends*. Nashville, TN: Ideals Children's Books, 1994. (4–8)
This book, written in verse, advocates harmony, friendship, cooperation, and acceptance of differences among children. The messages are ones that everyone should heed, but the unappealing, cartoon-like illustrations undermine the importance of the ideas. Hallinam's book, That's What a Friend Is, *also has a fine message about friendship, but the illustrations are mediocre at best. Consider reading just the texts of these books and asking the children in your class to make drawings to elucidate the messages.*

Hamanaka, Sheila. *All the Colors of the Earth*. New York: Morrow Junior Books, 1994. (3–8)
Exquisite full-page paintings and poetic language beautifully make the point that children come in all the colors of the earth. Girls and boys are equally active or involved, and there are as many girls as boys in the pictures.

Harper, Wilhelmina. Illustrated by William Wiesner. *The Gunniwolf*. New York: E. P. Dutton, 1978. (3–7)
A little girl forgets her mother's warnings and wanders into the jungle. She meets the gunniwolf, sings him to sleep, and runs back home to safety. Children will love singing the refrains along with the protagonist. The illustrations are cheerful and lighthearted, not frightening. For a second version of this tale, try the one by A. Delany.

Hart, Carole, Pogrebin, Letty C., Rodgers, Mary, and Thomas, Marlo (Eds.). *Free to Be You and Me*. New York: Bantam Books, 1987. (3–8)
This collection of poems, photos, songs, illustrations, and stories is a must for anyone who wants to encourage children to be whatever they can be,

regardless of race or sex. These pieces challenge gender stereotypes in ways that are both fun and illuminating.

Havill, Juanita. Illustrated by Anne Sibley O'Brien. *Jamaica's Find*. Boston: Houghton Mifflin, 1986. (3–6)

Jamaica, an African American girl, finds another child's stuffed dog and brings it home. Her understanding mother helps Jamaica solve the dilemma, and, as a result, Jamaica meets a new friend. The expressive and appealing illustrations enrich the story. Other books about this engaging girl are Jamaica Tag-Along *and* Jamaica and Brianna.

Hedderwick, Mairi. *Katie Morag and the Big Boy Cousins*. Boston: Little, Brown, 1987. (4–8)

In this book about Katie Morag and her grandmother, Katie joins her big-boy cousins in mischief making. In the end, it is Katie who makes things right. The grandmother single-handedly running her island farm is far from stereotypical.

————. *Katie Morag Delivers the Mail*. Boston: Little, Brown, 1984. (4–7)

A spirited girl and her independent grandmother combine their considerable forces to straighten out a mix-up in the mail deliveries. The detailed and expressive drawings are full of humor. The grandmother in her boots and overalls, ready to put a new part in her tractor, is a nontraditional delight.

Henkes, Kevin. *Chrysanthemum*. New York: Greenwillow Books, 1991. (4–8)

Chrysanthemum is a confident little mouse with a name she loves—until she gets to school. Even her loving and supportive parents can't keep her from wilting under the verbal assaults of the other girls. Finally, the problem is solved with the help of an adored and empathic teacher who is also named for a flower. The illustrations are filled with humorous details and buoyancy. Any child who has wished for a different name or has been teased unmercifully will love this enchanting story.

————. *Jessica*. New York: Greenwillow Books, 1989. (3–6)

Ruthie relies on her imaginary friend, Jessica, to help her get through the first days of school. Ruthie's problem is solved when she makes a new friend, who, not surprisingly, is also named Jessica. Appealing illustrations enhance this book about a same-sex friendship. For a book in which a boy is anxious about school, read Will I Have a Friend? *by Miriam Cohen.*

————. *Sheila Rae, the Brave*. New York: Greenwillow Books, 1987. (3–7)

In this warm and amusing story of sibling differences and love, two sisters, who are mice, discover that no one is always brave and self-sufficient. The personalities of both girls are wonderfully expressed in the delightful and funny illustrations.

Hess, Debra. Illustrated by Diane Greenseid. *Wilson Sat Alone*. New York: Simon & Schuster, 1994. (4–8)

Until a new girl comes to school, Wilson, a shy and solitary boy, has no friends . Unlike Wilson, this spunky girl makes friends easily. In a game of monsters, she roars at Wilson, and, surprisingly, he roars back. From then on, he is one of the group. The vibrant paintings show girls and boys interacting on every page.

Hessell, Jenny. Illustrated by Jenny Williams. *Staying at Sam's.* New York: Lippincott, 1989. (3–7)

The narrator of this amusing story visits his friend Sam's house for an overnight and comes to understand and accept that friends and families are different. The sprightly and colorful illustrations are full of the details of family life.

Hest, Amy. Illustrated by DyAnne Disalvo-Ryan. *The Mommy Exchange.* New York: Four Winds Press, 1988. (5–8)

A girl and a boy, who are best friends, switch homes for the weekend. After each child experiences another mommy and way of life, each discovers there's no place like home. The life-like illustrations enhance this amusing and engaging story.

_____. *The Purple Coat.* Illustrated by Amy Schwartz. New York: Four Winds Press, 1986. (6–8)

Gabby's grandfather, a tailor, encourages Gabby to try new things. Gabby reminds her grandfather of his advice when he hesitates to make her a purple coat rather than the usual navy blue one. The grandfather is loving and Gabby is assertive. The whimsical and detailed illustrations of the setting contribute to the message in this book.

Hines, Anna Grossnickle. *Grandma Gets Grumpy.* New York: Clarion Books, 1988. (4–8)

A modern grandmother takes care of her five grandchildren when the parents go out. Fun turns to mischief, but Grandma sets things right. Realistic and detailed pictures show girls and boys having fun together. There is even a page on which the narrator plays the doctor and her boy cousin plays the nurse.

_____. *It's Just Me, Emily.* New York: Clarion Books, 1987. (2–4)

In this simple story about a girl who plays a game of make-believe with her mother, everyday events and imaginary details are captured in enticing illustrations.

_____. *Daddy Makes the Best Spaghetti.* New York: Clarion Books, 1986. (3–7)

Corey and his father collaborate to prepare dinner for the family. After dinner, Corey and his mother do dishes and his father gives him a bath. The delightful illustrations add to the warmth of this story about a loving family that shares tasks. The fun-loving father clearly enjoys being with his son as much as his son enjoys being with him.

_____. *Bethany for Real.* New York: Greenwillow Books, 1985. (4–7)

Bethany and a boy are busy with their imaginative play when an older girl disrupts their fun. When Bethany and her new friend stand up to this interloper, she joins in the play. The simple illustrations are perfect for this book about pretending.

Hoban, Russell. Illustrated by Lillian Hoban. *Best Friends for Frances.* New York: Harper & Row, 1969. (4–8)

Two badgers, Frances and Albert, are best friends, but when Frances wants to do "boy things" with Albert, he objects. Eventually, Frances solves the problem and makes a friend of her little sister in the process. Albert, meanwhile, learns that girls can play ball and catch frogs and snakes. Regrettably, after the reconciliation of the two best friends, Albert brings Frances flowers and tells her he is her best boyfriend, rather than simply her best friend. The line drawings with pastel backgrounds provide a delightful accompaniment to this story of cross-gender issues.

_____. Illustrated by Lillian Hoban. *Bread and Jam for Frances.* New York: Harper & Row, 1964. (3–7)

Frances, a strong-willed badger who knows what she wants, eats only bread and jam for every meal—until she decides it's time to try something else. Her mother and father are patient and understanding. The illustrations and soft pastel backgrounds perfectly capture the tone of the story. Other stories about the engaging Frances include Bedtime for Frances, A Baby Sister for Frances, A Birthday for Frances, *and* A Bargain for Frances.

Hoffman, Mary. Illustrated by Caroline Binch. *Amazing Grace.* New York: Dial Press, 1991. (5–8)

Grace, an African American girl, wants the part of Peter Pan in the school play. But, because she's a girl and she's black, she is told she can't have the part. However, Grace, with encouragement from her wise grandmother, prevails. The watercolor illustrations beautifully capture the emotions of the characters. In a sequel, Boundless Grace, *the protagonist visits her father and his new family in Africa.*

Hoffman, Phyllis. Illustrated by Emily McCully. *Steffie and Me.* New York: Harper & Row, 1970. (5–7)

Two girls, one African American and one white, are best friends. Their teacher is nurturing and understanding, and the narrator's older brother is believable as both a tease and an advocate. The three color line drawings express the warmth and simplicity of their interactions.

Holabird, Katharine. Illustrated by Helen Craig. *Angelina Ballerina.* New York: Crown Publishers, 1983. (4–8)

Angelina, an appealingly exuberant little mouse, drives her parents to distraction with her constant dancing about. Although it is the father who solves the problem, it is Angelina who, through perseverance and hard work, realizes her dream of becoming a ballerina. The detailed illustrations are whimsical and amusing. Other Angelina books include Angelina on Stage, Angelina's Christmas, *and* Angelina at the Fair.

Howard, Elizabeth Fitzgerald. Illustrated by James Ransome. *Aunt Flossie's Hats (and Crabcakes Later)*. New York: Clarion Books, 1991. (4–8)
Two African American sisters learn about their family's past as their great-great aunt shows them her collection of hats. Full-page paintings with brilliant hues and life-like expressions enrich this story of intergenerational love.

_____. Illustrated by Robert Casilla. *The Train to Lulu's*. New York: Bradbury Press, 1988. (4–7)
Two young African American girls overcome their fears and take a long trip by themselves to meet their Aunt Lulu. The adventures on the train and at the station are realistically portrayed in stunning watercolors.

Hughes, Shirley. *Giving*. Cambridge, MA: Candlewick Press, 1993. (3–5)
An active and generous girl tells about various kinds of giving. She is equally comfortable with traditional and nontraditional play. The colorful, expressive illustrations capture the feelings of the protagonist and the other characters.

_____. *The Snow Lady*. New York: Lothrop, Lee & Shepard, 1990. (5–8)
In a book that shows cross-gender friendships throughout, the female protagonist, Sam, and her friend, Barney, build a snow woman who resembles Sam's fussy (and somewhat stereotypic) babysitter. But, when Sam realizes the possible consequences of their fun, she decides to take action. The detailed, realistic illustrations are as full of energy as Sam and her friends.

_____. *Alfie Gives a Hand*. New York: Lothrop, Lee & Shepard, 1983. (2–5)
Delightful, colorful illustrations of boys and girls interacting enhance this book about a boy who is afraid to go to a party without his blanket. Alfie is empathic and kind to a girl at the party who is afraid of a mask.

_____. *Moving Molly*. Englewood Cliffs, NJ: Prentice Hall, 1978. (3–6)
When Molly moves to the country, she has to be resourceful to combat her loneliness. Her problem is solved when, in an unlikely scenario, twins just her age move in next door. Molly plays actively with her new friends, one of whom is a boy. Colorful, realistic illustrations reinforce the story.

Hurd, Edith Thatcher. Illustrated by Emily Arnold McCully. *I Dance in My Red Pajamas*. New York: Harper & Row, 1982. (3–6)
When she visits her grandparents, the female protagonist, who is engaged and active throughout the book, particularly enjoys dancing to the music her grandmother plays on the piano. The illustrations are warm and realistic.

Hutchins, Pat. *My Best Friend*. New York: Greenwillow Books, 1993. (3–6)
Two African American girls are best friends, each with her own special strengths. The girl who excels at many activities needs her friend's support when bedtime comes. The girls are shown in overalls, riding bikes, climbing trees, and jumping, as well as painting pictures, eating spaghetti

together, and going to bed. Large bold brightly colored pictures enliven the book.

———. *The Doorbell Rang.* New York: Greenwillow Books, 1986. (2–5)
The children in this book represent both sexes and various ethnic groups, and they cooperate and problem solve together. However, the mother and grandmother seem to belong to another era. The illustrations are bold and colorful.

———. *Rosie's Walk.* New York: Macmillan, 1968. (3–6)
On her walk, Rosie remains blissfully oblivious to the dangers around her. Both boys and girls will enjoy the humorous illustrations in this wordless book. The Camel Who Took a Walk *by Jack Tworkov tells a similar story using words.*

Ichikawa, Satomi. *Nora's Surprise.* New York: Philomel Books, 1994. (4–7)
A Japanese girl has a series of mishaps with her toy and animal friends. The captivating full-page illustrations highlight the antics that go on in this fanciful tale. Other Nora books include Nora's Roses, Nora's Duck, *and* Nora's Stars.

Imai, Miko. *Lilly's Secret.* Cambridge, MA: Candlewick Press, 1994. (3–6)
Lilly, a cat, feels uncomfortable about her peculiar paws and thinks that Joe, a cat she admires, could never like her because of this flaw. However, Joe understands that physical perfection is not a requirement for friendship. The whimsical illustrations mirror the feelings of the characters in this book.

Isadora, Rachel. *Max.* New York: Macmillan, 1976. (4–8)
Max, "a great baseball player," joins his sister's ballet class and discovers that dancing is fun. The lively black and white drawings capture the enthusiasm of this spirited boy who isn't afraid to explore the world more fully.

Jahn-Clough, Lisa. *Alicia Has a Bad Day.* Boston: Houghton Mifflin, 1994. (5–8)
Alicia tells what it's like to have a bad day. She says she feels "lugubrious," and nothing she does makes her feel any better. Child-like paintings complement the mood of the story. Use this book along with Judith Viorst's popular Alexander and the Terrible, Horrible, No Good, Very Bad Day.

James, Betsy. *Mary Ann.* New York: Dutton Children's Books, 1994. (3–6)
Two friends are separated when one moves to another town. The girl who is left behind raises a praying mantis's eggs and overcomes her sadness in the process. The delightful illustrations are expressive and informative.

Jensen, Virginia Allen. Illustrated by Ann Strugnell. *Sara and the Door.* Reading, MA: Addison-Wesley, 1977. (2–4)
Sara, an African American child, slams the door on her coat and is trapped. She tries and fails repeatedly to free herself, but, in the end, she solves the problem all by herself. Expressive, black and brown drawings embellish this simple story of a girl's persistence.

Jewell, Nancy. Illustrated by Leonard Weisgard. *Try and Catch Me*. New York: Harper & Row, 1972. (4–8)

An imaginative, energetic, and self-reliant girl explores the outdoors. She is undaunted by a boy who teases her. He, of course, ends up wanting to be her friend. The simple story of a beginning cross-gender friendship comes alive in the colorful and ebullient illustrations.

Johnson, Angela. Illustrated by James E. Ransome. *The Girl Who Wore Snakes*. New York: Orchard Books, 1993. (5–8)

The African American protagonist loves snakes and wears them wherever she goes. In the satisfying conclusion of the story, she discovers that one of her aunts shares her passion. This book dispels the stereotypic idea that all females are afraid of snakes. The illustrations are as colorful, bold, and full of life as the protagonist.

————. Illustrated by David Soman. *When I Am Old with You*. New York: Orchard Books, 1990. (4–7)

A young African American girl imagines herself as an old woman—as old as her grandfather—doing the things they like to do together. The watercolor illustrations suggest the girl's comfort with old age and lovingly portray the warm relationship she shares with her grandfather.

Jonas, Ann. *Splash*. New York: Greenwillow Books, 1995. (3–7)

Animals splash in and out of a pond in this humorous math lesson featuring an African American girl as the protagonist. The brightly colored illustrations add to the fun.

————. *Color Dance*. New York: Greenwillow Books, 1989. (4–7)

Three girls and a boy dance together with colored scarves. As the scarves come together, the colors change. The illustrations reflect the flow of movement and the color changes.

————. *Where Can It Be?* New York: Greenwillow Books, 1986. (2–4)

The little girl in this story loses her special blanket and looks for it everywhere. In the satisfying ending, the doorbell rings and her friend delivers the prized blanket. Large, colorful illustrations with interesting details enhance this simple story. For a delightful story about an older boy whose parents want him to give up his beloved blanket, read Owen *by Kevin Henkes.*

————. *The Quilt*. New York: Greenwillow Books, 1984. (3–7)

A young girl studies the quilt her mother has made from scraps of clothes the girl has outgrown. When she falls asleep, the quilt comes to life in a somewhat disconcerting dream. Lovely illustrations imaginatively display the multicolored quilt and the magical dream.

Jones, Carol. *This Old Man*. Boston: Houghton Mifflin, 1990. (3–7)

In this up-to-date version of the song, a little girl and her grandfather are pictured acting out the verses. Contemporary and colorful illustrations highlight the words.

Joosse, Barbara M. Illustrated by Barbara Lavallee. *Mama, Do You Love Me?* San Francisco: Chronicle Books, 1991. (3–6)
A little Inuit girl tests her mother's love in this beautiful story. The vibrant and dramatic illustrations wonderfully depict the Inuit culture, the Arctic setting, and the mother/daughter relationship.

Keats, Ezra Jack. *Maggie and the Pirate*. New York: Four Winds Press, 1979. (5–8)
In searching for her stolen cricket, Maggie comes up against the "pirate." The brave and resilient Maggie mourns the loss of her stolen pet cricket with her friends Paco and Niki. And then the "pirate" makes a surprise visit! Haunting illustrations go hand in hand with this moving story of cross-gender friendships.

_____. *A Letter to Amy*. New York: Harper & Row, 1968. (4–7)
Peter worries that his friend Amy won't come to his birthday party and that, if she does, the boys at his party will make fun of his friendship with a girl. Peter's mother is loving and reassuring, and Amy joins the party with ease. Keats's colorful collages reflect the urban setting and the feelings of the characters.

Keller, Holly. *Geraldine's Baby Brother*. New York: Greenwillow Books, 1994. (3–6)
The captivating pig, Geraldine, faces the arrival of a baby brother. She lets everyone know how displeased she is with this state of affairs, but, in the end, she finds she can cope with the intruder. Papa is shown walking the baby, and he and the other relatives are sensitive to Geraldine's feelings.

_____. *Geraldine's Big Snow*. New York: Greenwillow Books, 1988. (2–4)
Geraldine, an enchanting pig, awaits the promised snowstorm. When the snow finally arrives, she goes out to slide down the highest hill in the park. This book complements the popular book The Snowy Day *by Ezra Jack Keats and gives a female perspective to the joys of snow.*

_____. *Geraldine's Blanket*. New York: Greenwillow Books, 1984. (3–6)
Girls (and boys) who are attached to blankets or other objects will empathize with Geraldine's predicament and applaud her ingenious solution. The bright illustrations are as appealing as the little girl pig. For a story about a boy who loves his blanket, read Owen *by Kevin Henkes.*

Kellogg, Steven. *Best Friends*. New York: Dial Books, 1986. (5–8)
Kathy feels that life isn't fair: Her best friend, Louise, gets both a great vacation and the only puppy born to the new neighbor's dog. Kathy is devastated until Louise comes up with a terrific plan. The brightly hued illustrations are as imaginative as the narrator and her friend.

Klein, Norma. Illustrated by Roy Doty. *Girls Can Be Anything*. New York: E. P. Dutton & Company, 1973. (5–8)
Marina, with the help of her parents, sets her friend Adam straight as she proves that women, as well as men, can be doctors, pilots, and leaders. The

book uses stewardess *instead of* flight attendant *and has somewhat dated illustrations, but the story of these two friends working out various roles is still worthwhile.*

Knutson, Kimberley. *Ska-tat!* New York: Macmillan, 1993. (3–6)
Three friends rush out of the library and into a day of falling leaves. The language and the bright collages bring the reader into the action, which involves energetic and exuberant cross-gender play.

Komaiko, Leah. Illustrated by Laura Cornell. *Annie Bananie.* New York: Harper & Row, 1987. (4–8)
Two girls, who are best friends, cope with their feelings when Annie Bananie must move away. Both girls are shown as imaginative, exuberant, and irrepressible. The humorous illustrations add to the zest of this book. Aliki's We Are Best Friends *features two boys with the same problem.*

Kraus, Robert. Illustrated by José Aruego and Ariane Dewey. *Herman the Helper.* New York: Simon & Schuster, 1974. (3–6)
Herman is a male octopus who helps everyone. Colorful, whimsical illustrations enhance the story of this nurturing and caring male, who learns to help himself as well as others.

————. Illustrated by José Aruego. *Leo the Late Bloomer.* New York: Simon & Schuster, 1971. (3–6)
Leo, a little lion who is less mature and capable than all his friends, feels sad. His father worries and watches, but his wise mother assures them both that Leo will bloom in his own good time. The delightful illustrations and words go together perfectly.

Kroll, Virginia. Illustrated by Rose Rosely. *New Friends, True Friends, Stuck-Like-Glue Friends.* Grand Rapids, MI: William B. Eerdmans, 1994. (3–5)
Clever rhymes and quirky illustrations demonstrate the many kinds of friends there are. Cross-gender friendships are shown throughout the book.

Lacome, Julie. *I'm a Jolly Farmer.* Cambridge, MA: Candlewick Press, 1994. (3–5)
Bold, brightly colored illustrations enhance this book about an imaginative, active, resourceful young girl who gives her dog, Fred, parts to play in her high-spirited fantasies.

Lane, Megan Halsey. *Something to Crow About.* New York: Dial Books, 1990. (3–6)
Two chicks, Cassie and Randall, are friends, but Randall is jealous of Cassie's accomplishments. Feelings of envy and pride are treated as normal, and, in the end, both characters discover that being different is "something to crow about." Charming, full-page, pastel illustrations capture the pains and pleasures of this cross-gender friendship.

Lasker, Joe. *Mothers Can Do Anything.* Chicago: Albert Whitman, 1972. (3–8)
This book shows mothers involved in a myriad of exciting occupations. But, sadly, the book focuses on mothers, not women in general. The black

and white and color illustrations combine to admirably demonstrate the message of the text.

Leaf, Munro. Illustrated by Robert Lawson. *The Story of Ferdinand*. New York: Viking, 1936. (3–6)
In this classic, a young bull's understanding mother respects his individuality. When Ferninand is taken to Madrid to fight in the bullring, he sits and smells the flowers. The peace-loving Ferdinand is immortalized in the black and white drawings.

Lee, Jeanne M. *Silent Lotus*. New York: Farrar, Straus & Giroux, 1991. (6–8)
The protagonist, a young Cambodian girl, cannot hear or speak. She is lonely and unhappy until she learns to communicate with others through dance and movement. The luminous illustrations portray the ancient art of temple dancing in the Cambodian culture.

Lester, Alison. *Isabella's Bed*. Boston: Houghton Mifflin, 1993. (5–8)
A sister and a brother discover the secret of their grandmother's bed and learn about her earlier life in South America. The words and the pastel illustrations in this unusual book elicit the elements of mystery, magic, and misfortune that pervade this intergenerational story.

_____. *Imagine*. Boston: Houghton Mifflin, 1989. (3–8)
A girl and a boy delight in make-believe play. They pretend that they are on a farm, in the jungle, in the ocean, on an ice cap, in a swamp with dinosaurs, on an African plain, and in the Australian bush country. Each page of their real play is followed by a full-page spread of their imaginary adventures. The astonishingly detailed and riveting illustrations will attract children to these pages over and over again.

_____. *Clive Eats Alligators*. Boston: Houghton Mifflin, 1986. (3–8)
Boys and girls are shown as distinct individuals in this delightful book. The cheerful illustrations show seven children (four girls and three boys) engaged in their favorite activities. For example, we see Rosie at the rodeo, Frank at the bookstore, and Nicky building her own tree house. For more capers with these seven children, try Tessa Snaps Snakes *and* Rosie Sips Spiders.

Lester, Helen. Illustrated by Lynn Munsinger. *Three Cheers for Tacky*. Boston: Houghton Mifflin, 1994. (4–8)
Tacky, a penguin who does not fit the mold, ends up stealing the show at the cheering contest, proving that he has his own special abilities. Both the illustrations and the words are lively and funny. Children, especially those who don't fit in, will enjoy this book about differences and acceptance. For another book about this character, read Tacky the Penguin.

Levinson, Riki. Illustrated by Julie Downing. *Soon, Annala*. New York: Orchard Books, 1993. (5–8)
Annala and her closely knit and loving family come to America in the early twentieth century. Warm illustrations capture the feel of immigrant

life in the new country and the traditional male and female roles of that era.

Levy, Elizabeth. Illustrated by Mordicai Gerstein. *Nice Little Girls.* Delacorte Press, 1978. (5–8)
The teacher in this book has a biased view about what girls and boys should do, but Jackie, an assertive girl, sets her and the other children straight. Jackie's parents are shown as nurturing and supportive. The message is strong, but the two-color cartoon-like illustrations are less effective.

Lillie, Patricia. *Jake and Rosie.* New York: Greenwillow Books, 1989. (3–6)
These best friends are active, imaginative, and inseparable. But one day Rosie disappears, and Jake becomes upset enough to cry. Predictably, Rosie returns, and all is well. Delightful illustrations celebrate this cross-gender friendship. There is one glitch: The author uses mailman *instead of* mailcarrier.

Lionni, Leo. *Tillie and the Wall.* New York: Alfred A. Knopf, 1989. (3–8)
Lionni uses his trademark collages to introduce Tillie, the mouse, and her companions. Tillie—who is a dreamer, a leader, and a problem solver—wants to find out what is on the other side of the wall. When her persistent efforts lead to a splendid discovery, everyone celebrates.

————. *Frederick.* New York: Pantheon, 1967. (3–8)
Frederick, a field mouse who marches to a different drummer, ends up being appreciated for his special talent. Using beautifully illustrated collages and a moving text, Lionni tells a story that celebrates an artistic and sensitive male. This is a Caldecott Honor Book. For another book by Lionni with a similar theme, read Matthew's Dream.

————. *Swimmy.* New York: Pantheon, 1963. (3–8)
Swimmy, a little fish, saves himself and his companions by showing them that, with a little cooperation, they can all outwit their predators. Distinctive collages illuminate this Caldecott Honor Book.

Little, Lessie Jones. Illustrated by Jan Spivey Gilchrist. *Children of Long Ago.* New York: Philomel Books, 1988. (4–8)
Simple poems and tender illustrations celebrate an African American girl's life in the rural South in the early 1900s.

Lobel, Arnold. *Frog and Toad Are Friends.* New York: Harper & Row, 1970. (4–8)
This chapter book includes five short humorous stories about the rewards of friendship. The illustrations are as irresistible as the two friends. Other books about this winsome pair are Frog and Toad Together, Frog and Toad All Year, *and* Days with Frog and Toad.

Lyon, George Ella. Illustrated by Stephen Gammell. *Come A Tide.* New York: Orchard Books, 1990. (5–8)
When Grandma predicts a flood, people leave their homes to escape the disaster. The next day, after surveying the damage, everyone begins the clean-

up chores. Touching watercolor illustrations reveal the feelings of dread, sadness, hope, and affinity evoked by the catastrophe.

————. Illustrated by Vera Rosenberry. *Together*. New York: Orchard Books, 1989. (3–6)
Two girls, one African American and one white, dream up fantastic adventures they can share together. The dramatic and exuberant watercolor illustrations reflect the spirited imaginings and close friendship of these two girls.

MacLachlan, Patricia. Illustrated by Mike Wimmer. *All the Places to Love*. New York: HarperCollins, 1994. (4–8)
This quiet story, with shimmering paintings of rural life, celebrates the love between family members and their love of the land. The males in this book are comfortable showing their feelings. The grandfather cries when his grandson is born, and the father and son express mutual affection. When another baby is born, she is welcomed into this loving world.

Malone, Nola Langner. *A Home*. New York: Bradbury Press, 1988. (3–6)
When Molly moves to a new home, she meets Miranda Marie, and the two girls enter into imaginative and exuberant play. After a brief falling out, they realize how much they like each other. This attractively illustrated book can take its place with other friendship stories.

Marshall, James. *George and Martha Round and Round*. Boston: Houghton Mifflin, 1988. (4–7)
Short vignettes recount the ups and downs of an enduring friendship between two hippos. As in any strong friendship, George and Martha have good times, fight and make up, and tease each other. But through it all, they remain constant friends. The funny drawings fit the amusing stories. Other books about this delightful cross-gender friendship are George and Martha, George and Martha Encore, George and Martha Rise and Shine, George and Martha One Fine Day, George and Martha Tons of Fun, *and* George and Martha Back in Town.

Marzollo, Jean. Illustrated by Jerry Pinkney. *Pretend You're a Cat*. New York: Dial Books, 1990. (2–5)
Children will want to try their own imitations after hearing the rhymes and seeing the illustrations of girls and boys pretending to be animals in this book. Both sexes and different ethnic groups are represented in the enticing illustrations.

Mayhew, James. *Katie and the Dinosaurs*. New York: Bantam Books, 1992. (4–7)
Katie, a curious, adventurous, and daring girl, leaves her grandmother resting on a museum bench and goes off on her own to explore. She opens a forbidden door and meets real dinosaurs. This fantasy will please dinosaur lovers of both sexes, who will enjoy both the exciting story and the dinosaur-laden illustrations.

McAlary, Florence, and Cohen, Judith Love. Illustrated by David A. Katz. *You Can Be a Woman Marine Biologist*. Culver City, CA: Cascade Pass, 1992. (6–8)
This book is one of a series about women in nontraditional careers, such as architecture, engineering, zoology, and paleontology. The informative texts are printed on brightly colored pages with black and white line illustrations.

McCloskey, Robert. *Blueberries for Sal*. New York: The Viking Press, 1948. (3–6)
While on a blueberry picking expedition in Maine, a mother and her little girl get mixed up with a mother bear and her cub. The line drawings in this Caldecott Honor book capture the setting and the expressions of the characters. For another Calecott Honor Book about Sal and her family, read One Morning in Maine.

McCully, Emily Arnold. *Mirette on the High Wire*. New York: G. P. Putnam's Sons, 1992. (4–8)
Mirette meets a world-renowned tightrope walker and helps him overcome his fear, and, in the process, realizes her dream to walk on the high wire. The riveting watercolor paintings evoke the circus atmosphere and the world of nineteenth-century Paris.

McDonald, Megan. Illustrated by Paul Brett Johnson. *Insects Are My Life*. New York: Orchard Books, 1995. (5–8)
The protagonist, a budding entomologist, has to cope with the people in her life who do not understand her love of bugs. In the end, she becomes friends with a girl who loves reptiles. Full-page, lighthearted, and expressive illustrations enliven the story.

McGilvray, Richard. Illustrated by Alan Snow. *Don't Climb Out the Window Tonight*. New York: Dial Books, 1993. (3–6)
As she conjures up the scary things that could be outside her window, a little girl wisely decides to stay in bed. The simple words of this story were written by a 7-year-old boy; the amusing illustrations were created by a man in his thirties. Both seem to be in touch with weird and wonderful creatures of the night.

McKean, Thomas. Illustrated by Chris L. Demarest. *Hooray for Grandma Jo!* New York: Crown Publishers, 1994. (4–8)
An energetic and irrepressible grandmother frolics with a lion, who in turn captures a burglar. Amusing illustrations go perfectly with this funny and fantastic story. In his book, Crictor, *Tomi Ungerer tells a similar yarn about Madame Bodot, an intrepid French schoolteacher, whose pet boa constrictor saves the day.*

McKissack, Patricia C. Illustrated by Jerry Pinkney. *Mirandy and Brother Wind*. New York: Alfred A. Knopf, 1988. (5–8)
In this dynamic Caldecott Honor Book, stunning paintings highlight the story of a dynamic, young African American girl and her friendship with a sensitive boy in the rural South during the early 1900s.

————. Illustrated by Rachel Isadora. *Flossie and the Fox*. New York: Dial Books, 1986. (4–8)

This African American folktale features a clever girl who outwits a wily fox in order to deliver a basket of eggs to a neighbor. The rich dialect and the luxuriant illustrations combine to make this an enchanting book for young children.

McPhail, David. *Annie & Co.* New York: Henry Holt, 1991. (6–8)

Annie sets out with a wagon and tool kit to fix whatever needs fixing. Her resourcefulness, inspiration, and intelligence help her solve a myriad of problems. The soft-focus pastel illustrations are perfect for this enchanting story.

————. *Emma's Vacation*. New York: E. P. Dutton, 1987. (3–5)

Emma, a girl bear with a mind of her own, puts her foot down and insists that she and her parents enjoy the outdoors on their vacation rather than spend one more day at an amusement park. Endearing illustrations of this personable little bear add to the subtle humor. Emma also stars in Fix It *and* Emma's Pet.

Merriam, Eve. Illustrated by Linda Graves. *The Wise Woman and Her Secret*. New York: Simon & Schuster, 1991. (6–8)

In this fairy tale, the wise old woman and a young girl share the secret of wisdom: to be curious, to look closely, to use all ones senses, and "to keep on wandering and wondering." Beautiful paintings fill every page surrounding the text.

————. Illustrated by Eugenie Fernandes. *Mommies at Work*. New York: Simon & Schuster, 1989. (3–7)

In this reissue of an earlier book, mothers are shown doing all kinds of different work both inside and outside the home. It would be a stronger book if it were about women *at work, but this is a good start, and the new illustrations are far more appealing than those in the earlier version.* Boys & Girls, Girls & Boys *by the same author has a similar nonsexist message, but the cartoon-style illustrations are busy and unappealing. We hope to see a reissue of this second book with new illustrations.*

Miller, Margaret. *Can You Guess?* New York: Greenwillow Books, 1993. (2–4)

Striking color photographs show multiethnic girls and boys engaged in everyday activities. The guessing game text and format will engage readers of both genders.

Miller, William. Illustrated by Cornelius Van Wright and Ying-Hwa Hu. *Zora Hurston and the Chinaberry Tree*. New York: Lee & Low, 1994. (5–8)

In this book about the African American writer, Zora Hurston, her childhood and the world she later wrote about come to life. Zora is shown as an assertive girl who would rather wear overalls and climb trees than be the little lady her father wants her to be. Her mother encourages Zora to dream. The colorful and expressive illustrations evoke the time and place.

Moon, Nicola. Illustrated by Alex Ayliffe. *Lucy's Picture*. New York: Dial Books, 1994. (3–6)

At her preschool, Lucy works independently and diligently to make a collage her blind grandfather can enjoy through touch. Ayliffe's colorful collage illustrations show a diverse group of boys and girls interacting positively.

Moore, Elaine. Illustrated by Dan Andreasen. *Grandma's Garden*. New York: Lothrop, Lee & Shepard, 1994. (3–6)

A young girl and her grandmother work together to plant Grandma's garden. Grandma, dressed in jeans, is independent, knowledgeable, and active. Realistic illustrations depict the warm relationship between these two down-to-earth females.

Morgan, Allen. Illustrated by Brenda Clark. *Sadie and the Snowman*. New York: Scholastic, 1985. (2–4)

Although we would be happier if the protagonist were building a snowwoman or snowperson, at least a girl is doing the work and devising a clever way to save her snowman. Appealing illustrations of Sadie and the snow embellish the simple story.

Morris, Ann. Photographed by Ken Heyman. *Loving*. New York: Lothrop, Lee & Shepard, 1990. (3–8)

In simple words and stunning photos, girls and boys from around the world are shown in loving relationships with their mothers and fathers.

Munsch, Robert N. Illustrated by Michael Martchenko. *The Paper Bag Princess*. Toronto: Annick Press, 1980. (4–8)

In a delightful reversal, Elizabeth, a princess, rescues Prince Ronald. She is brave and clever and quick to reject Ronald when she sees that he places too much emphasis on appearance. The humorous illustrations highlight Elizabeth's accomplishments. Another book by Munsch, Angela's Airplane, *features a curious and adventurous girl who becomes a pilot.*

Neitzel, Shirley. Illustrated by Nancy Winslow Parker. *The Jacket I Wear in the Snow*. New York: Greenwillow Books, 1989. (2–4)

A young girl names the clothes she needs to wear outside to play in the snow. Straightforward, attractive illustrations work well with the simple text. Read this book with Ezra Jack Keats's The Snowy Day, *which has a boy as the main character.*

Nikola-Lisa, W. Illustrated by Michael Bryant. *Bein' with You This Way*. New York: Lee & Low, 1994. (3–6)

An African American girl gathers together a group of friends at the park. As this diverse group of boys and girls plays together, they discover that their similarities are more important than their differences. The rap language and the vibrant illustrations join together to celebrate friendship and cooperation.

Nye, Naomi Shihab. Illustrated by Nancy Carpenter. *Sitti's Secrets*. New York: Four Winds Press, 1994. (5–8)

Mona travels with her father to a small Arab village to visit her grandmother. The warm relationship of the girl and her grandmother and the portrayal of the Arabic culture are nicely interwoven. The soft focus illustrations and the poetic language in this book are graceful and expressive.

Ormerod, Jan. *Moonlight*. New York: Lothrop, Lee & Shepard, 1982. (3–6)
Watercolor illustrations reflect the warmth of this delightful bedtime story about a little girl who finds lots of reasons not to go to sleep. Her parents are equally involved in chores and child care. Children and parents of both sexes will relate to this wordless book.

Peterson, Jeanne Whitehouse. Illustrated by Sandra Speidel. *My Mama Sings*. New York: HarperCollins, 1994. (4–8)
An African American mother sings old songs to her young son throughout the day. But when she has problems at work, the sensitive and caring young boy makes up a special song for her. Heartwarming illustrations reflect the love between the two.

Pfanner, Louise. *Louise Builds a Boat*. New York: Orchard Books, 1989. (4–8)
Louise, a girl of imagination and talent, builds an extraordinary boat. Children will learn about parts of a boat when they hear the words and study the sprightly and whimsical illustrations. In an earlier book, Louise Builds a House, *this ingenious girl creates a fantastic dwelling.*

Pinkney, Gloria Jean. Illustrated by Jerry Pinkney. *The Sunday Outing*. New York: Dial Books, 1994. (4–8)
Ernestine and her great aunt share special outings to the train station, and together they devise a way for Ernestine to go on a train trip to visit relatives in the South. This caring African American family is shown in lightly sketched and softly washed paintings.

Piper, Watty. Illustrated by George and Doris Hauman. *The Little Engine That Could*. Platt & Munk, 1930. (2–6)
The little female engine saves the day when the engine of the train carrying toys and goodies to the children on the other side of a mountain breaks down. Children have chanted, "I think I can, I think I can," along with the valiant little engine since the book was published in 1930. The vintage illustrations work nicely with the text.

Polacco, Patricia. *Chicken Sunday*. New York: Philomel Books, 1992. (5–8)
A white girl is best friends with two African American brothers and their grandmother. The children work together to resolve problems that arise when they decide to earn money for a gift for the grandmother. This moving story about cross-gender, intercultural, and intergenerational friendships is enhanced by the vivid and sympathetic illustrations.

————. *Thunder Cake*. New York: Philomel Books, 1990. (4–8)
The narrator tells how her Russian grandmother helped her conquer her fear of thunderstorms. After the young girl braves the brewing storm and barnyard perils to collect the ingredients for a thunder cake, she realizes, with the help of her wise grandmother, how courageous she has been.

Colorful and sensitive illustrations reflect the moods of the characters and the ominous quality of the oncoming storm.

Pomerantz, Charlotte. Illustrated by Nancy Winslow Parker. *Here Comes Henny*. New York: Greenwillow Books, 1994. (4–8)
This hilarious verse about a mother hen, her chicks, and nutritious snacks will capture the attention of both boys and girls. The illustrations are as funny as the words. Piggy in the Puddle, *another book by the same author, will also make children laugh.*

Porte, Barbara Ann. Illustrated by Maxie Chambliss. *When Aunt Lucy Rode a Mule*. New York: Orchard Books, 1994. (5–8)
This story of several female generations, as told by Aunt Lucy to her nieces, is full of the family's interesting, active, and strong women. The grandfather in the family is shown wearing an apron and serving the lunch he prepared. The illustrations are as lively as the girls and women.

Provensen, Alice, and Provensen, Martin. *A Book of Seasons*. New York: Random House, 1976. (3–6)
Delightful and detailed illustrations highlight the simple text in this book about girls and boys enjoying the changing seasons. Girls and boys play together, and girls are as active as boys. Other books by the Provensens that show cross-gender interactions in a country setting include Our Animal Friends at Maple Hill Farm *and* The Year at Maple Hill Farm.

Quinlan, Patricia. Illustrated by Lindsay Grater. *Anna's Red Sled*. Toronto: Annick Press, 1989. (5–8)
In this nostalgic story, a mother and daughter recapture a meaningful time from the past. The quiet watercolors reflect the special mother/daughter relationship and the winter scenes.

Rattigan, Jama Kim. Illustrated by G. Brian Karas. *Truman's Aunt Farm*. Boston: Houghton Mifflin, 1994. (4–8)
In this amusing story, Truman gets a most unusual present from his Aunt Fran. Truman trains the aunts in his farm to be as wonderful as his own unique aunt. The capricious illustrations capture the humor of the play on words and make the improbable events seem believable.

———. Illustrated by Lillian Hsu-Flanders. *Dumpling Soup*. Boston: Little, Brown, 1993. (4–8)
Marisa, the central character in this book, joins her Asian American relatives at a Hawaiian New Year's Eve celebration. Many dumplings are needed to make enough dumpling soup for the whole rollicking family, and Marisa gets to help for the first time. The engaging and expressive full-page brightly colored illustrations reflect the festive mood, but it is worth noting that the females in the family do all the food preparation, while the males set up the fireworks.

Rayner, Mary. *One by One: Garth Pig's Rain Song*. New York: E. P. Dutton, 1994. (2–5)

Five little girl and five little boy pigs march singly, in pairs, and in groups to get out of the rain. The repetition in the rhymes and the colorful and detailed illustrations of the pigs' antics will appeal to both sexes.

Reiser, Lynn. *Tomorrow on Rocky Pond.* New York: Greenwillow Books, 1993. (4–7)
A young girl tells the reader about the canoe trip she anticipates taking with her family. The females and the males in the family are all portrayed as active and enthusiastic about the outdoors. The colorful, detailed drawings of the girl's encounter with nature add to the story.

Rice, Eve. *Benny Bakes a Cake.* New York: Greenwillow Books, 1981. (2–4)
Benny helps his mother bake his birthday cake. But when his dog eats it, he is inconsolable. He cries and cries (something rarely seen in a book with a boy protagonist), but in the end, Mama and Papa have a telephone conversation, and the problem is solved. The simple illustrations fit this story of ordinary family life.

Ringgold, Faith. *Tar Beach.* New York: Crown Publishers, 1991. (5–8)
Cassie Louise Lightfoot flies from the rooftop of her apartment building in Harlem on a magical flight over New York City. Elements of African American history and of Ringgold's life are dramatized in the words and the astonishing and brilliantly colored paintings that fill the pages of this extraordinary book. Aunt Harriet's Underground Railroad *features Cassie and her brother in another magical journey that tells the Harriet Tubman story in a unique way.*

Rockwell, Anne. Illustrated by Lizzy Rockwell. *Apples and Pumpkins.* New York: Macmillan, 1989. (2–5)
A little girl goes to a pumpkin farm and brings home a pumpkin to carve. The bold, clear illustrations add to the book's appeal.

_____. Illustrated by Harlow Rockwell and Lizzy Rockwell. *My Spring Robin.* New York: Macmillan, 1989. (2–5)
While searching for the robin she saw last year, a little girl discovers many signs of spring. Bold, colorful illustrations enliven the text.

_____. *When We Grow Up.* New York: E. P. Dutton, 1981. (3–7)
Six girls and eight boys consider what they want to be when they grow up. The six girls choose nontraditional occupations. The boys are more traditional in their choices with two exceptions: one wants to be an artist and the other wants to be a teacher like his own male teacher. The typical Rockwell illustrations complement the text.

Rockwell, Anne, and Rockwell, Harlow. *The First Snowfall.* New York: Macmillan, 1987. (2–4)
The protagonist in this simple and colorfully illustrated book is a girl who shovels a path, builds a snowman (unfortunately, not a snowperson or snowwoman), and goes to the park to play in the snow with her parents.

Rockwell, Harlow. *My Nursery School*. New York: Greenwillow Books, 1976. (3–5)
> *A father takes his daughter to nursery school. The teachers are male and female, and the multiethnic children are engaged in a variety of activities together. Susan builds a tower, and Jim uses scissors, paper, and glue. Characteristic Rockwell illustrations depict a typical nursery school.*

———. *My Doctor*. New York: Harper & Row, 1973. (2–4)
> *A young boy tells about a routine visit to his (female) doctor. The waiting room scenes show girls and boys playing together and both boys and girls with books. The straightforward, realistic illustrations will reassure young patients.* My Dentist *features a young girl telling about her visit to her (male) dentist.*

Rogers, Fred. Photographed by Jim Judkis. *Making Friends*. New York: G. P. Putnam's Sons, 1987. (3–5)
> *A girl and a boy learn about friendship—the good times and the difficult moments. The photographs of the friends sensitively portray the girl and the boy and the range of their emotions.*

Rose, Deborah Lee. Illustrated by Irene Trivas. *Meredith's Mother Takes the Train*. Niles, IL: Albert Whitman, 1991. (2–5)
> *Colorful, animated illustrations show what Meredith and her mother are doing when they are apart—Meredith at day care and mother at work in the city. The pictures of the day-care setting show girls and boys playing cooperatively together, resting, and eating together. The mother's work world features equal numbers of females and males interacting as peers.*

Rosenberg, Maxine B. Photographed by George Ancona. *My Friend Leslie: The Story of a Handicapped Child*. New York: Lothrop, Lee & Shepard, 1983. (4–8)
> *In this book, two girls, one with multiple handicaps, are friends. The girl with handicaps is shown as capable, friendly, and fun to be with. The photographs are both truthful and positive.*

Rylant, Cynthia. Illustrated by Diane Goode. *When I Was Young in the Mountains*. New York: Dutton Children's Books, 1982. (4–8)
> *The narrator tells the story of her childhood in Appalachia. The tender, pastel illustrations recall an earlier era in this special setting.*

Scheffler, Ursel. Illustrated by Ulises Wensell. *A Walk in the Rain*. New York: G. P. Putnam's Sons, 1986. (2–5)
> *In a subtle role reversal, it is Grandmother who takes her grandson, Josh, on a discovery-filled walk in the rain, while Grandfather reads a story to them when they return home. The illustrations reflect the loving relationship between Josh and his grandparents.*

Schlank, Carol Hilgartner, and Metzger, Barbara. Illustrated by Janice Bond. *Elizabeth Cady Stanton: A Biography for Young Children*. Beltsville, MD: Gryphon House, 1991. (4–8)

Historically accurate and sensitive illustrations depict the life of Elizabeth Cady Stanton from birth to her leadership role in the women's rights movement. The book focuses on Elizabeth's childhood as a rebel, a thinker, and an achiever, and shows that times have, in fact, changed. For another biography about a remarkable woman by the same authors, read A Clean Sea: The Rachel Carson Story.

Scott, Ann Herbert. Illustrated by Glo Coalson. *Hi!* New York: Philomel Books, 1994. (2–4)
Margarita tries to get the people at the post office to respond to her greetings. But everyone, except the woman at the counter, is preoccupied. Margarita's persistence pays off in this simple story. The sensitive and realistic illustrations reveal Margarita's feelings.

_____. Illustrated by Meg Kelleher Aubrey. *Grandmother's Chair.* New York: Clarion Books, 1990. (3–6)
As they look at old photographs together, a grandmother shares the history of the little chair that she will give to her 4-year-old granddaughter. The illustrations beautifully depict the lives of the women and girls of four generations.

Sendak, Maurice. *Outside Over There.* New York: Harper & Row, 1981. (4–8)
While Ida is left in charge of her baby sister, the goblins kidnap the baby. Ida sets out to rescue her sister, and the adventure that follows is weird and dreamlike. The paintings that illustrate this Caldecott Honor Book are an aesthetic treat full of marvelous details.

Seymour, Tres. Illustrated by Wendy Anderson Halperin. *Hunting the White Cow.* New York: Orchard Books, 1993. (4–8)
The girl who narrates this story about the family's renegade cow succeeds in catching the cow—for a brief time. (The men have all failed miserably.) Large double-spread pastel illustrations beautifully depict the details of this determined young girl's life in rural Kentucky. The cow is another strong-willed and determined female!

Shannon, Margaret. *Elvira.* New York: Ticknor & Fields, 1993. (4–8)
Like Ferdinand in the Munro Leaf story, Elvira, a young dragon, doesn't want to fight and be a "normal" member of the group, but wants to sit on the grass and make daisy chains. Her parents don't understand her, and she runs away to join the princesses. In the end, she discovers she can be herself. The pictures of Elvira and the dragons are lively and humorous. A warning: Elvira's desire to wear frilly dresses and be attractive is overemphasized as a way of being different.

Sheppard, Jeff. Illustrated by Felicia Bond. *The Right Number of Elephants.* New York: Harper & Row, 1990. (3–6)
A little girl is the main character in this amusing counting book. The humorous illustrations will entice children to count the elephants.

Simon, Norma. Illustrated by Dora Leder. *Mama Cat's Year.* Morton Grove, IL: Albert Whitman, 1991. (3–6)

By watching Mama Cat's behavior, the narrator and his family can predict the changing seasons. Engaging pastel illustrations show the family and their cat enjoying the different times of the year. The family shares work and play, and boys and girls interact in positive ways.

_____. Illustrated by Dora Leder. *Cats Do, Dogs Don't.* Niles, IL: Albert Whitman, 1986. (3–6)
Multiethnic girls and boys interact throughout this book about the differences between pet cats and dogs. The lively illustrations show appealing children and pets. Another book by this author, Where Does My Cat Sleep? *features a girl with her pet.*

Skofield, James. Illustrated by James Graham Hale. *'Round and Around.* New York: HarperCollins, 1993. (3–5)
In this book, a nurturing father and son share many loving moments as they talk about things that go around in circles. The illustrations reflect the warmth of this father/son relationship, but, unhappily, the father is smoking a pipe.

Small, David. *Imogene's Antlers.* New York: Crown Books, 1985. (4–7)
Imogene, a little girl who wakes up with antlers, handles the situation with aplomb. The amusing illustrations will make both boys and girls smile.

Soentpiet, Chris K. *Around Town.* New York: Lothrop, Lee & Shepard Books, 1994. (4–8)
A girl and her mother share a wonderful day in New York City. The realistic double-page illustrations depict the pleasures of urban life and show boys and girls interacting.

Soya, Kiyoshi. Illustrated by Akiko Hayashi. *A House of Leaves.* New York: Philomel Books, 1986. (2–4)
A little Asian girl, who is caught out in the rain, looks for shelter. Soft, appealing illustrations of the girl and the creatures she sees enhance this quiet story.

Spier, Peter. *Oh, Were They Ever Happy!* New York: Doubleday & Company, 1978. (3–8)
When their parents leave home for a day, the children (both sisters and brothers) get together and paint the house. The rainbow-colored result delights the children and shocks the parents. The humorous and detailed illustrations add to the fun.

Steig, William. *Brave Irene.* New York: Farrar, Straus & Giroux, 1986. (4–8)
Brave Irene confronts a series of disasters when she goes to deliver the ball gown her sick mother has made for the duchess. The illustrations vividly convey Irene's valiant struggle and the happy outcome.

Stinson, Kathy. *Bare Naked Book.* Toronto: Annick Press, 1986. (2–5)
The bodies of boys, girls, men, women, and babies are shown in this realistic, straightforward book about different bodies. The illustrations are clear and appealing and show the physical differences between the sexes.

_____. *Red Is Best*. Illustrated by Robin Baird Lewis. Toronto: Annick Press, 1982. (2–4)
A little girl loves and chooses her favorite color red whenever she can. Young children of both sexes will respond to the feelings of the protagonist and to the sprightly illustrations that feature, as you would expect, the color red.

Stoeke, Janet Morgan. *A Hat for Minerva Louise*. New York: Dutton Children's Books, 1994. (2–5)
A curious and resourceful chicken finds a pair of mittens to keep her warm. The bright, cheerful illustrations highlight the simple straightforward text. For another story about this dauntless chicken, read Minerva Louise.

Thomas, Joyce Carol. Illustrated by Floyd Cooper. *Brown Honey in Broomwheat Tea*. New York: HarperCollins, 1993. (4–8)
The poems and golden brown illustrations in this book celebrate the African American heritage and family. Lovely pictures of girls and women fill these pages.

Trivizas, Eugene. Illustrated by Helen Oxenbury. *The Three Little Wolves and the Big Bad Pig*. New York: Margaret K. McElderry Books, 1993. (3–8)
In a side-splitting reversal of the three little pigs story, the wolves build what they hope will be three increasingly secure dwellings. The big bad pig outwits them—until the end, when an unforeseen solution turns the enemies into friends. The full-page watercolor illustrations are filled with amusing details. Another successful reversal story, Deep in the Forest *by Brinton Turkle, has the bear cub visiting Goldilock's home.*

Tsutsui, Yoriko. Illustrated by Akiko Hayashi. *Anna's Secret Friend*. New York: Viking Kestrel, 1987. (3–6)
In this Japanese picture book, Anna moves with her parents to a new home. She is lonely until she and another girl become friends. The pastel illustrations show the two girls riding bikes and playing ball together and the children at Anna's new school involved in cross-gender play.

Turkle, Brinton. *Do Not Open*. New York: E. P. Dutton, 1981. (3–6)
Miss Moody, who loves storms, is a champion beachcomber. When she finds a bottle and lets out an ugly creature, she uses her wits to put things right. The bold illustrations conjure up the gutsy protagonist and her life by the sea. For another story about an intrepid female, read The Little Old Lady Who Was Not Afraid of Anything *by Linda Williams. (Both books could be used at Halloween.)*

Tusa, Tricia. *Miranda*. New York: Macmillan, 1985. (5–8)
Miranda, a young pianist, falls in love with boogie-woogie. Her parents object to her playing that kind of music, but she suggests a compromise and solves the problem. The busy black and white illustrations with red touches may not appeal to all readers.

Udry, Janet. Illustrated by Maurice Sendak. *Let's Be Enemies*. New York: Harper & Row, 1961. (3–5)
Two boys, who are friends, have a falling out, but come back together in the end. This story makes a good companion to Charlotte Zolotow's The Hating Book.

————. Illustrated by Marc Simont. *A Tree Is Nice*. New York: Harper & Row, 1956. (3–6)
A young girl plants and nurtures a tree. The attractive illustrations in this Caldecott Medal winner convey what makes trees special. However, the number of boys in the book far outnumbers the girls, and the boys, not the girls, are active.

Van der Beek, Deborah. *Alice's Blue Cloth*. New York: G. P. Putnam's Sons, 1989. (3–5)
Alice, an active and imaginative girl, capers with the blue cloth and her cat, Tom, in this appealing story. The realistic illustrations will delight children.

VanLaan, Nancy. Illustrated by Nadine Bernard. *Round and Round Again*. New York: Hyperion Books, 1994. (4–8)
The young girl narrator's mother in this modern tall tale is an inveterate and marvelously creative recycler. The fun-filled and humorous illustrations spill over onto every page.

Van Leeuwen, Jean. Illustrated by Juan Wijngaard. *Emma Bean*. New York: Dial Books, 1993. (4–6)
A stuffed toy rabbit named Emma Bean is the constant companion of a girl named Molly. Luminous and expressive illustrations embellish this captivating story of a girl's first five years.

Vincent, Gabrielle. *Bravo, Ernest and Celestine*. New York: Greenwillow Books, 1981. (3–7)
Celestine comes up with the solution to the problem of a leaky roof in this story of a happy collaboration. Pastel watercolors reveal the characters love and respect for one another. This book is one in a series about this enchanting pair.

Viorst, Judith. Illustrated by Kay Chorao. *My Mama Says There Aren't Any Zombies, Ghosts, Vampires, Creatures, Demons, Monsters, Fiends, Goblins, or Things*. New York: Aladdin Books, 1973. (4–7)
A boy, who is frightened by monsters and other such creatures, has a hard time believing that his mother knows what she is talking about when she says they don't exist. The illustrations of the scary things are more amusing than frightening.

Vulliamy, Clara. *Ellen and Penguin*. Cambridge, MA: Candlewick Press, 1993. (3–5)
Ellen, a shy little girl with a toy penguin, finds it hard to join the activities at the playground until she meets another girl with a toy monkey. The real-

life illustrations reveal the protagonist's feelings, but, sadly, the largest picture in the book shows an all-girl cliquish tea party. Shy Charles *by Rosemary Wells vividly portrays a male who won't talk to anyone, except in a crisis.*

Waddell, Martin. Illustrated by Jill Barton. *Little Mo.* Cambridge, MA: Candlewick Press, 1993. (2–6)
Little Mo, a female polar bear, perseveres in her efforts to learn to skate on the ice. In the end, she is sliding, gliding, and whizzing along with joy. The ebullient illustrations capture the setting and mood.

———. Illustrated by Dom Mansell. *My Great Grandpa.* New York: G. P. Putnam's Sons, 1990. (3–7)
A spunky little girl tells about her experiences with her great grandpa. She takes him for a ride in his wheelchair through the neighborhood and later helps her granny care for him at home. Although the females are in traditional nurturing roles, the relationships are loving and realistic, and the narrator is active and assertive. The full-page illustrations are colorful and lively.

———. Illustrated by Jonathan Langley. *Alice, the Artist.* New York: E. P. Dutton, 1988. (4–7)
In this imaginative and amusing story, Alice gets advice from her friends on what to put in her picture. In the end, Alice makes her own decision. The friends, active multiethnic girls and boys, and their suggestions for Alice, are delightfully illustrated in colorful detail.

Ward, Leila. Illustrated by Nonny Hogrogian. *I Am Eyes: Ni Macho.* New York: Greenwillow Books, 1978. (3–6)
A young girl who lives in Kenya starts her day saying, "Ni macho," which in Swahili means, "I am eyes." And then through her eyes, the reader sees the young girl's African world unfold. Simple poetic language and delicately colored and black and white illustrations merge to create this graceful book about a girl and another culture.

Weber, Bernard. *Ira Sleeps Over.* Boston: Houghton Mifflin, 1972. (4–7)
Ira is in a quandary as to whether to take his teddy bear on an overnight visit to his friend's house. But the problem is solved when the two boys discover that each of them needs a special cuddle toy at times. The straightforward illustrations capture the vulnerability of the two boys.

Wells, Rosemary. *Edward Unready for School.* New York: Dial Books for Young Readers, 1995. (2–6)
Edward, an apprehensive and timid bear, is resistant to going to nursery school. After a week, his wise teachers decide that the desolate Edward is not ready for school. The watercolor illustrations, which show many cross-gender interactions, perfectly capture Edward's vulnerability and fear. In Edward's Overwhelming Overnight, *he is not ready to spend the night at a friend's house, and in* Edward in Deep Water, *he is loath to attend a swimming party without his water wings.*

_____. Illustrated by Mark Graham. *Lucy Comes to Stay*. New York: Dial Books, 1994. (4–7)

Mary Elizabeth brings home a new puppy named Lucy. As Lucy grows up, Mary Elizabeth takes care of her in a loving, inventive, and responsible way. The heartwarming illustrations show the caring relationships, but we would be happier if Mary Elizabeth wore slacks and sneakers as well as dresses and fancy shoes.

_____. *Timothy Goes to School*. New York: Dial Books, 1981. (3–6)

Timothy, an endearing raccoon, has a hard time liking school until he meets Violet, a kindred spirit, who becomes his friend. Pastel colors and appealing line drawings join with the simple text to create a sensitive and humorous book with a heartwarming cross-gender friendship.

_____. *Benjamin and Tulip*. New York: Dial Books, 1973. (3–6)

Tulip, who is anything but the sweet, little, girl raccoon Aunt Fern thinks she is, bullies Benjamin time and again. The humorous illustrations and the predictable story line are a winning combination. This is a good book to read along with any that show boys as bullies.

_____. *Noisy Nora*. New York: Dial Press, 1973. (3–6)

Although Nora, the mouse, is incredibly noisy, she gets little attention from her preoccupied parents until she disappears. Children will love the ending when Nora comes out of hiding saying, "But I'm back again," as the contents of the closet spill out "with a monumental crash." The verses and drawings are perfect together.

Westcott, Nadine Bernard. *The Lady with the Alligator Purse*. Boston: Little, Brown, 1988. (3–8)

In a rollicking retelling of the familiar rhyme, the lady with the alligator purse cures Tiny Tim by giving him pizza! The colorful illustrations are exuberant and full of humorous details.

Wetterer, Margaret K. Illustrated by Karen Ritz. *Kate Shelley and the Midnight Express*. Minneapolis, MN: Carolrhoda Books, 1990. (5–8)

In this true story, a young girl risks her life to give a warning that prevents a terrible train wreck. Soft-washed illustrations dramatically recall this act of courage in a book that children will find riveting.

Wild, Margaret. *Our Granny*. New York: Ticknor & Fields, 1994. (4–7)

This engaging book celebrates the individuality of grandmothers of all sizes, shapes, colors, and styles. The full-page illustrations are as colorful and unique as the grandmothers.

_____. Illustrated by Dee Huxley. *Mr. Nick's Knitting*. New York: Harcourt Brace, 1989. (4–8)

Miss Jolley and Mr. Nick are knitting partners and very good friends. Humorous and poignant full-page and brightly colored illustrations join with the text to create a splendid book about a cross-gender friendship.

Williams, Sherley Anne. Illustrated by Carole Byard. *Working Cotton*. New York: Harcourt Brace Jovanovich, 1992. (6–8)

This book recreates a day in the life of a young African American girl who works with her family in the cotton fields. The moving illustrations in this Caldecott Honor Book highlight the hardships of a migrant girl's life.

Williams, Vera B. *"More More More," Said the Baby*. New York: Greenwillow Books, 1990. (2–4)

In this Caldecott Honor Book, three multiethnic babies (two of whom are girls) ask for more loving attention. A mother, father, and grandmother are all eager to comply with their particular beloved child's demands. (A caveat: The way the father is shown throwing his baby in the air could harm a baby.)

_____. *A Chair for My Mother*. New York: Greenwillow Books, 1982. (4–8)

An African American family (Rosa, her mother, and her grandmother) all save money in a jar so Rosa's waitress mother can have a comfortable chair to sit in after work. The illustrations in this Caldecott Honor Book are colorful and sensitive. The sequels about these three resourceful females, Something Special for Me *and* Music, Music for Everyone, *will please their fans.*

Winthrop, Elizabeth. Illustrated by Mary Morgan. *Asleep in a Heap*. New York: Holiday House, 1993. (3–6)

Julie, an irrepressible and energetic little girl, tires out her family. They all fall asleep waiting for her to wilt. In the end, she falls asleep on top of her sleeping family. The colorful, lighthearted illustrations add to the humor.

_____. Illustrated by Tomie dePaola. *Maggie and the Monster*. New York: Holiday House, 1987. (3–6)

Maggie is not afraid of the little monster who shows up each night, but she wants her to go away. Maggie solves the dilemma, when she follows her mother's advice and asks the monster what she wants. The illustrations are inviting and humorous.

_____. Illustrated by Lillian Hoban. *Tough Eddie*. New York: E. P. Dutton, 1985. (3–6)

Eddie is a little boy with a tough guy side, but he loves his dollhouse too. At first, he's ashamed of his dollhouse, but, by the end of the story, he is thinking about bringing it to school for show and tell. The appealing illustrations reveal the feelings of the characters. A cautionary note: Eddie and two friends are shown playing with toy guns.

Wright, Betty Ren. Illustrated by Gail Owens. *The Cat Next Door*. New York: Holiday House, 1991. (4–8)

A young girl grieves for her beloved grandmother who has died. When the cat next door shows up with a "splendiforous surprise," the granddaughter is able to accept her grandmother's death. The muted, pastel illustrations recall the caring relationship between the vibrant grandmother and her sensitive granddaughter and the good times the two have shared.

Yashima, Taro. *Umbrella*. New York: Viking Press, 1958. (3–6)
A little Japanese girl finds it hard to wait for a rainy day and the chance to use her new umbrella and boots. Her conviction that she should "walk straight like a grown up lady" seems outdated, but, overall, this Caldecott Honor Book with its soft focus and sensitive illustrations is charming.

Yolen, Jane. Illustrated by John Schoenherr. *Owl Moon*. New York: Philomel Books, 1987. (4–7)
In this Caldecott Medal winning book, a little girl and her caring father go on a nighttime search for an owl. The outstanding illustrations evoke the winter night and the shared joy of the girl and her father.

Young, Ed. *Lon Po Po: A Red-Riding Hood Story From China*. New York: Philomel Books, 1989. (4–8)
Three girls open their door after hearing a voice claiming to be their granny. But, of course, it's not granny; it's a wolf. Not to worry: The ingenious girls get the best of the scoundrel. Lovely illustrations grace this Caldecott Medal winning book.

Young, Ruth. *Starring Francine and Dave: Three One-Act Plays*. New York: Orchard Books, 1988. (5–8)
These two friends complicate the process of making a sandwich, lemonade, and sharing chocolate cake in ways that will tickle readers and/or actors. Francine is the leader in this cross-gender friendship. The whimsical cartoon-like illustrations are just right.

Zalben, Jane Breskin. *Miss Violet's Shining Day*. Honesdale, PA: Boyds Mills Press, 1995. (3–6)
When Miss Violet discovers music, she also discovers the rewards of perseverance and hard work. Graceful, detailed illustrations enhance the story.

Ziefert, Harriet. Illustrated by Laura Rader. *Pete's Chicken*. New York: Tambourine Books, 1994. (4–8)
Pete, a young rabbit, has an abundance of self-esteem until his classmates make fun of his drawing of a multicolored chicken. Even his mother's appreciation of his drawing is not enough. Finally, though, Pete reaffirms his right to be his own person. The brightly colored illustrations and the simple text celebrate Pete's individuality.

_____. Illustrated by Anita Lobel. *A New Coat for Anna*. New York: Alfred A. Knopf, 1986. (5–8)
At the end of World War II, money and merchandise are in short supply, so Anna's mother trades her possessions for the wool and the skills of the craftspeople to make Anna a much needed new coat. The story is informative and the two female characters are resilient and resourceful. Vibrant illustrations realistically depict the time and place.

_____. Illustrated by Susan Bonners. *Sarah's Questions*. New York: Lothrop, Lee & Shepard, 1986. (3–7)

A little girl, full of curiosity, asks her mother all kinds of how and why questions when they go on a walk together. The patient mother takes her daughter seriously and answers all her questions. The illustrations reveal the warm feelings each of the characters has for the other.

Zolotow, Charlotte. Illustrated by Anita Lobel. *This Quiet Lady*. New York: Greenwillow Books, 1992. (2–6)

The little girl in this story explores old photographs that reveal her mother's life from childhood to motherhood. The continuity of family is reflected in the straightforward text and in the warm, rich illustrations.

_____. Illustrated by James Stevenson. *I Know a Lady*. New York: Greenwillow Books, 1984. (3–6)

An independent, active old woman who lives alone is a good friend to the little girl narrator and her companions. The illustrations reveal the passing seasons and the quiet intergenerational friendship.

_____. Illustrated by William Pene du Bois. *William's Doll*. New York: Harper & Row, 1972. (3–7)

Although the males in the book think William should play with "boy toys," William's grandmother wisely gives him the doll he covets. She explains that caring for a doll will help William be a nurturing father someday. The warm illustrations capture William's feelings.

_____. Illustrated by Ben Shecter. *The Hating Book*. New York: Harper & Row, 1969. (4–7)

Two girls have a misunderstanding, but when they talk about what caused the trouble, they become friends again. The mother in the book is wise and empathic. Expressive illustrations support the text of this natural companion to Let's Be Enemies *by Janet Udry and* Best Friends *by Miriam Cohen.*

_____. Illustrated by Maurice Sendak. *Mr. Rabbit and the Lovely Present*. New York: Harper & Row, 1962. (3–6)

*A little girl and a talking rabbit work together to assemble just the right birthday present for the little girl's mother. This charmingly illustrated Caldecott Honor Book can be read along with another similar and popular preschool book with a male protagonist—*Ask Mr. Bear *by Marjorie Flack.*

RESOURCES

There are many good books that can be ordered from the materials and equipment catalogs listed in the Resources section in Chapter 2. In addition, you may wish to request the following book catalogs—ones we have found to have particularly good selections or to emphasize antibias literature.

Chinaberry Books
2780 Via Orange Way, Suite B
Spring Valley, CA 92078
1-800-776-2242

Great Owl Books
41 Watchung Plaza, Suite 112
Montclair, NJ 07042
1-800-299-3181

Gryphon House
P.O. Box 207
Beltsville, MD 20704
1-800-638-0928

Just Girls: Books That Celebrate Girls
P.O. Box 34487
Bethesda, MD 20827
1-800-465-5445

Listening Library, Inc.
One Park Ave.
Old Greenwich, CT 06870
1-800-243-4504

CHAPTER SIX
BUILDING COMPATIBLE PARTNERSHIPS WITH PARENTS

Recognizing Where Parents Are Coming From and Enlisting Their Support for Your Program

As you get to know the parents of the children in your class, you will find that they are as different from one another as their children are. You will want to show the parents that you appreciate them as unique individuals and respect their differences and their varying points of view, just as you respect the individuality of each of their children.

In relation to gender, the parents in your group will come with a host of different expectations, depending on which sex they are and what their experiences as males or females in their particular culture and class have been. They will have conscious and unconscious attitudes about their own and the other gender and about the value and the possibility of cooperation between the sexes.

You will surely find some parents who are "on the same wavelength" as you are in relation to gender issues. But you will also undoubtedly find a few parents for whom gender issues are trivial and others to whom gender equity and cross-gender play are new and alien concepts. Many parents will have given little thought to how gender stereotyping and lack of interaction and cooperation between girls and boys affect their young children. However, most parents, providing they feel you are supportive and care about them and their children, will be open to learning new ideas and behaviors that can positively shape their children's lives. And of course, you will endeavor to help all the parents come to an understanding and acceptance of your goals for encouraging gender equity and fostering cooperative play. In some instances, though, parents will remain committed to their own views even after much discussion and sharing of ideas. In the end, you will have to decide what is in the best interest of the children and your program.

In this chapter, we suggest ways you can work with parents to gain their understanding of and endorsement for your gender-related goals. We start by sharing ways to introduce your program to parents and we elaborate on ways to communicate with them. Next, we discuss ways to meet the challenge of working with parents whose convictions and attitudes may be at variance with your goals for gender equity. We end the chapter with a discussion of ways to encourage and enhance parent involvement in the planning and implementing of your program goals for gender equity and cooperative play.

INTRODUCING YOUR PROGRAM TO PARENTS

To successfully carry out a program for children and their families that is committed to a *Together and Equal* philosophy, you will need to help parents understand your program's goals and objectives. You will also want to make parents feel that their contributions toward realizing these goals will be vital and valued.

Initial Contact with Parents

Your first contact with a parent or parents is likely to be by phone. Give parents time to ask questions and share information about themselves and their families and briefly explain your program to them. Try to establish in this conversation whether your program is likely to meet their needs. If they are interested in learning more about your program, you will want to schedule an on-site visit.

Introductory On-Site Visits

At this visit, schedule enough time to get acquainted with the parents and to allow them to begin to get to know you. Give them an opportunity to share information about themselves and their families and give them a brief overview of your program's philosophy and goals, including those relating to gender. After parents observe your program in action, they will be better able to determine whether your program is right for them. Be sure to try to find a time after the parent visit to answer questions that arise. Be careful not to rush these important initial contacts. If parents feel comfortable with you and understand your program goals and policies right from the start, you will be establishing the foundation for a good working relationship.

Preliminary Home Visits

Preliminary home visits can give you an opportunity to get to know new families and to help children and their parents make the transition from home to school. By making the effort to visit and get to know the families, you will communicate interest and caring and will begin to establish good relationships with the children and parents.

You may also decide to go over program goals, policies, and other written materials with the parents during the home visit. Remember that communication works both ways—be careful to listen to any comments and concerns parents articulate. During this exchange, you will begin to learn about parent expectations, attitudes, and beliefs, including those related to gender equity and cooperative play.

Orientation Meetings

Depending on your program, you may decide to have an orientation meeting to explain your program philosophy and policies to the parents of the children in your class. An orientation meeting can be helpful if you are meeting a large number of parents at one time. However, we do urge that you not limit yourself to a group meeting but plan to schedule times to get to know the individual parent's concerns and expectations.

Written Materials for Parents

After a phone conversation or a visit, you might want to mail or give the parents a copy of your program brochure and mission or goal statements. Later, after parents have enrolled their children in your program, you can give them any supplemental materials you may have: a more detailed handbook for parents, a calendar of events, a handout on visiting and helping in the classroom, and so on.

Having your program goals and policies written out in a form parents can refer to throughout the year can be helpful for them and for you. As you write these pieces, keep the language clear and straightforward. Remember that your goal is to *communicate* with the parents, not to overwhelm them with print. Of course, your brochures, handbooks, and mission statements will include information about many aspects of your program. But because of the focus of our book, we address only the goals that refer to gender equity and cooperation issues in our discussion of what to include in your written materials for parents. We supply some sample statements regarding gender and cooperation for you to consider. You may, of course, adapt any of our suggestions to fit the needs of your particular program.

For example, a *gender statement* in a brochure or mission statement might say something like this:

> In this program, we want girls and boys to like and respect one another and to work and play cooperatively. *All* children are encouraged to participate in *all* areas of the classroom: the house corner, the block area, the art center, the sand and water tables, the table games area, the workbench, the library corner, and the dress-up/dramatic play area. There are no areas or activities delegated for boy or girl play only. For example, boys can pretend to be fathers in the house corner, and girls can be builders in the block area. We want *all* children to feel that they can be who they are and aspire to become whatever they choose to be regardless of their gender.

You may wish to include more specific information about your rules and policies in a parent handbook or a list of guidelines. The following are *statements relating to cooperation and gender* for you to consider including in your written materials.

- These are our two school rules relating to gender:
  All children can play with all toys and in all activity areas of the classroom.

  No children can be excluded from play because of a physical characteristic, such as gender, skin color, or disability.
- We strongly endorse cooperation rather than competition in our classroom(s) and we foster cooperative play between the sexes.
- We discourage stereotyping according to gender. A comment such as "Boys don't play with dolls" or "Girls can't run fast" will be challenged and discussed.
- We encourage all children to come to school prepared for active and messy play. Sneakers or rubber-soled shoes are safest. We recommend slacks, overalls, jeans, and t-shirts for all children—in short, clothes that are practical and safe. We strongly urge children to wear clothing that will not restrict their choices in play. (For example, girls who wear dresses often hesitate to hang upside down on the climber for fear of being teased.) Although we are not suggesting that you get into a battle over whether your child can wear his favorite baseball shirt or her special new dress from Grandma, we do encourage you to send your child to school in gender-neutral clothing when possible.
- Our school is well equipped with a variety of toys and materials. Therefore, we like children to leave their toys at home, except in the case of a security toy or a special book. Competition, rather than cooperation, can result if children try to outdo one another with the toys they bring from home.
- You may notice the anatomically correct dolls in our house corner. We believe that children will learn from these dolls that anatomy, not clothes or choice of activity, determines gender. We also believe that matter-of-fact acceptance of sex differences leads to a healthier attitude about any differences between people.

Parent/Child Orientation

You will want to plan how to ensure as smooth a transition from home to school as possible. We suggest that you invite small groups of parents and children to visit the classroom, become familiar with you and any other staff members in the setting, and get to know one another. To set the stage for cooperative play between boys and girls, make sure you include both sexes in this visit.

When a new child joins your class during the year, invite the child and her or his parent(s) to come in for a short visit or several short visits. Talk to the children in your classroom about the new friend who will be joining them. And during the new child's first days, be on the lookout for ways to gently encourage the group to include this new friend.

Be careful to be as attentive to the parents' feelings as you are to the children's. Separation can be hard for parents, too, and parents will be reassured if they know they are welcome to stay with their children until you and they decide that their children are ready to be on their own.

COMMUNICATING WITH PARENTS

To strengthen parent/teacher interactions, we suggest that you make communicating with parents a primary goal in your planning. Remember that parents like to hear about what their children are experiencing and learning in your class. When you take a minute or two to talk with a parent, you are letting that parent know he or she is important.

If parents feel valued by you and are comfortable with you and your overall program, they will be better able to ask questions about specific areas of the program they do not understand and make comments about their concerns and beliefs. For example, parents who feel valued will be more likely to ask about, listen to, and consider your explanations about the importance of gender equity and cross-gender play. And parents who have developed a sense of trust and feel at ease talking with you will be more likely to openly discuss and even disagree with some of your ideas on gender issues.

General Questions to Ask Yourself about Your Communications with Parents

- *Am I welcoming and friendly? Do I show the parents that I care about them and am glad to see them?* If you don't indicate your genuine caring for the parents as individuals, your communication techniques will be compromised.

- *Do I listen carefully to what the parent has to say? Am I careful to make sure that I am engaged in a conversation—not giving a lecture?* Remember that communication is a two-way proposition and that your goal is to get to know the parent.

- *Do I avoid educational/child development jargon? In relation to gender equity and cooperation issues, do I make sure the words I am using are familiar? Do I state the program goals and philosophy clearly in simple easy-to-understand vocabulary?* Too often, teachers forget that the words they use with such abandon can turn off or even frighten parents. Remember that your aim is to get your message across in a nonthreatening way.

- *Do I communicate in a way that lets parents know I respect their rights to different opinions? Do I let them know that I welcome an exchange of points of view and the opportunity to discuss an issue more fully?* If you listen to parents and respect their rights to have ideas and opinions, they will be more inclined to listen to your suggestions and respect your beliefs.

- *Do I avoid becoming defensive when a parent challenges or criticizes me or my program?* This is a hard one, since nobody likes to be challenged or criticized. But it is important to communicate to parents that you have heard their message and that you will give their opinions your thoughtful consideration.

Daily Interactions

Parents and children should be greeted warmly when they enter the classroom. (Be careful not to routinely give more attention to boys or fathers than you do to girls or mothers. And remember to be nonjudgmental if you must comment on extrinsic characteristics such as a haircut or a new outfit when you greet a parent or child.) If a parent has time to stay and visit briefly, encourage this contact. Many parents will feel worthwhile if they are invited to help in a specific area or with an activity; other parents will need more time to simply watch what is going on before they feel comfortable to interact or help out. Just as you are sensitive to their children's needs, you will want to be sensitive to how parents feel. Be sure to let parents know that your program has an "open-door" policy and that they are welcome to drop in at any time.

Try to speak with parents as they arrive at dismissal time. Most will be eager to hear about their children and what went on that day. By giving parents an opening for a parent/child conversation, you can help eliminate the frustration both parents and children feel when parents ask, "What did you do today?" and their children can only come up with, "Played" or "Nothing."

You might also find it helpful to post a large notice for the parents about special activities the children took part in on a particular day. For example, your message might read, "Today, the children had fun playing parachute games together. Since boys and girls need to cooperate to successfully play these games, we learned about the importance of working together for a common goal." By posting a message such as this, you can communicate what the children did that day and show an example of how you plan for cooperative play between girls and boys.

Naturally, if a child has an upsetting experience on a particular day, talk with the parent about the incident right away. For example, if Juanita and Akiko had a major falling out, tell the parents what happened and how you handled it. Likewise, if a child achieves a milestone or has a particularly meaningful experience, be sure to share this. For instance, be sure to tell Ben's parent(s) that he had a good time dancing with the other children for the first time and let Katie's parent(s) know that she made it to the top of the climber that day.

Try to have a special place (a "mailbox") for each child's parents to receive your notices, letters, newsletters, and private notes. If you feel you are too busy at dismissal time to communicate with parents, make an effort to put notes into the mailboxes telling something meaningful about their children's activities. For example, a simple note such as, "Today, Tykeesha used the unit blocks to build a house with two windows and a door" or "Cedric helped make applesauce and wash up the cooking utensils afterwards" can help keep the lines of communication open and show parents that children of both sexes play with blocks and cook.

If a child is physically hurt, be sure to tell the parent what happened and what you did to take care of the wound or bump. You may want to keep simple "accident report" forms on hand, fill one out at the time of an "accident," and put the form in the parent mailbox. If you employ a system such as this, you can ensure that the incident is not overlooked in the confusion at dismissal time. A sample completed form might look like this:

Child's name: Juan

Date and time: 10/2/96, 10:05

What happened: Juan fell off a tricycle and scraped his knee.

How treated: Cleaned with antibacterial soap and water and covered with adhesive bandage.

Child's response: <u>Juan cried briefly, but was reassured by hugs and</u> <u>enjoyed choosing a colored bandage.</u>

This sample report communicates two messages: It tells about the injury and it reinforces the idea that it is OK for a boy to cry and to be hugged and comforted.

If you seldom see a child's parent(s) because of work schedules, illness, or other reasons, make an effort to keep in touch by telephone. A parent may be particularly grateful for a call telling about how much fun Lola had making a giant floor puzzle with Damion that day. Point out how nice it was to see these two children playing cooperatively together. Try not to use the telephone only to talk about problems that have come up.

If gender issues surface when you talk with parents, try to address them at that point. If the needs of the group preclude a discussion on the spot, be sure to follow up with a phone call or a mini-conference with the parent involved. Use concrete examples to make your points and refer to your policy statements if necessary. For example, if a parent observes her daughter building with three boys in the hollow block area and says, "Marcella is such a tomboy!" or if a parent says, "Does my son ever play anywhere besides in that house corner?" you can use these comments as opportunities to do some on-the-spot gentle teaching about your program goals for gender equity and nonsexist attitudes. If a parent says something dramatically at odds with your program, such as, "I don't want my son dancing around with scarves like a girl!" you will want to schedule a private time to talk with that parent. If, in any of these instances, you sense that other parents have similar attitudes, you might decide to use these comments as a starting point for a discussion at a parent meeting or as the basis for an article in your newsletter. (Be careful not to single out any parent or child, but to speak of the concern in general.) Whichever way you decide to follow up on comments like these, we are sure you will find it worth your time and effort.

OTHER WAYS TO SPREAD THE WORD ABOUT GENDER EQUITY AND COOPERATION

Throughout the year, you will want to address the topics of cooperative play and gender equity in as many ways as possible. Use your parent bulletin board and parent newsletter to convey your messages. Letters to parents about specific issues and situations related to gender issues can also be a way to communicate your goals.

A Bulletin Board for Parents

Cartoons, newspaper articles, comic strips, quotes from experts, quips by the famous and infamous, and examples of sexist and nonsexist advertisements can be used to present your message about gender stereotyping and cooperative versus competitive interactions. Cut out and display these items on your parent bulletin board. Often, a clever cartoon illuminating an attitude about gender or a blatantly sexist advertisement will underscore a point you have made or will clarify a point you have failed to make in conversations with parents. Sometimes, an article written by someone else will give credence to what you have been advocating.

Be sure to encourage parents to clip and share messages they find in their newspapers and magazines about gender equity, gender stereotyping, and cooperation or lack of cooperation between the sexes. If parents feel welcome to contribute to their bulletin board, they will be more likely to read it and heed it.

Following are two examples of short, germane, and easy-to-read items of the kind you might want to write up for your parent bulletin board. (These are only samples; you will, of course, find your own stories and comment on them.)

Out of the Mouths of . . .

The actor Jack Nicholson is alleged to have said on the birth of a son, the first boy after several daughters, "We finally got it right!" Even in jest, this is a damaging message to send to those older sisters and to any other female who hears the remark! And it places a special burden on that little boy to live up to his father's expectations—whatever they may be.

When It All Starts

A mother we heard about tried an experiment. When she took her infant out for a ride in the carriage, passersby would invariably ask, "Is it a boy or a girl?" When she said, "It's a girl," the responses were inevitably, "Oh, how sweet she is" and "Oh, look at how delicate she is!" When she answered, "It's a boy," the responses were, "Oh, what a big boy he is" and "Aren't you handsome, big guy?" Enough said?

Advertisements are a great source of material about gender equity and sex-role stereotyping. You will not have trouble finding sexist ads. It is harder to find ads that support gender equity, but we urge you to look for these as well. You may need to comment on an advertisement and explain why you approve or disapprove of its message about gender and cooperation. (For an easy place to find sexist ads, check out the "No Comment" page on the inside back cover of *Ms.* magazine.)

Following are examples of advertisements we have found in popular magazines and described as something you could use for a sample bulletin board display. We have highlighted our comments.

A Put Down of Both Sexes

The New York Times Magazine (February 26, 1995) ran a full-page ad with an illustration of a blond woman and a man with a wolf's head standing next to her. The ad, which promotes Giorgio Armani clothing, says, "Millie had a way of bringing out the beast in Kurt." **Both men and women are demeaned by this ad!**

An Ad We Like

An advertisement we like is this one from the March 1995 *Parents' Magazine* that shows an African American father with his toddler. The child is wearing a Huggie diaper. **It is important, in our opinion, that the father and his child are spending time together. (And the ad implies that the father is comfortable changing his child's diapers.)**

The Road to Success?

Hofstra University took out a full-page ad in the March 12, 1995, edition of *The New York Times Magazine* that shows preteen children playing soccer and emphasizes the importance of the competitive edge. **The ad buys into the myth that in order to be successful, competition rather than cooperation is imperative.**

Kudos to Dimetapp

This advertisement from the February 1, 1995, *Woman's Day* states that even doctors' kids catch colds, and pictures an African American pediatrician hugging **her** daughter. **(We like the fact that Dimetapp used a photo of a real pediatrician and her daughter instead of models for this ad.)**

When you have a large enough collection of gender-related clippings, you might decide to devote an entire bulletin board to ideas about the importance of gender equity and cross-gender cooperation. But even if you do not choose to use the whole bulletin board for an examination of gender issues and cooperation, be sure to keep the ideas alive by posting thought-provoking items on these topics for parents to see and consider.

Since a picture can be worth a thousand words, you can use photos of the children you teach playing and working cooperatively together to help parents see your program goals in action. Try to get good snapshots of children of both sexes playing cooperatively in all areas of the room. For example, include pictures of girls and boys engaged in active indoor and outdoor play, dramatic play, block building, art activities, cooking projects, and science activities. Take pictures of both boys and girls reading books, playing musical games, and participating in movement activities and dance. Photos posted prominently on a parent bulletin board can bring parents together in a congenial shared experience.

Parent Newsletters

A parent newsletter can be used to keep parents in touch with activities that are going on in your classroom. You may wish to report on projects or trips that have taken place and/or include a calendar of events to let parents know about activities you are planning for the future. You can also use your parent newsletter as a way to present information about child development.

We see the newsletter as another way to educate parents about gender issues and the value of cooperation between the sexes. You can use short articles or editorials on gender-related topics, summaries of parent meeting discussions about these issues, and reviews of pertinent books for children and adults. You may want to include brief accounts of cooperative play and conflict resolution that have taken place in your classroom. Parents may also be grateful if you print the words to particularly popular songs, rhymes, and fingerplays you teach—including the revised gender-equitable versions. You may also decide to reproduce some of the most thought-provoking clippings from your parent bulletin board in order to emphasize a point and to give parents and other family members who may not have seen the bulletin board an opportunity to read these pieces. As with the bulletin board, it is important for parents to feel that they can contribute to their newsletter. Involve them as much as possible in everything from writing articles to doing layout and collating pages.

Following are some sample gender-related columns, articles, and reviews for your newsletter.

No Hitting, Please!
by Tom Ciardi, Teacher

Sometimes parents feel that it is normal for boys to hit one another but that it is wrong for boys to hit girls. This implies that boys are stronger than girls and that girls have to be treated differently because they are "the weaker sex." Girls are often expected to be "ladylike" and not hit anyone, whereas boys may be told to hit an aggressor back so as not to be a "sissy." We believe that these sexist attitudes are damaging to children's self-esteem and undermine cooperation. In our program, hitting by anyone is considered unacceptable, regardless of the child's sex. Instead, we encourage all children to use words to solve their differences. You may have heard one of us telling a child who is angry to "Use your words. Tell _____ that you don't like that." We believe that talking about disagreements can lead to peaceful solutions in which children solve problems together and no one gets hurt. Wouldn't it be nice if world leaders did more of this?

Parent Meeting Report
by Rami Holman, Parent of Hannah

In our parent meeting on gender histories, we discussed how our attitudes about gender come about. We discovered that many of us were "programmed" by our parents to be good little girls or tough little boys. Some of us were fortunate enough to be encouraged to follow our own dreams. All of us found that our gender bias influences how we treat our own kids. Even when we *think* we want equality between the sexes, it requires real work to break away from familiar, but sexist, roles and behaviors. I have decided to work hard to make sure my daughter learns she can be assertive, strong, and independent, as well as caring and nurturing!

Book Review
by Luisa Ramirez, Teacher

Halmoni and the Picnic is a book we liked enough to buy for our program. It is by Sook Nyul Choi and tells the story of a Korean girl and her grandmother who have immigrated to New York City. The grandmother is lonely and misses the old country, but her granddaughter and her school friends come up with a plan to help her feel more at home.

Book Review
by Chris Greene, Parent of Meg

I recommend a book I just finished called *The Little Girl Book: Everything You Need to Know to Raise a Daughter Today* by David Laskin and Kathleen O'Neill. It has a lot of good suggestions on how to raise girls in a nonsexist environment. I think parents of boys would find it worth reading too.

An Example of Cooperative and Nonsexist Play in Our Classroom
by Susan Stein, Teacher

We wish you could have been in our room the other day to see how well the children worked together to make a bus big enough for all the children who wanted to ride on it. When the bus builders ran out of hollow blocks, an argument about who would get seats broke out. Then Kate suggested that the children use chairs for extra seats, and the problem was solved. Tio and Martha made tickets for all the riders, and both girls and boys took turns driving the bus.

How to Raise Kids Who Are Free to Be Themselves
by Simon Barone, Parent of Stephen

Set a good example by being nonsexist yourself. Grab a dishcloth, Dad, and Mom, fix that broken flashlight.

When you read to your kids, choose books about strong, smart, caring, and sensitive males and females.

Allow your child to be an individual! Think of your kid as a great person—not just as a girl or a boy.

Encourage both girls and boys to solve problems. Get in the habit of asking, "What do you think?" Be sure to really listen to your child's answer.

Dads, make parenting a priority: Spend quality time with your kids!

Letters to Parents

You can use letters to communicate with parents about needs, events, concerns, or issues that come up during the year. A letter can be another way to state your program goals for gender equity and cross-gender cooperation. This sample letter invites fathers and mothers to volunteer to help with program activities.

Dear Parents:

We often need volunteers to help us enrich our program. Please check off which areas you could help with, and return the letter to us. We welcome **both fathers and mothers equally** as volunteers **in all areas**.

____ Newsletter articles
____ Newsletter production (typing, layout, etc.)
____ Photographing children in activities
____ Tape recording children's books for our listening corner
____ Assisting with field trips
____ Repairing and painting toys and equipment
____ Helping to plan parent meetings
____ Serving on the family activities committee
____ Playing a musical instrument for the children
____ Sharing your work/career with the children
____ Helping with classroom activities
____ Sharing your family traditions and customs
____ Other _____

Thanks in advance for being willing to help out in our program.

Julia Kaseman, teacher

The following sample letter addresses gender equity and a program need at the same time:

Dear Parents:

We are planning to introduce the workbench and tools to your children next week. We would like to invite any interested parents to give us some extra help at this time. For safety reasons, the workbench must be supervised at all times. If you can help out, please let us know.

When children use tools and work with wood, they have an opportunity to learn the names and functions of each of the tools and to learn about the properties of wood. They also have the chance to further develop hand/eye coordination and small and large muscle facility and strength. As they decide what to make and how best to do it, they will be using their minds to make decisions and solve problems. And when they accomplish a task they have never attempted before, they will experience feelings of self-worth and confidence.

Children can learn a great deal when they work at the workbench. Too often, however, the workbench is viewed as the exclusive domain of the boys, just as repair work and construction are often viewed as male responsibilities. It is important to stress that both girls and boys can work with tools, and that both men and women are builders, construction workers, carpenters, woodworkers, and repair persons.

We feel confident that you will help us encourage both girls and boys to learn to use tools and enjoy the process of woodworking. We would like both mothers and fathers to help us in order to model for children that both sexes can and do work with tools.

Please volunteer!

Thanks for your support,

Melanie Irwin and Ron Taylor, teachers

Evaluations by Parents

You will want to find out what parents are thinking and feeling about your program in order to determine how well you are accomplishing your program goals. By asking parents for feedback, you accomplish two things: Parents will feel that their opinions are valued and you will receive information that will be helpful in future planning.

After each parent meeting or planned family activity, you might decide to ask parents to fill out anonymous evaluations of the event. You can print a feedback form in your newsletter to give parents a chance to tell you if and how it meets their needs. In addition to this specific feedback, we recommend asking parents to evaluate your total program twice a year. We have included a sample of an anonymous evaluation you may find helpful as a guideline for preparing your own. (We highlighted those comments on the evaluation form which relate to our emphasis on gender equity and cooperation.)

Sample Program Evaluation for Parents

Dear Parents:

You can help us make our program stronger. Please take a few minutes to fill out this evaluation form. Your signature is optional.

On a scale from 1 to 5, with 5 being excellent, please rate the following:

The setting is comfortable and appealing.
Rating _____   Comment _____

Staff members follow health and safety precautions.
Rating _____   Comment _____

Staff members are warm and friendly.
Rating _____   Comment _____

Materials and activities are interesting and varied.
Rating _____   Comment _____

Children are treated as individuals, not as representatives of their gender, race, or ethnic group.
Rating _____   Comment _____

Girls and boys are encouraged to play cooperatively together.
Rating _____   Comment _____

Staff members keep the lines of communication open.
Rating _____   Comment _____

Individual expression is encouraged in art, music, block building, and dramatic play.
Rating _____   Comment _____

Books, reading, and language arts are valued.
Rating _____   Comment _____

Both girls and boys are listened to and asked to contribute ideas.
Rating _____   Comment _____

Conflicts are handled in a fair and nonjudgmental way.
Rating _____   Comment _____

Boys and girls are expected to be equally responsible for solving problems.
Rating _____   Comment _____

Girls and boys participate in all areas and activities.
Rating _____   Comment _____

The overall program promotes social, emotional, physical, and cognitive learning.
Rating _____   Comment _____

Suggestion Box for Parents

Place a suggestion box where all parents have easy access to it. Encourage parents to feel free to slip in notes to express a concern, ask a question, or convey approval. Your suggestion box can double as a place for parents to return evaluation forms.

ENCOURAGING AND ENHANCING PARENT INVOLVEMENT

Parent involvement is key to a strong early childhood program. To help parents understand that they are an integral part of your program, you will want to make them feel welcome, listen to their ideas and concerns, and talk with them about their children and your program. In addition to keeping communication open and ongoing, we believe that planned meetings and activities for parents are vital components of a strong parent involvement program and are excellent vehicles for furthering your goals of promoting gender equity and cross-gender cooperation in your group.

In this section, we suggest ways to reach out to parents through parent meetings and through parent participation in program activities. These activities include special parent and child activities such as field trips, picnics, shared suppers, and family nights, as well as parent conferences.

Parent Meetings

We suggest that you have a series of parent meetings to discuss your program goals. Some large programs have a parent group leader whose job it is to work with parents, but in many more settings, the job of parent group leader falls to the person who works directly with the children. For the purposes of clarity, we will assume that you are the group leader.

Of course, you will want to have meetings that focus on your goals for gender equity and cooperation between girls and boys. However, it is always a good idea to find out which meetings parents want most and what they want to discuss and explore. You may want to form a small parent committee to work with you to find out what topics appeal to the parents. The committee might decide to interview parents for suggestions for parent meetings or to send out a list of possible topics (including some of the ones we suggest) asking parents to check those that sound most interesting.

Using methods such as these, you may find that parents are much more interested in one topic than they are in another. Start where the interest is high and try to stimulate additional interest in topics you consider important as you go along. (For good information on how to run parent meetings, read "Successful Parent Meetings" by Suzanne M. Foster in *Young Children* 50(1) (1994).) We include here some sample parent meetings related to gender issues and cross-gender cooperation for you to consider using or adapting.

Sample Parent Meeting Format

We have had success with the following format for leading parent meeting discussions. To set the stage for equal and open dialogue, arrange the group's chairs in a circle. Of course, you can adapt our format or use another method that you have devised.

1. Present the topic for discussion.
2. If the group is larger than five, divide the group into small groups and ask each small group to choose a recorder/reporter. For an easy way to form small groups, ask the members of the large group to count off by twos, threes, or fours (depending on the size of the large group) and then meet with the parents whose numbers match theirs. In a small group, everyone gets a say, and the less vocal are not overwhelmed by the size of the group.
3. The members of each small group will discuss the topic using the questions or materials you have prepared.
4. Ask the groups to come back together. Each recorder/reporter will share the main ideas from their small groups. You may wish to record the ideas from each group of parents on a blackboard or chart for all to see and comment on. Guide any discussion that comes up in the large group. At this time, you can respond briefly, but with sensitivity, to comments the parents have brought up.

Sample Parent Meetings on Gender Equity and Cooperation

Are Our Goals the Same?

In this meeting, you and the parents will discuss your program goals for gender equity and cooperation between boys and girls. Start by going over the goal statements and gender-related rules that are written in your various parent handouts. Display these statements on a blackboard or on a large piece of paper taped to the wall, or prepare handouts with the written goals.

The small groups will work together on the following questions before coming together to share their ideas with the whole group:

Do you agree with and support the goal statements related to gender and cooperation? Why or why not?

What, if any, other statements related to gender and cooperation are needed?

What do you do with your child(ren) to encourage gender equity and foster cooperation?

By giving parents an opportunity to think about and discuss these sometimes controversial ideas about gender and cross-gender cooperation, you show parents that you care about their opinions, and you help parents understand why you believe gender equity and cooperation are important. Moreover, you will find out which parents support your goals, which parents disagree with specific goals, and which parents seem uncertain or confused. After this parent meeting, you are bound to be in a better position to work effectively with individual parents on these issues.

Exploring Gender Histories
In this parent meeting, the parents will recall, share, and note the similarities and differences in their experiences as females or males. Since the parents you work with will represent a variety of backgrounds and come with different perspectives, they will benefit from hearing other points of view as they discuss how their experiences relate to their attitudes and beliefs about gender issues.

We recommend that you divide your parent group into small groups of three or four for this meeting. You will find that in a small group even shy parents are willing to talk about their past experiences in relation to gender. Give each of the parents a list of questions to discuss. Each parent in the small group should have a chance to respond to each of the following questions:

What were your feelings about growing up as a male/female?

How did you feel about the other sex?

How are your views on gender different from those your parents held?

How has your gender influenced your life choices?

How do you feel about competition and cooperation?

Do you think women and men can work as equal partners?

When the small groups have finished discussing the questions, ask each recorder/reporter to share the main points from the small group discussion with the large group. Chart the responses of the small groups to show similarities and differences that are revealed through the discussions. As you listen to the reports from the small groups, remember to accept what people say about their experiences and attitudes as valid for them. Do not jump right in to try to change someone's ideas. Use any ideas and attitudes that limit gender equity and stifle cooperation as a basis for planning future strategies for working with parents around these issues.

After parents have had a chance to think and talk about their gender histories with other parents, they will note commonalties and differences and become more aware of the connection between past experiences and gender bias. As you know from your own explorations into your gender history, awareness is an important first step toward change.

Hot Topics Related to Gender Equity and Cooperation

For a meeting or meetings on gender issues and issues of friendship and cooperation, bring in some hot topics for parents to discuss in small groups. (These should be hypothetical situations, not real problems that parents have shared with you. Be sure that you do not breach confidentiality or seem to be talking about someone in the group in a veiled way.)

Pass out index cards with one or more different hot topics. Then ask the parents to discuss the situation described and try to come up with possible solutions. After the parents in the small groups discuss the hot topics, call everyone back to the large group. The recorders/reporters will read the hot topics and summarize the comments from their small groups. You will facilitate any further discussion in the large group.

Sample Hot Topics for Parent Meetings

Jack is a father of two young sons. He has changed their diapers and read bedtime stories to them over the years, but when either of them gets hurt and cries inconsolably, he soon becomes anxious and annoyed. He comforts his son for a minute, but then finds himself saying, "Hey, cut out the waterworks. This bump is no big deal." (How is he tied to the traditional male role model? Should he do something different here? Will his sons grow up to be sissies if he lets them cry?)

Mary sees her son putting on a dress and heels in the dramatic play area. Her thoughts immediately turn to gay bars and AIDS. She is only partly satisfied by the teacher's comment, "Joe is interested in trying out how different roles feel. Last week he dressed up like a firefighter." (How would you feel if Joe were your son? Do you feel that Joe's behavior is "normal"?)

Shandola's mother works as a paralegal and has time with her daughter on mornings, evenings, and weekends. She finds her job exciting and fulfilling, but she feels guilty and distressed when Shandola says, "I wish you didn't go to work. I wish you stayed home like Tara's mom does." (How can Shandola's mother deal with her daughter's and her own feelings?)

Alison's father wants her to become computer literate like her older brother, so he has bought some computer games for her to play. However, she is not particularly interested in this activity; she would rather play with her dollhouse or make pictures with her colored markers. (What might be the reasons for Alison's behavior? What should Alison's father do?)

Marlene says she notices that she is harder on her son than on her daughter when they misbehave, and that she is more nurturing when her daughter is sick than when her son is. (Is this an OK way to deal with her children? What could she do differently?)

Luis says his daughter wants to wear frilly dresses and patent leather shoes to school. He tells her she cannot play well in these clothes, but dressing for school is now a battle. (What can Luis do to begin to solve this problem?)

As parents discuss these hot topics, they will be involved in trying to find solutions to problems they may have experienced. They will see that problems often have no easy answers and that there may be several constructive ways to handle a situation.

Nonsexist Toys and Books
A parent meeting focusing on nonsexist toys and books that promote gender equity and cooperation can occur anytime during the year, but we have found that parents often like to discuss these issues before they shop for holiday gifts. Show the whole group examples of popular nonsexist toys and books as well as a few examples of blatantly and subtly

sexist toys and books. In this way, you can demonstrate the contrast between what you advocate and what you urge parents to avoid. (See the resources at the end of Chapter 2 and the What to Look For in Books section in Chapter 5 for information about these topics.)

After you have introduced the topic, you will want to have small group discussions using questions about toys and books for children. Pass out index cards with one or more of the following questions for the parents in each group to discuss:

> What toys are generally considered appropriate for boys? For girls? Is it OK for girls to play with toys that are considered toys for boys, and vice-versa? Would you feel comfortable buying a "boy toy" for a girl and a "girl toy" for a boy? If so, which kinds of toys would you buy/not buy? Why?

> Would you buy a book about a girl for a boy, and vice-versa? If not, why not? If you liked a book that had some obvious stereotypes about males and/or females, would you buy it? If so, why? What could you do about the stereotypes in the book?

> What toys have you noticed are popular with both sexes? Why do you think these toys are appealing to both boys and girls? Will children return to these toys over and over again? If so, why? What toys have limited appeal to both sexes or to either sex? Why do children quickly lose interest in these toys?

The sharing that occurs as the groups report back can be helpful for everyone. In addition, many parents will appreciate a bibliography of nonsexist books such as ours (see Chapter 5) and a listing of catalog 800 numbers (such as the ones given in Resources in Chapters 2, 4, and 5). Also give parents an opportunity to browse through your book and toy catalogs and books such as *The New York Times Parent's Guide to the Best Books for Children* by Eden Ross Lipson; *Books Kids Will Sit Still For* by Judy Freeman; *Buy Me! Buy Me!: The Bank Street Guide to Choosing Toys for Children* by Joanne F. Oppenheim; and *The Right Toys: A Guide to Selecting the Best Toys for Children* by Helen Boehm. (Although the photographs in the book by Boehm are dated and sometimes reveal stereotypes, the ideas about toys are useful.)

Coping with Superheroes and Barbie Dolls
We have found that parents are eager to discuss their children's fascination with and demand for current action figures, Barbies, TV character spinoffs, and war toys. (In preparing for this meeting, refer to our

discussion in Coping with Superheroes and Barbie Dolls in Chapter 1.)
Ask the parents to form small groups to discuss the following questions:

Should children be allowed to play with toy guns and other toy
weapons? If not, why not? If so, under what circumstances?

How can parents deal with the constant requests for current fad
toys? Are these toys good/harmful for children? Why? Do children
play with them?

What, if any, is the value of superhero play? Are there ways to
change repetitious and violent superhero play into more creative
play? How familiar are you with the superhero stories?

Do you think children should be discouraged from playing with
Barbie dolls? If so, why? If not, what is the value of this play?

Since TV influences what toys children want and how they play,
should TV viewing be limited? And if so, what can you put in its
place? What sexist and nonsexist messages do children get from TV
spinoffs? (For example, have you noticed that nearly all the engines
in the *Thomas the Tank Engine* series are males and that the less
important and less powerful box cars are females?) How can we
counteract these kinds of sexist messages?

As parents discuss these questions, they may find solace in the discovery that many other parents share their concerns. Those who have
not given much thought to the messages in toys and the power of TV
will become more aware of how these influence their children's desires
and behavior.

Additional Possible Topics for Parent Meetings

Have a meeting using one or two open-ended questions for parents
to discuss in small groups. Here are two suggestions:

How can I be a more gender-sensitive parent?

What can I, as a parent do to promote gender equity and help
girls and boys feel OK about themselves and each other?

Consider publishing the discussion results in your newsletter.

Invite a parent or a group of parents to read and report on different articles and books that relate to gender issues. (See our bibliography in Chapter 7 for some suggested titles.)

Invite parents to read and review children's books for the parent
group, paying particular attention to whether the books are free of

gender stereotyping and show females and males cooperating. (You may wish to suggest titles or distribute books from which the parents may choose.)

Parent Participation in Program Activities

Classroom Visits

To increase parent involvement and understanding of your program goals (in this case, those related to gender equity and cooperation), invite parents to visit your classroom. Some parents are comfortable reading a story to one or two children or helping a child with a difficult puzzle. Other parents want to jump right in and take part in larger group activities. Some parents like to come in to help in a specific interest area such as block building or water play. Others are comfortable helping with a cooking activity, an art project, a woodworking enterprise, or a science experiment. When possible, have parents counteract a stereotype by helping in an area that is considered primarily the domain of the other sex. For example, ask Momar's father if he is willing to assist with a cooking project or ask Cassandra's mother if she is amenable to helping with a science activity. As parents work with both girls and boys in these activities, they will observe firsthand that all activities are open to both sexes.

Special Parent/Child Activities

Field Trips

Many parents like to go on field trips with the children. Take advantage of any interest and invite parents to go with your group on trips to places such as a public library, a farmers' market, a pizza parlor, or a museum exhibit. You can even invite a parent to go with a staff member and a small group on a walk around the neighborhood. Whenever you go on a trip with parents and children, be alert to opportunities to promote your goals for gender equity and cooperation between the sexes. For example, try to point out to the children and parents any instances you see of women and men working together cooperatively or working in nontraditional jobs.

Birthdays

Most parents like to celebrate their children's birthdays at school. Suggest that parents bring simple treats for snack or dessert time and that they spend some time sharing in their children's activities. Parents who are reluctant visitors will find it hard to resist a birthday celebration. Remember that no matter what brings the parents into the classroom, you can use the visit as an opportunity to share your goals and observations regarding gender equity and cooperation.

Career Education

The parents of the children in your class may be involved in a wide variety of careers. Encourage parents to visit your group to tell the children about their work and demonstrate the "tools of their trade." Some parents may be able to invite you and your group to have a firsthand view of their work world. The more parents you can involve, the more children will see that both sexes participate in a range of work. You may not find many examples of nontraditional work in your group of parents, but you can alert children to wider possibilities simply by asking some questions. For example, if a father who is a mail carrier visits your group, be sure to ask him at some point if women are mail carriers too.

Potluck Supper

Invite parents and families to a potluck supper. Ask parents to bring ethnic specialties or family favorites to share. Be sure to have committees with fathers, as well as mothers, involved in food preparation, setting the tables, and washing dishes. Have fathers and mothers equally involved in reading stories or playing quiet games with the children while the clean-up crew of both men and women do those chores.

Family Picnic

In warm weather, plan a picnic for parents and children. Be sure to involve mothers and fathers equally in the food preparation and the supervision of children, including siblings. Use the playground facilities for regular outdoor activities. This is also a good time to get parents and children involved in playing win-win games together.

Parents' Night

Consider a parents' night, which can involve parents whose work keeps them from taking part in their children's daytime program. We suggest that you set up the room as it would be on a regular day and then let the children and parents participate in a simulated routine. Your classroom arrangement, bulletin board and other displays, and the activities you have available for the boys and girls in your group to share with their parents should send a clear message that this environment fosters gender equity and cooperative play.

Grandparent Visits

Invite grandparents (or other older people) to visit your program to take part in activities or read stories. Set aside a special time when these older people can tell stories about their lives. Children will be fascinated with the differences between the past and the present generations.

Parent Conferences

Schedule at least two parent conferences during the year and arrange for special conferences as needed. Parents want to hear how their children are doing and how you view their children. As you talk with parents, start by asking them to share any observations or concerns they have about their particular child and/or the program. If you and the parents share a concern about their child, plan how best to work together to solve the problem. If you have a concern about the child that the parent has not brought up, share it in a caring and respectful way. Of course, you will focus on the child's strengths and share positive observations with parents.

A conference can also serve as a time to discuss any positive developments or problems that have come about as a result of your focus on gender/cooperation. Sometimes parents want to limit their children's activities—who they can play with and what they can play. For example, if a parent says, "I don't want Sholinda playing with Philip" or "I don't want my daughter roughhousing," you will need to address the problem. First, try to learn why the parents feel the way they do and let them know that you understand their point of view. Listen to what they have to say and summarize their comments, saying something like, "This is what I hear you saying . . . ." Next, try to explain your position in ways that are meaningful to them. In most instances, if parents are treated with courtesy and consideration, you and the parents will be able to resolve the problem, and they will be willing to go along with your program goals. However, if a conflict about gender issues cannot be resolved, you may need to respect the parents' stand and try to negotiate a compromise that stays within the confines of what you generally believe to be best for the children.

TO SUM UP . . .

When you involve parents in your program—whether through home and classroom visits, planned family activities, written communications, or parent meetings—you are setting the stage for mutual growth and understanding. Parents who feel they are contributing to the program as well as learning from it will have a larger investment in its success. As you form partnerships with the parents of the children you teach, you will be setting the groundwork for effecting change without alienating parents. Parents who feel valued and whose ideas are listened to will be better able to work with you to ensure a program with equal opportunities for girls and boys and one that fosters cooperation rather than distance from or hostility between the sexes. Those who respect you and value you will find it easier to embrace the concepts and practices regarding gender equity and cross-gender cooperation that you advocate.

CHAPTER SEVEN
HEIGHTENING YOUR AWARENESS

Self-Evaluation, Staff Development, and Continuing Education

As a good teacher, you will want to evaluate your interactions with children and parents on a regular basis. In addition to informal evaluation of your teaching on a daily basis, engage in planned self-appraisal to become more aware of yourself as a teacher, of your impact on children and parents, and of your growth as a professional.

Whether you work with a large staff or arrange to get together with others who work in small programs, you will find it invaluable to share and discuss observations and concerns regularly in a supportive collegial setting. As a result of your self-evaluation and this interchange of ideas with other professionals, you will grow in your ability to implement a quality program.

We encourage you to use individual self-evaluation as a means to uncover and eliminate your own gender bias and stereotyping behavior in the classroom and to come up with new ways to promote your goals for gender equity and cross-gender cooperative play. We also urge you to work together with your colleagues to uncover your unconscious attitudes regarding gender and to develop strategies for correcting any bias that creeps into your teaching as a result. As you and your colleagues share your experiences in attempting to meet gender-related goals and devise new approaches for dealing with problems that arise, you will feel supported in your efforts to make changes.

In this chapter, we suggest ideas and models for self-evaluation and staff development meetings. We also include a bibliography of articles, books, and resources that focus on gender issues and/or nonsexist teaching.

GUIDELINES FOR SELF-EVALUATION

You may find it helpful to begin your self-evaluation by observing what is happening in your classroom. For example, pay attention to which children stay in one area for a majority of the time, which children move easily from one activity to another, who plays with whom, which children solve problems, and which children take leadership roles. You may decide to observe each child individually for a period of time to see where, how, and with whom that child plays; you may also decide to keep a roster showing who plays in which activity areas and with whom. To help you observe which activities children choose and what interactions occur between girls and boys, we have included some sample observation tools.

Individual Observation

Child's name: _____

Date and time: _____

Activity: _____

With whom: _____

Is play cooperative?_____ Parallel?_____ Confrontational?_____

Additional comments:

Group Observation

Fill in the names of the children who are engaged in activities in these areas at a given time. (If a child is just watching others in the area, note that.)

Activity Areas	9:30 AM	10:00 AM	10:30 AM	11:00 AM
Hollow Block Area				
Unit Block Area				
House Corner				
Library Corner				
Art Area				
Manipulative Play Center				
Sand and Water Area				
Science Center				
Woodworking Center				
Indoor/outdoor Active Play Areas				
Music and Movement Area				

Observation Focusing on Cross-Gender Interactions

For more in-depth information on the number and type of cross-gender interactions, try using questions such as the following ones as you observe the children in action. (If you spend a day focusing on cross-gender interactions, you may find it helpful to keep paper and pencils in several convenient locations around the room in order to easily jot down your observations at the time they occur.)

Who is playing with whom? For how long? Where?

Which girls and boys are playing in same-sex groups? Where? For how long?

Which boys and girls are playing cooperatively? Where? For how long?

Are any confrontations between boys and girls taking place? Where? Why?

Are girls and boys solving differences or problems on their own?

Are children engaging in any stereotyping or sexist behavior?

Which children are taking the roles of leaders, followers, or observers?

After you have observed classroom interactions and behavior patterns, you will have ideas about where you need to plan for changes. For example, if girls are avoiding the blocks or boys are shunning dramatic play, you can plan activities to encourage cross-gender participation in these areas. If you notice that Mikey almost never takes a leadership role, you can choose him to be a leader when the opportunity arises, or if Shauna is usually an observer rather than a player, you can look for ways to help her become involved.

Self-Evaluation

When you have finished the classroom observations, it is then time to evaluate how good a job you are doing promoting gender equity and cooperation between the boys and girls you teach. Set aside a block of time when you are not responsible for children to think about the following questions:

Have I set up my room in a way that will encourage cross-gender play?

Do I encourage both sexes to feel free to explore all areas and activities? Do I plan activities that will encourage girls and boys to work and play cooperatively in all areas of the room?

Do the materials I use with children encourage cooperation and gender equity? Are the pictures I display free of gender bias and sex-role stereotyping?

Do I have a good collection of nonsexist books on the children's bookshelves? Do I have as many books with female protagonists as I do those with male protagonists? Am I careful to read to the children as many books about females as I do about males? Do I discuss with the children any examples of sexism that appear in books?

Do I make an effort to eliminate stereotypes from the fingerplays, songs, rhymes, chants, and games I teach the children?

Do I give as much attention to girls as to boys? Do I respond to boys and girls with equal interest and enthusiasm? Do I ask girls what they think as often as I ask boys?

Am I careful to be even-handed in my approach to the behavior of boys and girls? (For example, am I careful not to tolerate more rough play in boys than in girls, or more silly play in girls than in boys?)

Do I avoid gender bias when I delegate tasks to girls and boys?

Do I avoid making assumptions about the future lives of boys and girls?

Am I careful to avoid stereotyping and using sexist language?

Do I avoid making judgmental comments on children's appearance? (Saying, "You had a haircut, Kevin!" acknowledges an event in the child's life. Saying, "You have such beautiful hair, Rosalie" overemphasizes appearance.)

Am I sensitive to ethnic and cultural beliefs about gender roles as I try to help parents understand the importance of gender equity and cooperative play between boys and girls?

Do I treat fathers and mothers as equally important?

Do I constantly remind myself to treat all the children and their parents as unique individuals rather than as representatives of their gender?

Evaluating Supportive Intervention

Although you will want to allow children to solve problems on their own whenever possible, in some instances you will need to intervene to further your goals for gender equity and cross-gender cooperation. To evaluate the ways you intervene to support these goals, think about the following questions:

Do I correct stereotyping behavior and confront excluding behavior in a way that leaves the children feeling good about themselves?

If I need to intervene in a confrontation between a girl and a boy or between boys and girls, do I deal with the problem fairly and treat girls and boys as individuals rather than as members of their sex?

Do I listen well to both sexes and help both boys and girls listen to each other and express their needs and feelings in words? (For example, "Piya, you need to listen to Aaron. He wants to tell you how that makes him feel.") If a child doesn't know the words, do I suggest some possibilities? (For example, "Moira, you can tell Hu, 'I want that truck.'")

Do I reflect back to children that they have handled a situation involving cooperation or gender well? (If two children have found a way to include a child who is being excluded from play, do I describe their behavior without resorting to excessive praise? For example, "Noako and Francisco, you figured out a way to let Rico play too. Look how happy he is to be the pizza delivery person.")

If you find that you can answer yes to the self-evaluation questions, you are well on your way to providing a program that encourages girls and boys to feel good about themselves and each other and to feel free to be who they are. If you answer no, think about how to make changes in your teaching and/or your program. Set a few manageable goals for ways to change, and check your progress over the next few weeks.

You may also wish to talk about your self-evaluation with a colleague (or a group of colleagues) to get support and suggestions. In addition, if you and a colleague are both committed to gender equity, you may find it extremely helpful to observe each other's programs and teaching. Often, a colleague can see something you are doing that is particularly effective or something that limits your success in achieving your goals. Of course, you and your colleague should agree ahead of time to point up any "blind spots" in a nonjudgmental way.

If you have access to a video camera, you may want to ask someone to film a few hours of your teaching and your program. Later, you can review the video on your own to see if you can find instances where you fostered or failed to foster cooperation and gender equity. You can also use the video to get another perspective on the children you teach.

IN-SERVICE MEETINGS

You will want to be part of an in-service group in order to work on ways to implement your goals involving gender equity and cooperation between girls and boys. If you are part of a large program, you already have a built-in staff support group; if you work alone or have a small program, you will want to find a way to meet with other colleagues who work in similar situations.

As part of an in-service group, you will have a chance to talk with colleagues whose backgrounds, experiences, and ideas are likely to be different from yours. As you share your diverse points of view and feelings, you and your colleagues will work through differences and come to recognize the value of different perspectives.

To effectively plan your in-service meetings, you and your colleagues will want to set up a planning committee to ensure that the meetings address issues that are important to the group members, that the meetings occur regularly, and that each meeting is organized to use time effectively. The planning committee may also want to ask different members of the in-service group to take turns organizing and facilitating the in-service meetings.

Whoever is designated as the facilitator will organize the meeting, explain the agenda, divide the group into smaller groups as needed, provide materials, keep track of the time, and expedite any large group discussion. The facilitator should be sure to allow enough time for the full group to hear, discuss, and sum up the main ideas from any small group discussions. To set the stage for more equal and open exchange, the facilitator should ask group members to arrange their chairs in a circle.

On the following pages, we include some ideas for in-service meetings related to gender issues and cross-gender cooperation that you and your colleagues may find helpful to consider as you plan your meetings. Of course, you can adapt any suggestions to meet your particular group's needs.

Sample In-Service Meetings on Gender Issues and Cooperation

Sharing Gender Histories

In this in-service meeting, you and your colleagues will recall, share, and discuss the differences in your experiences as males or females and look at how these events shaped your attitudes and beliefs regarding gender. If you and your colleagues represent varying ethnic and cultural traditions, as well as different economic and educational backgrounds, each of you can use your new understandings of these unique perspectives to help promote your gender-related goals in ways that respect differences.

After the small groups are formed and a recorder/reporter is chosen for each group, the facilitator will hand out lists of the following questions for participants to discuss one at a time. The recorder/reporter will take notes on the discussion to share when the full group reconvenes. The facilitator might choose to chart the responses of staff members to show similarities and differences that are revealed through individual answers to the questions. Each member of the group should have a chance to respond to each of the following questions:

> What were your feelings about growing up as a female/male?
>
> How are your views on gender different from those of your parents?
>
> How has your gender affected your life at home, at school, at work?
>
> How do you perceive the other sex?
>
> What do you consider the advantages/disadvantages of being male/female?
>
> How do you feel about competition, cooperation, and partnership?
>
> How are your ideas on cooperation and gender similar to or different from those of the parents/children with whom you work?

As you and your colleagues share gender histories, you will become more aware of how life experiences influence attitudes toward gender and cooperation. This enhanced awareness should help you be more sensitive to the diversity within the group of parents and children with whom you work. It will also help you be better able to deal with their varied responses to your efforts to advance gender equity and further cooperation between girls and boys.

What's in a Word?

In this in-service meeting, you and your colleagues will look at the ways you describe yourselves. Then you will look at how you describe females and males in general. The facilitator will divide the groups as needed and will ask each participant to write down the first 10 words that come immediately to mind as best describing herself or himself. These lists should then be set aside.

Next, the facilitator will ask the members of each small group to work together to quickly generate two lists using the first words that come to mind, being careful not to censor "incorrect" responses. The first list will include as many words as possible that describe females, the second as many words as possible that describe males. The recorder will jot down the words that members call out. (The facilitator will allow approximately three minutes for this activity.)

The facilitator will then ask members of each group to designate which words on their two lists conform to male/female stereotypes and which words are gender neutral. For example, a group might designate *nurturing* as a female characteristic, *aggressive* as a male attribute, and *generous* as gender neutral.

Then, the facilitator will ask everyone to return to their individual lists and mark the words that conform to female/male stereotypes and those that are gender neutral. The facilitator will leave some time for members of the small groups to talk about the attributes they used to describe themselves.

When the large group reconvenes, the recorders/reporters will share lists and comments from the small groups. The facilitator will lead a brief discussion about the words on the different lists and how these words relate to gender bias.

As you take part in this activity, you may be surprised at how often a word has become a stereotype and how few words are truly gender neutral. Through recognizing the pervasiveness of gender stereotyping, you may be better able to work toward goals that make it acceptable (even normal) for more descriptors to be gender neutral.

Do You Practice What You Preach?

In this in-service meeting, you and your colleagues will discuss your program goals for gender equity and cooperation between girls and boys and ways to implement these goals. The facilitator will post any gender/cooperation statements from your program materials (brochures, mission statements, handbooks, and the like) where they can be read and reviewed by all the staff members.

If needed, the facilitator will ask the participants to form smaller groups. The groups will work together on the following questions:

Do you agree with and support the statements related to gender and cooperation? If you have any reservations, what are they?

Are any statements ambiguous? How would you rephrase them for clarity?

What, if any, other statements are needed?

If you agree with these goals, policies, and rules, how do you implement them? Give concrete examples such as, "I make sure that when we play games, girls are leaders as often as boys are" or "When I assign the cubbies to children, I make sure that each child will be next to at least one member of the other sex."

After this meeting, you and your colleagues will be clearer about how seriously you are committed to furthering program goals. You are also likely to get new ideas from colleagues who share practical suggestions for encouraging gender equity and cooperative play.

Hot Topics on Gender Issues

The planning committee for in-service will ask group members to write up descriptions of some real or hypothetical situations relating to gender issues that have occurred or could occur in classrooms. A meeting (or meetings) to discuss these hot topics will have meaning for you and your colleagues and will lead to lively discussions.

The facilitator will divide the group as needed and give each small group index cards with one or more different hot topics. The group members will discuss the situation described on each card and try to come up with possible solutions. After each small group discusses its hot topic(s), the large group will reconvene and share topics and solutions.

Sample Hot Topics for In-Service Meetings

Nancy and Joel have a boy in their classroom who undresses the anatomically correct dolls. He announces to other children, "This doll has a penis and that one has a vagina." A parent who is visiting observes this behavior and says, "That kid has a dirty mouth. How come you don't stop that?" (What should Nancy and Joel tell this parent? Should they allow the boy to continue this play?)

Yentl's Dad bursts into the room one morning and tells Selma, the teacher, that he does not want Yentl playing with Ramon anymore, because Ramon is too rough and tough and always chasing Yentl on the playground. Selma has observed Yentl teasing Ramon and inviting him to chase her on frequent occasions. (What should she say to this angry father? How should she handle the interactions between Yentl and Ramon?)

Bobby likes the dramatic play area and often dresses up in ballet slippers and a long satin skirt. He dances and prances around in this outfit, and says, "I'm going to the store. See you later, guys." Bobby's parents have never seen him in this outfit, but his teachers, Miho and Rebekah, are wondering what will happen when they do. They expect that Bobby's parents would order him to take off the clothes and never dress up like that again. (How can the teachers prepare for this confrontation? Are their expectations rational or colored by bias?)

Jasmine waits each day for her best friends, Emily and Lauren, to arrive, and then the three head straight for the house corner area. They have "taken over" the house and direct all the play. When Kareem enters their space, he is immediately told to go out to the store for groceries or medicine. When he says he wants to be the daddy, they say, "We don't have a dad in this family." (How should the teachers, Shirley and Phyllis, react? Should they let this play continue or should they intervene?)

At snack or meal time, the children rush to the tables and save seats for their friends. Children are told, "You can't sit here; this table is for boys/girls." As a result, there are girls at one table and boys at the other. (How can the teacher, Christopher, change this situation to encourage cross-gender interaction at snack or meal time?)

Colin and Jessica often build together, paint side by side, and play together in the house corner. The teachers, Buzz and Louisa, are pleased to see this cross-gender interaction. Recently, however, they have heard some children calling Jessica and Colin "love-birds." Finally, the name calling has escalated to the point where Toby, one of the class leaders, has begun to get other children to join him in taunting Colin, singing, "Colin's got a girlfriend, Colin's got a girlfriend!"

   Colin angrily denies it, yelling, "You shut up. I do not have a girlfriend. I don't even like Jessica." Of course, Jessica is upset by this betrayal. (What should the teachers do to support Colin's and Jessica's friendship? How can they help the other children recognize the value of cross-gender friendships?)

Anayo and Emma are sick and tired of the superhero play that goes on in their classroom. They find it repetitive, rough and noisy, and often exclusive. They are at the point of banning this play but feel there must be a better way to handle the situation. Clearly, the children who are enthralled with this play would resist a ban. (What should Anayo and Emma do? Can they redirect this play or come up with ways to change and extend it? Or should they ban the play completely?)

Lucas hangs back whenever his teachers, Rafael and Amber, put on music for movement or dance activities. The other girls and boys are enthusiastic about participating in these activities, and Rafael models that males like to dance. When either Amber or Rafael asks

Lucas to join in, Lucas looks at the floor and acts embarrassed. (Should Rafael and Amber leave Lucas alone, provide an alternative activity, or continue their efforts to get him involved?)

Ernie feels he has made a bad situation worse. He noticed that the boys in his class were taking over the climber and the girls seemed afraid to encroach on the boys' territory. Because he wanted the girls to have a chance to use the climber, Ernie decided to declare one day a week as "girls only" day on the climber. The day was instituted after he explained to the class that it is important for everyone to have a chance to use their muscles. The girls used their "girls only" days playing actively on the climber.

But now the boys are demanding "boys only" days, and the girls are insisting on more "girls only" days. Ernie wants to promote cooperative play between boys and girls, not gender-segregated battlegrounds. (Did he make a mistake suggesting the "girls only" day? What should he do now?)

Kathy and Armand usually find that they work well as team teachers. However, they have different degrees of commitment to the program's goals for gender equity and cooperative play. Armand says, "What's so bad about the boys all playing with the blocks while the girls do their thing in the art area? After all, boys and girls are different. Look at how often a girl plays with a truck, or how often a boy picks up a doll on his own. Aren't you trying to change girls and boys into what you think they should be?"

Kathy has strong feelings about the way women have been treated over centuries. She wants to be sure that no doors are closed to girls. "I don't care if a girl is into dolls and frills as long as she knows she has other options," she argues. "And, if I don't try to encourage her to build with blocks, she might miss out on an important learning experience." (Do Armand and Kathy each have a valid point of view? Where does either argument fall short? How can these two work out their differences?)

As you and your colleagues wrestle with these problems, you will be invigorated by the stimulating exchange of ideas, and as you work with colleagues to develop strategies for coping with gender issues, you will discover that many problems have no simple solutions and that what works in one setting may not work in another. You will also realize that there are several constructive ways to deal with a situation, not just one right way.

Improving Communication with Parents

You and your colleagues may find it helpful to plan an in-service meeting around ways to communicate and interpret your program goals for gender equity and cooperation between the sexes to parents who represent a variety of ethnic groups, cultures, and social, educational, and economic backgrounds. You can also use staff development meetings to discuss how best to work with parents whose resistance to letting go of entrenched beliefs and rigid attitudes regarding gender issues makes you feel ineffective and frustrated.

The facilitator will ask group members to share examples of their experiences in working with parents in situations that involve gender issues. The facilitator will divide the group as needed and ask group members to discuss both successes and problems they have with parents around gender issues. Group members will propose possible solutions to any unsolved problems. When the full group reconvenes, the reporters from each of the small groups will summarize what took place in their discussions, and the facilitator will lead any further discussion.

As you and your colleagues share problems and successes you are having with the parents in your programs, you will all have an opportunity to vent your feelings and gain support from each other. You may also garner new ideas for ways to be more effective in reaching your gender-related goals and discover possible solutions to problems you face.

Developing Your Cultural Sensitivity

In the event that the members of a particular culture seem to have opinions and attitudes that are at odds with your gender goals, your in-service group may find it invaluable to invite colleagues, parents, and/or community members from that culture to talk to your group about their beliefs and customs. (To avoid any gender bias, you will want to invite representatives of both genders to share their perspectives.)

As you come to better understand and respect the beliefs of parents from a particular culture, you will undoubtedly find it easier to talk with them about your goals for gender equity and cross-gender cooperation. And you will become more sensitive to parents as you work to seek mutually acceptable resolutions regarding gender issues.

Taking on Issues

You and your colleagues may decide to have an in-service meeting to work on ways to promote gender equity in the larger community. At this meeting, your in-service group will generate ways to take on issues and bring about changes.

Prior to the meeting, the facilitator will ask group members to bring in the names of companies that sell toys and materials that support or neglect gender equity, companies that use sexist or nonsexist advertisements and packaging, TV networks that encourage gender equity and cooperation and those that perpetuate sexist stereotypes through their programming, and organizations that support or neglect gender equity. The group members will organize the materials they have brought to the meeting and decide what tasks to take on. The facilitator will keep track of the volunteers for various tasks.

Following are a few ways you and your colleagues could decide to take action in your community:

Write letters to thank companies that produce nonsexist toys and materials and to urge those that are remiss to stock nonsexist toys and materials.

Write letters to thank companies that use nonsexist advertising and packaging and to urge those that use sexist advertising and packaging to stop the practice.

Patronize companies and stores that sell nonsexist toys and materials and let their owners know why you are choosing them.

Boycott companies that advertise and sell sexist products and let their owners know why you are not buying their products.

Support women-owned businesses.

Support legislation that favors gender equity.

Write to TV network executives to praise them for airing specific programs that promote gender equity and cooperation and to complain about specific programs that are sexist and violent.

Write letters to thank newspapers for articles that promote gender equity and cooperation and to protest biased articles.

Locate organizations that work on gender issues and write for their free materials.

Check to see if your local library has a selection of nonsexist books. If there is a dearth of good titles, you can urge the librarians to add appropriate books. Be prepared to share a list of nonsexist book titles. Do the same with bookstore owners.

Work on strategies for involving parents in some of these activities.

When you and your colleagues have decided on which issues to tackle, you will want to figure out how to provide follow-up on the actions you take. Your in-service group may decide to hold another meeting to check on progress and plan how to continue these efforts.

Additional Possible Topics for In-Service Meetings

Have a meeting in which you and your colleagues search through magazines and newspapers for items to use on your bulletin boards and in your newsletters. Look for items related to gender issues: sexist and nonsexist advertisements, gender-related cartoons, and pertinent quotations. Then you and your colleagues can create appropriate captions to go with the items and arrange bulletin board displays or newsletter contributions to use in your program(s). (See Other Ways to Spread the Word about Gender Equity and Cooperation in Chapter 6.)

Set up a meeting in which you and your colleagues bring in non-sexist fingerplays, rhymes, chants, and songs, as well as win-win games to teach each other. You can also share ways you have changed popular circle-time activities to make them gender equitable. (See Songs, Rhymes, and Fingerplays and Win-Win Games in Chapter 4.)

Have a meeting in which every group member brings in several children's books that promote gender equity, show females in a positive light, feature nontraditional roles, or highlight coopera-tion between the sexes. Read and discuss the books. You can also bring in examples of sexist books and discuss whether they should be removed from your shelves, adapted, or used for discussions with children. (See Chapter 5.)

Plan a meeting in which you and your colleagues discuss a book you have all read prior to the meeting. For example, the group could decide to read and discuss *The Second Sex* by Simone de Beauvoir, *In a Different Voice* by Carol Gilligan, or *Failing at Fairness: How America's Schools Cheat Girls* by Myra and David Sadker.

TO SUM UP . . .

In this chapter, we have suggested ways you can work alone and with colleagues to look at and evaluate your growth as a facilitator for gen-der equity and cooperation between the sexes. We urge you to make time for this fundamental aspect of teaching, since your attempts to change your behavior and your program will be reinforced by ongoing self-scrutiny and insightful feedback from colleagues.

BIBLIOGRAPHY FOR BUILDING AWARENESS OF GENDER ISSUES

In our own explorations into gender issues, nonsexist teaching, and cooperation between children and as preparation for writing this book, we found the following books and articles useful background reading— even when we did not agree with everything we read. Of course, this short bibliography is by no means exhaustive, but we hope you will find this list helpful as you continue your reading on these subjects.

Abraham, Kitty G., and Lieberman, Evelyn. "Should Barbie Go to Preschool?" *Young Children* 40(2) (1985):12–14.

Abramson, Shareen, Robinson, Roxanne, and Ankenman, Katie. "Project Work with Diverse Students: Adapting Curriculum Based on the Reggio Emilia Approach." *Childhood Education* 71(4) (1995):197–202.

American Association of University Women and the National Educational Association. *How Schools Shortchange Girls*. A joint report. Washington, DC, 1992.

Belenky, Mary Field, Clinchy, Blythe McVicker, Goldberger, Nancy Rule, and Tarule, Jill Mattuck. *Women's Ways of Knowing*. New York: Basic Books, 1986.

Benderly, Beryl Lieff. *The Myth of Two Minds: What Gender Means and Doesn't Mean*. New York: Doubleday, 1987.

Benditt, John (Ed.). "Gender and the Culture of Science." *Science* 260 (1993):383–430.

Berk, Laura E. "Vygotsky's Theory: The Importance of Make-Believe Play." *Young Children* 50(1) (1994): 30–39.

Bettelheim, Bruno. "The Importance of Play." *The Atlantic* 259(3) (1987):35–46.

Bos, Bev. *Together We're Better: Establishing a Coactive Learning Environment*. Roseville, CA: Turn the Page Press, 1990.

Bredekamp, Sue (Ed.). *Developmentally Appropriate Practice in Early Childhood Programs Serving Children Birth Through Age 8*. Washington, DC: National Association for the Education of Young Children, 1987.

Byrnes, Deborah A. and Kiger, Gary (Eds.). *Common Bonds: Anti-Bias Teaching in a Diverse Society*. Wheaton, MD: Association for Childhood Education International, 1992.

Carlsson-Paige, Nancy, and Levin, Diane E. *Who's Calling the Shots? How to Respond Effectively to Children's Fascination with War Play and War Toys*. Philadelphia, PA: New Society Press, 1990.

Cherry, Clare. *Think of Something Quiet: A Guide for Achieving Serenity in the Early Childhood Classroom*. Carthage, IL: Fearon Teacher Aids, 1981.

Chesler, Phyllis, *Women and Madness*. New York: Doubleday, 1972.

Clemens, Sydney G. *The Sun's Not Broken, A Cloud's Just in the Way*. Beltsville, MD: Gryphon House, 1983.

Cohen, Monroe D., and Martin, Lucy Prete. *Growing Free: Ways to Help Children Overcome Sex-Role Stereotypes*. Washington, DC: Association for Childhood Education International, 1976.

Corbett, Susan M. "Teaching in the Twilight Zone—A Child Sensitive Approach to Politically Incorrect Activities." *Young Children* 49(4) (1994):54–58.

Cray, Elizabeth. *Kids Can Cooperate: A Practical Guide to Teaching Problem Solving*. Seattle, WA: Parenting Press, 1984.

Derman-Sparks, Louise. *Anti-Bias Curriculum: Tools for Empowering Young Children*. Washington, DC: National Association for the Education of Young Children, 1989.

Dinwiddie, Sue A. "The Saga of Sally, Sammy, and the Red Pen: Facilitating Children's Social Problem Solving." *Young Children* 49(5) (1994):13–19.

Douglas, Susan J. *Where the Girls Are: Growing Up Female with the Mass Media.* New York: Times Books, 1994.

Ehrenreich, Barbara. *The Hearts of Men: American Dreams and the Flight from Commitment.* Garden City, NY: Anchor Press, 1983.

Faludi, Susan. *Backlash: The Undeclared War Against American Women.* New York: Crown Publishers, 1991.

French, Marilyn. *The War Against Women.* New York: Summit Books, 1992.

Friedan, Betty. *The Feminine Mystique.* New York: Dell, 1963.

Galinsky, Ellen, and David, Judy. *The Preschool Years.* New York: Times Books, 1988.

Garcia, Maria. *Gender Equity Module: Ensuring Unbiased Behavior in an All-Girl Environment.* New York: Girl Scouts of the U.S.A., 1994.

George, Felicia. "Checklist for a Non-Sexist Classroom." *Young Children* 45(2) (1990):10–11.

Gilligan, Carol. *In a Different Voice: Psychological Theory and Women's Development.* Cambridge, MA: Harvard University Press, 1982.

Gilman, Charlotte Perkins. *The Charlotte Perkins Gilman Reader.* Edited by Ann J. Lane. New York: Pantheon Books, 1980.

Gilmore, David D. *Manhood in the Making: Cultural Concepts of Masculinity.* New Haven, CT: Yale University Press, 1990.

Gorman, Christine. "Sizing Up the Sexes." *Time* (Jan. 20, 1992): 42–51.

Gould, Lois. "Stories for Free Children: X." *Ms.* (1980):61–64.

Gronlund, Gaye. "Coping with Ninja Turtle Play in My Kindergarten Classroom." *Young Children* 48(1) (1992):21–25.

Honig, Alice Sterling. "Sex Role Socialization in Early Childhood." *Young Children* 38(6) (1983):57–70.

Honig, Alice Sterling, and Wittmer, Donna Sasse. "Helping Children Become More Prosocial: Ideas for Classrooms, Families, Schools, and Communties." *Young Children,* 51(2) (1996): 62–70.

Kaplan, Joel, and Aronson, David. "The Numbers Gap." *Teaching Tolerance* (Spring) (1994):20–27.

Kessler, Shirley, and Swadener, Beth Blue (Eds.). *Reconceptualizing the Early Childhood Curriculum: Beginning the Dialogue.* New York: Teachers College Press, 1992.

Kimmel, Michael. *Manhood in America: A Cultural History.* New York: Free Press, 1996.

King, Edith W., Chipman, Marilyn F., and Cruz-Janzen, Marta. *Educating Young Children in a Diverse Society.* Boston: Allyn and Bacon, 1994.

Klemm, Bonita, Kuykendall, Jo, Greenberg, Julie, Carlsson-Paige, Nancy, and Levin, Diane E. "Various Viewpoints on Violence." *Young Children* 50(5) (1995):53–63.

Kohl, Mary Ann, and Potter, Jean. *Science Arts: Discovering Science Through Art Experiences.* Bellingham, WA: Bright Ring Publishing, 1993.

Kostelnik, Marjorie J., Wirren, Alice P., and Stein, Laura C. "Living with He-Man: Managing Superhero Fantasy Play." *Young Children* 41(4) (1986):3–9.

Kuschner, David. "Put Your Name on Your Painting, But . . . the Blocks Go Back on the Shelves." *Young Children* 45(1) (1989):49–56.

Laskin, David, and O'Neill, Kathleen. *The Little Girl Book: Everything You Need to Know to Raise a Daughter Today.* New York: Ballantine Books, 1992.

Levin, Diane E., and Carlsson-Paige, Nancy. "The Mighty Morphin Power Rangers: Teachers Voice Concern." *Young Children* 50(6) (1995):67–72.

Lott, Bernice. *Women's Lives: Themes and Variations in Gender Learning.* Pacific Grove, CA: Brooks/Cole, 1987.

Mann, Judy. *The Difference: Growing Up Female in America.* New York: Warner Books, 1994.

Marder, Brenda. "Evelyn Fox Keller '57 Reflects on Gender and Science." *Brandeis Review* 12(3) (1993):22–25.

McCracken, Janet Brown. *Valuing Diversity: The Primary Years.* Washington, DC: National Association for the Education of Young Children, 1993.

Meyerhoff, Michael K. "Of Baseball and Babies: Are You Unconsciously Discouraging Father Involvement in Infant Care?" *Young Children* 49(4) (1994):17–19.

Miedzian, Miriam. *Boys Will Be Boys.* New York: Anchor Books, 1993.

Mikel-Brown, Lyn, and Gilligan, Carol. *Meeting at the Crossroads: Women's Psychology and Girl's Development.* Cambridge, MA: Harvard University Press, 1992.

Miller, Jean B. *Toward a New Psychology of Women.* Boston: Beacon Press, 1976.

Mincer, Jillian, and Raffalli, Mary. "Persistent Sexism in American Education." *Education Life* (*The New York Times*, Jan. 9, 1994):26–27.

Minnich, Elizabeth Kamarck. "A View of Beginnings." *Transforming Knowledge*, pp. 1–14. Philadelphia: Temple University Press, 1990.

Moynihan, Cynthia Russet, and Crumpacker, Laurie (Eds.). *Second to None: A Documentary History of American Women.* Lincoln: University of Nebraska Press, 1994.

Neugebauer, Bonnie (Ed.). *Alike and Different: Exploring Our Humanity with Young Children.* Washington, DC: National Association for the Education of Young Children, 1992.

Noddings, Nel. "The Gender Issue." *Educational Leadership: Journal of the Association for Supervision and Curriculum Development* 49(4) (1991–1992):65–70.

Notman, Malkah T., and Nadelson, Carol C. (Eds.). *Women and Men: New Perspectives on Gender Differences.* Washington, DC: American Psychiatric Press, 1991.

Nourot, Patricia Monighan, and VanHoorn, Judith L. "Symbolic Play in Preschool and Primary Settings." *Young Children* 46(6) (1991):40–50.

Orenstein, Peggy. *School Girls: Young Women, Self-Esteem, and the Confidence Gap.* New York: Doubleday, 1994.

Paley, Virginia Gussin. *You Can't Say You Can't Play.* Cambridge, MA: Harvard University Press, 1992.

_____. *Boys and Girls: Superheroes in the Doll Corner.* Chicago: University of Chicago Press, 1984.

Parry, Anne. "Children Surviving in a Violent World—'Choosing Non-Violence.'" *Young Children* 48(6) (1993):13–21.

Pogrebin, Letty Cottin. *Growing Up Free: Raising Your Child in the 80's.* New York: McGraw-Hill, 1980.

Powlishta, Kimberly K. "Gender Segregation Among Children: Understanding the 'Cootie Phenomenon.'" *Young Children* 50(4) (1995):61–69.

Prutzman, Priscilla, Stern, Lee, Burger, M. Leonard, and Bodenhamer, Gretchen. *The Friendly Classroom for a Small Planet: A Handbook on Creative Approaches to Living and Problem Solving for Children.* Philadelphia: New Society Publishers, 1988.

Ramsey, Patricia G. *Making Friends in School: Promoting Peer Relationships in Early Childhood.* New York: Teachers College Press, 1991.

Rogers, Cosby S., and Sawyers, Janet K. *Play in the Lives of Children.* Washington, DC: National Association for the Education of Young Children, 1988.

Rossi, Alice S. (Ed.). *The Feminist Papers from Adams to de Beauvoir.* New York: Columbia University Press, 1973.

Sadker, Myra, and Sadker, David. *Failing at Fairness: How America's Schools Cheat Girls.* New York: Charles Scribner's Sons, 1994.

Secunda, Victoria. *Women and Their Fathers: The Sexual and Romantic Impact of the First Man in Your Life.* New York: Delacorte Press, 1992.

Shannon, Jacqueline. *Why It's Great to Be a Girl—50 Eye-Opening Things You Can Tell Your Daughter to Increase Her Pride in Being Female.* New York: Warner Books, 1994.

Sheldon, Amy. "Kings Are Royaler Than Queens: Language and Socialization." *Young Children* 45(2) (1990):4–9.

Silverstein, Olga, and Rashbaum, Beth. *The Courage to Raise Good Men.* New York: Viking, 1994.

Sprung, Barbara. *Perspectives on Non-Sexist Early Childhood Education.* New York: Teachers College Press, 1978.

Sprung, Barbara, Froschl, Merle, and Campbell, Patricia B. *What Will Happen If . . . Young Children and the Scientific Method.* New York: Educational Equity Concepts, 1985.

Steinem, Gloria. *Moving Beyond Words.* New York: Simon & Schuster, 1994.

————. *Revolution from Within.* New York: Little, Brown, 1992.

Tannen, Deborah. *You Just Don't Understand: Women and Men in Conversation.* New York: William Morrow, 1990.

Tavris, Carol. *The Mismeasure of Woman: Why Women Are Not the Better Sex, the Inferior Sex, or the Opposite Sex.* New York: Simon & Schuster, 1992.

Thorne, Barrie. *Gender Play: Girls and Boys in School.* New Brunswick, NJ: Rutgers University Press, 1993.

Wainrib, Barbara Rubin (Ed.). *Gender Issues Across the Life Cycle.* New York: Springer, 1992.

Wichert, Susanne. *Keeping the Peace: Practicing Cooperation and Conflict Resolution with Preschoolers.* Philadelphia: New Society Press, 1989.

Wittmer, Donna Sasse, and Honig, Alice Sterling. "Encouraging Positive Social Development in Young Children." *Young Children* 49(5) (1994):4–12.

Wolf, Naomi. *The Beauty Myth: How Images of Beauty Are Used Against Women.* New York: William Morrow, 1991.

RESOURCES

American Association of
University Women
1111 Sixteenth St. N.W.
Washington, DC 20036-4873
1-800-225-9998

International Women's History Archive
2325 Oak St.
Berkeley, CA 94708
1-510-524-1582

National Committee on Pay Equity
1126 16th St., N.W., Suite 411
Washington, DC 20036
1-202-331-7343

National Council for Research on
Women
530 Broadway, 10th Floor
New York, NY 10012
1-212-274-0730

National Organization for Women
(N.O.W.)
1000 Sixteenth St. NW, Suite 700
Washington, DC 20036
1-202-331-0066

National Women's Hall of Fame
76 Fall St.
Seneca Falls, NY 13148
1-315-568-8060

National Women's History Project
7738 Bell Rd.
Windsor, CA 95492-8518
1-707-838-6000

Organization for Equal Education of the
Sexes
P.O. Box 438
Blue Hill, ME 04614
1-207-374-2489

UNICEF
Office of Evaluation and Research
3 UN Plaza
New York, NY 10017
1-212-702-7279

Women's Action Alliance
370 Lexington Ave.
New York, NY 10017
1-212-532-8330

Women's Educational Equity Act (WEEA)
Publishing Center
Education Development Center
55 Chapel St., Suite 222
Newton, MA 02158-1060
1-800-225-3088

Women's Rights National Historical Park
P.O. Box 70
116 Fall St.
Seneca Falls, NY 13148
1-315-568-2991